Federalism and
democratisation in Russia

MANCHESTER
UNIVERSITY PRESS

Federalism and democratisation in Russia

CAMERON ROSS

Manchester University Press

Manchester and New York

distributed exclusively in the USA by Palgrave

Published by Manchester University Press
Oxford Road, Manchester M13 9NR, UK
and Room 400, 175 Fifth Avenue, New York, NY 10010, USA
www.manchesteruniversitypress.co.uk

Distributed exclusively in the USA by
Palgrave, 175 Fifth Avenue, New York,
NY 10010, USA

Distributed exclusively in Canada by
UBC Press, University of British Columbia, 2029 West Mall,
Vancouver, BC, Canada V6T 1Z2

British Library Cataloguing-in-Publication Data
A catalogue record for this book is available from the British Library

Library of Congress Cataloging-in-Publication Data applied for

ISBN 0 7190 5869 4   *hardback*
     0 7190 5870 8   *paperback*

First published 2002

10 09 08 07 06 05 04 03 02   10 9 8 7 6 5 4 3 2 1

Typeset in 10 on 12 pt Palatino
by SNP Best-set Typesetter Ltd., Hong Kong
Printed in Great Britain
by Biddles Ltd, Guildford and King's Lynn

Contents

List of tables, boxes and appendices

Tables

Boxes

Appendices

Abbreviations

AO	autonomous okrug (Avtonomnyi Okrug)
AOB	autonomous oblast (Avtonomnaya Oblast')
APR	Agrarian Party of Russia (Agrarnaya Partiya Rossii)
ASSR	autonomous soviet socialist republic (Avtonomnaya Sovet-skaya Sotsialisticheskaya Oblast')
CDPSP	*Current Digest of the Post-Soviet Press*
CDSP	*Current Digest of the Soviet Press*
CO	Honour and Fatherland (Chesti i Ochestvo)
CPSU	Communist Party of the Soviet Union (Kommunisticheskaya Partiya Sovetskovo Soyuza)
DVR	Russia's Democratic Choice (Demokraticheskii Vybor Rosii)
GDP	gross domestic product
GRP	gross regional product
IP	industrial production
KEDR	Ecological Party of Russia (Ekologicheskaya Partiya Rossii)
KPRF	Communist Party of the Russian Federation (Kommunisticheskaya Partiya Rossiiskoi Federatsiya)
KRO	Congress of Russian Communities (Kongress Russkikh Obshchin)
LDPR	Liberal Democratic Party of Russia (Liberal'no Demokraticheskaya Partiya Rossii)
NDR	Our Home is Russia (Nash Dom-Rossiya)
NPR	People's Party of Russia (Narodnaya Partiya Rossii)
NPSR	National Patriotic Union of Russia (Narodno Patrioticheskii Soyuz Rossii)
OVR	Fatherland–All Russia (Otechesvo-Vsya Rossiya)
PL	party list
PST	Party of Independent Workers (Partiya Samoupravleniya Trudyashchikhsya)
RF	Russian Federation

RKRP	Russian Communist Workers' Party (Rossiiskaya Kommunis-ticheskaya Rabochaya Partiya)
RP	Republican Party (Respublikanskaya Partiya)
RSFSR	Russian Soviet Federative Socialist Republic (Rossiskaya Sovet-skaya Federativnaya Respublika)
RSP	Russian Socialist Party (Russkaya Sotsialisticheskaya Partiya)
SM	Single member
SPS	Union of Right Forces (Soyuz Pravo Sil')
USSR	Union of Soviet Socialist Republics (Soyuz Soveticheskikh Sotsialisticheskikh Respublik)
TIK	Territorial Election Commissions (Territorial'naya Izbiratel-'naya Komissiya)
VTsIOM	All-Union Centre for Public Opinion Research (Vserossiiskii Tsentr Izucheniya Obshchestvennovo Mneniya)
Zhir	Zhirinovsky bloc

1

Introduction

Democracy and democratisation

Since the early 1970s a 'third wave' of democratisation has swept the world. In the period 1972–94 the number of democratic political systems doubled from 44 to 107. And by the mid-1990s 58 per cent of the world's states had adopted democratic governments.[1] These momentous developments have led political scientists to re-examine the theoretical literature on democratisation, and to compare the current transitions in the post-communist bloc with earlier transitions in Latin America and Southern Europe. From my reading of this literature three major schools can be identified.

One school has focused on the *preconditions* necessary for the emergence of stable democracy:

1 modernisation, industrialisation, urbanisation, education, capitalism and wealth;[2]
2 the nature of classes and the class structure, with a focus on the positive role of the bourgeoisie or the proletariat;[3]
3 a democratic political culture and civil society;[4]
4 the importance of institutional factors,[5] electoral systems,[6] type of regime – parliamentary or presidential,[7] the development of strong parties, and a stable party system;[8]
5 a unified state, agreed borders and the absence of ethnic and religious conflict;[9]
6 external factors: a peaceful international environment, the impact of globalisation.[10]

A second school has centred its research on the transition process. Here scholars argue that the very nature of the transition itself largely determines the success or failure of democratisation.[11] 'Revolutions from above' are contrasted with 'revolutions from below'. A major focus for this school is the role of elites and the importance of elite unity, settlements and pacts.[12] From this perspective, democratic transitions and breakdown can best be understood by examining changes in the internal relations of national elites. For Higley and Gunther, 'what principally distinguishes unconsolidated from consolidated democracies, is in short, the absence of elite consensual unity'.[13] For a democratic system to persist and flourish, elites must engage in 'politics as bargaining' rather than 'politics as war'. Democratic transitions are the result of negotiated pacts between actors in the dominant elite leading either to sharing with, or conceding power to, ascendant elites.[14]

A third school focuses on the period after the collapse of the old regime and the problems associated with the consolidation of democracy, which we discuss further below.[15]

In contrast to the first school with its stress on socio-economic and other structural preconditions, the second and third schools stress the independent role of individual actors and human agency and the ability of elites to craft democracy, even where pre-conditions are unfavourable.[16]

Each of these three approaches has made a positive contribution to the field. However, there are two major omissions in the transition literature. First, the focus of all three schools has largely been on national-level politics. None of the above authors has devoted more than passing attention to the importance of democratisation at the regional and local levels. Second, the relationship between federalism and democracy has largely been overlooked in the transition literature.[17]

This study seeks to redress this imbalance by moving the focus of research from the national level to the vitally important processes of institution building and democratisation at the local level and to the study of federalism in Russia. I believe that the insights garnered in the study of the democratisation process of separate countries can be applied equally fruitfully to individual regions within countries, especially in such a large and diverse country as Russia.

Many authors have alluded to the unique nature of Russia's dual transition and its difficult task of simultaneously reforming its economy and polity. But there is in fact a third transition under way in Russia that is of no less importance, the need to reconfigure central–local relations and to create a stable and viable form of federalism. Federal states are much more difficult to set up than unitary ones. And forging a new federal system at the same time as privatising the economy and trying to radically overhaul the political system has clearly made Russia's transition triply difficult.

Defining democracy

There are many competing definitions of democracy. Perhaps the most famous is that of Robert Dahl who lists the following eight 'institutional guarantees' which citizens must enjoy before a country can be classified as a democracy:

> 1) Freedom to form and join organisations, 2) freedom of expression, 3) right to vote, 4) eligibility for public office, 5) right of political leaders to compete for support, 5a) right of political leaders to compete for votes, 6) alternative sources of information, 7) free and fair elections, 8) institutions for making government policies depend on votes and other expressions of preference.[18]

Dahl groups these eight factors into the following three essential attributes of a democratic polity:

> 1) Meaningful and extensive *competition* among individuals and organized groups (especially political parties) for all effective positions of government power, at regular intervals and excluding the use of force;
> 2) a 'highly inclusive' level of *political participation* in the selection of leaders and policies, at least through regular and fair elections, such that no major (adult) social group is excluded;
> 3) a level of *civil and political liberties* – freedom of expression, freedom of the press, freedom to form and join organizations – sufficient to ensure the integrity of political competition and participation.[19]

Dahl argued that there was no country where all of his eight conditions were fully satisfied thus; he preferred to call such states 'polyarchies', leaving the term democracy for the non-existent, ideal type.[20]

Dahl's eight conditions for polyarchy have been criticised for not taking into consideration the importance of such institutional features as 'parliamentarism or presidentialism, centralism or federalism, majoritarianism or consensualism' and for its silence over the degree to which governments 'are responsive or accountable to citizens between elections, and the degree to which the rule of law extends over the country's geographic and social terrain'.[21] Thus, O'Donnell argues that two further conditions must be met before a country can be considered democratic: '1) elected officials should not be arbitrarily terminated before the end of their constitutionally mandated terms; 2) elected authorities should not be subject to severe constraints, vetoes, or exclusion from certain policy domains by other, nonelected actors, especially the armed forces'.[22]

Beetham takes up many of these issues in his excellent studies of democracy. For Beetham there are two major features of democracy, 'political equality' and 'popular control'. Political equality 'is realised to the extent that there exists an equality of votes between electors, and equal right to stand for public office, an equality in the conditions for making one's voice heard and in treatment at the hands of legislators'.[23]

Popular control has four major dimensions which build on and extend many of Dahl's original eight preconditions for polyarchy:

> 1) The popular election of the parliament or legislature and the head of government; 2) Open and accountable government, and the continuous

political, legal, and financial accountability of government directly, to the electorate; 3) Guaranteed civil and political rights or liberties: freedoms of speech, association, assembly and movement, and the right to due legal process; 4) A lively civil society.[24]

Democratic consolidation

During the past quarter of a century, more than sixty countries around the world have made the transition from authoritarian rule to some kind of democratic regime. But as Schedler notes, 'sustaining democracy is often a task as difficult as establishing it'.[25] Thus, political scientists have turned their attention to democratic consolidation. As Beetham notes, 'the process of consolidating democracy which begins where the transition to democracy ends, i.e., with the inauguration of a new government at the first free and fair elections . . . is a much more lengthy and difficult process than the transition itself'.[26]

The installation of democratic institutions and the ratification of a democratic constitution are but the first of many essential steps on the path to consolidation. Thus, as O'Donnell notes, a democracy may only be considered consolidated, 'when a society frees itself from the spells cast by authoritarian demagogues and rejects all alternatives to such democracy so as to no longer imagine any other possible regime'.[27] And in a similar vein for Linz and Stepan consolidation comes about, when 'democracy as a complex system of institutions, rules, and patterned incentives and disincentives has become, in a phrase, "the only game in town"'.[28]

Consolidation, however, should not be mistaken for merely the stability or longevity of a regime. Consolidation requires a deepening and broadening of democracy, a 'depth of institutionalisation reaching beyond the electoral process itself'.[29] As Schedler notes, 'it implies constructing all those big organisations that make up the characteristic infrastructure of modern liberal democracies: parties, and party systems, legislative bodies, state bureaucracies, judicial systems, and systems of interest intermediation'.[30] And consolidation is only completed, 'when the authority of fairly elected government and legislative officials is properly established (i.e., not limited) and when major political actors as well as the public at large expect the democratic regime to last well into the foreseeable future'.[31]

But how do we know a consolidated democracy when we see one, and what are the preconditions that are necessary for the creation of a consolidated democracy? In answer to the first question, Huntington put forward his two 'turnover test', whereby a democracy can be said to be consolidated when there have been two consecutive changes of government through free and fair elections.[32] However, there are problems here when the same party is democratically elected repeatedly over a number of elections, as was the case in Japan or Italy. If there are free and fair elections but no turnover of parties does this mean a democracy is not consolidated? Surely not!

In answer to the second question, most scholars agree that the preconditions needed to consolidate a democracy may not necessarily be the same as those which brought it about in the first place. Linz and Stepan, following Rustow, stress that no democracy can be consolidated until consensus has been reached over national unity and any contested boundaries of the state have been settled. 'Consolidated democracy needs a state ... no state no democracy'.[33] Second, they argue no state can consolidate its democracy unless it already satisfies all of Dahl's criteria for democracy listed above. With these preliminary conditions in place Linz and Stepan posit five addition prerequisites which a democratic state must satisfy before it can be considered consolidated:

> 1) the development of a free and lively civil society; 2) a relatively autonomous political society; 3) throughout the territory of the state all major political actors ... must be effectively subjected to a rule of law that protects individual freedoms and associational life; 4) there must be a state bureaucracy that is usable by the new democratic government; 5) there must be an institutionalised economic society.[34]

Finally, as Gitelman notes, 'democracy should not be seen as an absolute, but as a spectrum'. Some states are more democratic than others 'and the same system may vary over time in the extent to which it is democratic'.[35] Moreover, as we shall show in this study, levels of democracy and authoritarianism in different regions within one country may also vary considerably.

Federalism

Writing in 1987 Elazar noted, that a 'federalist revolution' was sweeping the world 'changing the face of the globe in our time'.[36] And as a result of this largely unnoticed revolution some 40 per cent of the world's population now reside in federal states, and another third live in polities that are governed by some form of federal arrangements. Moreover, as Smith observes, with the collapse of communism, federalism has been, 'propelled into occupying a more central place by the resurgence of nationalist and ethnic tensions which have paralleled, if not taken sustenance from the end of the Cold War'.[37]

Following Watts, it is important to distinguish between: 'federalism', 'federal political systems' and 'federations'. Federalism is a normative concept, an ideology which advocates, 'multi-tiered government combining elements of shared-rule and regional self-rule'.[38] Federal political systems, on the other hand, are descriptive terms referring to a broad category of non-unitary states ranging from quasi-federations and federations, to confederacies (including: federacies, associated statehood, condominiums, leagues and joint functional authorities). Federations are thus but one species of the genus 'federal political system'. In federations according to Watt's classic definition:

> 1) neither the federal nor the constituent units of government are constitutionally subordinate to the other, i.e., each has sovereign powers derived from the constitution rather than another level of government;
> 2) each is empowered to deal directly with its citizens in the exercise of legislative, executive and taxing powers and
> 3) each is directly elected by its citizens.[39]

Structural prerequisites for federations

How can we test if a country is a federation or not? In light of the above discussion, scholars of federalism have put forward the following structural prerequisites which states must meet before they can be classified as federations:[40]

> 1) The existence of at least two-tiers of government, both tiers of which have a formal constitutional distribution of legislative, executive and judicial powers and fiscal autonomy,
> 2) Some form of voluntary convenant or contract among the components – normally a written constitution (not unilaterally amendable and requiring for amendment the consent of a significant proportion of the constituent units),
> 3) Mechanisms to channel the participation of the federated units in decision-making processes at the federal level. This usually involves the creation of a bicameral legislature in which one chamber represents the people at large and the other the component units of the federation,
> 4) Some kind of institutional arbiter, or umpire, usually a Supreme Court or a Constitutional Court to settle disputes between the different levels of government,
> 5) Mechanisms to facilitate intergovernmental collaboration in those areas where governmental powers are shared or inevitably overlap.[41]

Decentralism and noncentralism

Elazar alerts us to yet another vitally important factor in defining federal systems, the differences between the decentralisation to be found in unitary states and the noncentralisation of federal regimes. Decentralisation 'implies a hierarchy – a pyramid of governments with gradations of power flowing down from the top'.

Noncentralisation, on the other hand, 'is best conceptualised as a matrix of governments ... where there are no higher or lower power centres, only larger or smaller arenas of decision making and action'.[42] Thus, in federations, in contrast to unitary states, regional autonomy is not only devolved but constitutionally guaranteed.[43] The federal government cannot usurp powers which have been constitutionally devolved to the federal subjects. As Elazar observers, federal systems such as the United States, Switzerland and Canada have such noncentralised systems. Each has, a national government that functions powerfully in many areas for many purposes, but not a central government controlling all the lines of political communication and decision making. In each, the states, cantons or provinces are not creatures of the federal government but, like the latter, derive their authority directly from the people. Structurally, they are substantially immune to federal interference.[44]

Structure, process and culture

Another important distinction to be made is that between structure and process. Here we refer to the formal structural features of federations, as defined above, and the actual operational procedures put into practice by federal governments. As Elazar stresses, 'the structure of federalism is meaningful only in polities whose processes of government reflect the federal principle'.[45] In other words, federal structures may be in place in a polity, and federal principles may be enshrined in a country's constitution, but there may still be no federalism in operation – as was the case, for example in the Soviet Union (see chapter 2). Here, we need to add a cultural dimension to the five structural definitions provided above. A democratic and legalistic culture is required for a democratic federation. As Watts notes, a recognition of the supremacy of the constitution over all orders of government and a political culture emphasising the fundamental importance of respect for constitutionality are therefore prerequisites for the effective operation of a federation.[46]

As I shall show in this study, Russia has adopted all of the key structural trappings of a federation and the Constitution does indeed enshrine many of the key principles of federalism and democracy, but in practice, neither the federal authorities nor the federal subjects have fully lived up to these federal principles. Moreover, in the absence of a democratic political culture in Russia there can be no real federalism. Russia is a federation without federalism.

Symmetrical and asymmetrical federations

Federations may be further sub-divided into symmetrical and asymmetrical federations. As we discuss below, the Russian Federation has one of the highest levels of asymmetry in the world. Stepan makes the interesting observation that all multinational democracies (with the exception of

Switzerland) are constitutionally asymmetrical, and all federations that are constitutionally symmetrical are mononational.[47]

The Russian Federation is the largest multinational country in the world incorporating 128 officially recognised ethnic groups and nationalities. As box 1.1 shows there are 89 federal subjects, 57 of which are territorially defined entities, and 32 of which are ethnically defined, including 21 ethnic republics and 11 national autonomies. Thus, it is hardly surprising that Russia is also constitutionally asymmetrical. However, as Smith notes, it is not asymmetry per se, but rather, the extent of Russia's asymmetry that marks it out from other federations.[48]

There are three types of asymmetry in federal states: (1) socio-economic; (2) political; and (3) constitutional. And whilst elements of the first two are present in all federations, this is not the case with the third type. Russia possesses high levels of asymmetry in all three areas.

Socio-economic asymmetry

Socio-economic asymmetry is, of course, present in every federation, referring as it does to such factors as, the number of federal subjects, their size, population, economic status, and wealth. Whilst it is impossible to avoid some degree of socio-economic asymmetry, where there are high levels of inequality between regions, tensions and even outright conflict between federal subjects may arise. Such tensions are liable to be particularly rife in those federations where one subject has a predominant position, such as was the case with the Russian Soviet Federative Socialist Republic (RSFSR) in the USSR, and is currently the case with Moscow city within the Russian Federation (see table 1.1 and chapter 5).

The 89 different components of the Russian federation vary widely in the size of their territories and populations. Thus for example the republic of Sakha has a territory which is 388 times the size of the republic of North Osetiya. The population of Moscow (8.5 million) is 443 times greater than that of the sparsely populated Yevenk Autonomous Okrug.[49] The thirty-two ethnically defined 'subjects' also vary considerably in their ethnic composition (see chapter 4).

Box 1.1   Federal structure of the Russian Federation

Ethnically defined subjects (32)	*Territorially, defined subjects (57)*
21 Ethnic republics	6 Krais
10 Autonomous okrugs	49 Oblasts
1 Autonomous oblast	2 Federal cities (Moscow and St Petersburg)

Table 1.1 Asymmetry of population of fully fledged constituent units in federal systems

	No. of units	Largest unit	% of federation	Smallest unit	% of federation	Population difference between largest and smallest units
Russia	89	Moscow	5.8	Yevenk AO	0.01	443.0
India	25	Uttar Pradesh	16.4	Sikkim	0.05	342.6
Switzerland	26	Zurich	17.2	Appenzell	0.20	84.2
Canada	10	Ontario	37.8	Prince Edward	0.46	81.5
United States	50	California	11.9	Wyoming	0.18	65.8
Spain	17	Andalucia	17.9	La Rioja	0.68	26.4
Germany	16	N. Rhine Wesphalia	21.8	Bremen	0.84	26.0
Australia	6	New South Wales	33.7	Tasmania	2.67	12.6
Malaysia	13	Perak	12.8	Perlis	1.06	12.0
Belgium	3	Flemish region	57.6	Brussels	9.52	6.0
Austria	9	Vienna	19.6	Burgenland	3.51	5.6
Pakistan	2	East Pakistan	54.0	West Pakistan	44.16	1.2

Source: Ronald Watts, *Comparing Federal Systems* (Montreal; Kingston; London; Ithaca: McGill-Queen's University Press, 2nd edn, 1999), p. 64 (amended version with my figures for Moscow and Yevenk added to the original table).

There are also considerable variations amongst the subjects of the federation in their levels of industrial development, per capita income and expenditure, average wages and other socio-economic indices such as the numbers of unemployed and the percentage of citizens living below the poverty line (see chapter 5). Thus, for example, in the mid-1990s the level of per capita income in the oil rich Yamala-Nenetsk Autonomous Okrug was 178 times greater than in the republic of Ingushetiya. The volume of gross regional products per capita in Yamalo-Nenetsk is 36 times higher than in Ingushetiya. In comparison, the volume of national income varies by only 1.3 times in the USA. And income per capita varies only 1.5 times in the German Lander.[50]

In 1999 unemployment varied across the Russian Federation from 5.6

per cent in Moscow city to 51.8 per cent in refugee flooded Ingushetiya. The disproportionate economic strength of Moscow city is graphically illustrated by the fact that tax payments from the city regularly comprises about one-third of the total tax revenues going to the federal budget (see chapter 5).

Political asymmetry

Political asymmetry refers to the inequalities of representation and political status which federal subjects gain either from their socio-economic status or which they may develop from more overtly political factors such as patron–client relations. Federal subjects which are economically powerful will usually also have more political status. This is clearly seen in Russia where rich donor subjects (regions which pay more taxes into the federal coffers than they receive back in income from the federal budget) have been able to make more political demands on the centre than the impoverished 'recipient regions' who depend on the centre for economic survival (see chapter 5).

Constitutional asymmetry

Constitutional asymmetry, which is not found in all federations, refers to 'constitutionally embedded differences between the legal status and prerogatives of different sub-units within the same federation'.[51] One example is the case of the Canadian Federation, where the province of Quebec has been granted exclusive powers over language, education and immigration policy, which for other Canadian provinces are the exclusive power of the federal government. Other countries with such constitutional asymmetries are: Belgium, India, Malaysia and Spain.[52]

Constitutional asymmetry is also a major feature of Russian federalism. Even although the Russian Constitution declares that all subjects are constitutionally equal (article 5) in fact the twenty-one ethnic republics have been granted far greater powers than the other subjects of the federation. Such constitutional inequalities have fundamentally undermined the authority of the Constitution and led to power struggles between the ethnic republics and the other territorially defined subjects. There have also been attempts by some regions to unilaterally elevate their status to that of the republics. Russian nationalists have pressed for Russia's dual ethno-territorial form of federalism to be abolished in favour of a new federation based solely on territorial criteria (see chapters 2 and 3). And bilateral treaties signed between some privileged subjects and the federal government has widened constitutional asymmetry even further (see chapter 3).

Origins and types of federations

The origins of federal states and the specific ways in which they were formed are of crucial importance in determining the 'character of the distribution of powers' in federations. Federal states may emerge 'from below' through the voluntary amalgamation of independent states (e.g., the US, Switzerland and Australia), or on the contrary they may result from top-down constitutional changes made to unitary states to prevent their collapse (India, Belgium, Spain). Stepan calls the former types which emerge from below as 'coming together federalism' and the latter top-down varieties as 'holding-together federalism'.[53] Stepan also defines a third category, 'putting together federalism', which entails 'a heavily coercive effort by a nondemocratic centralizing power to put together a multinational state, some of the components of which had previously been independent states'.[54] The USSR was a classic example of this type of federalism. Those federations which arise out of bottom-up bargaining ('revolutions from below') generally cede more powers to their federal subjects than those which come about as the result of top-down bargaining amongst elites ('revolutions from above'). As we discuss in chapter 3 Russia's Constitution was imposed from above. Yeltsin's 'Presidential' Constitution of December 1993 granted the federal government sweeping powers over all of the major aspects of the economy and polity (article 71), and whilst aticle 72 lists a number of concurrent powers to be shared between the federal government and the regions, no exclusive powers were given to the federal subjects. The regions were only granted residual powers (article 73).

Federalism and democracy

Scholars of federalism have also stressed the positive relationship between federalism and democratisation. For Watts, federalism is inherently democratic as it presumes, 'the voluntary consent of citizens in the constituent units, non-centralisation as a principle expressed through multiple centres of political decision making, open political bargaining ... the operation of checks and balances to avoid the concentration of political power, and a respect for constitutionalism'.[55]

For King, federation and democracy are but two sides of the same coin, and for true federalism to function relations between the centre and regions must be grounded in constitutional law and democratic representation. In particular, the constituent units of the federation must be incorporated into the decision-making procedures of the central government, on some 'constitutionally entrenched basis'.[56] King posits four essential attributes of a democratic federation:

(a) Its representation is preponderantly territorial; (b) and this territorial representation is characteristically secured on at least two sub-national levels; (c) the regional units are incorporated electorally, perhaps otherwise, into the decision procedure of the national centre; and (d) the incorporation of the regions into the decision procedure of the centre can only be altered by extraordinary constitutional measures, not for example by resort to a simple majority vote of the national legislature, or by autonomous decision of the national executive.[57]

Thus, King, Watts, Elazar and others signal what has tended to become accepted as the norm, 'only those states whose governments are subordinate to constitutional law and which therefore practice democracy are judged as true federations'.[58] We shall return to a discussion of federalism and democracy in the conclusion.

Outline of study

In this study I argue that Russia's weak and asymmetrical form of federalism has played a major role in thwarting the consolidation of democracy. Just as founding elections and the 'freezing' of party systems are highly important for the subsequent trajectory of transitional societies, I would argue that the 'freezing' of a particular set of federal (both constitutional and unconstitutional) relations over the period 1991 to 1993, has been of no less importance in shaping the present contours of Russia's semi-authoritarian form of governance. The result has been the formation of a highly asymmetrical federation with a weak federal state and powerful federal subjects. And political and economic relations have now superseded legal and constitutional procedures as the basis of centre–periphery relations.

Below I discuss the major factors which have been instrumental in bringing about the current chronic weakness of 'state capacity' at the federal level and which, in turn, have thwarted the development of democracy in Russia. I also argue that it is too simplistic to test the level of democratisation in Russia by merely studying national level politics. As we shall see (in chapters 6–7 and 9) there are many different kinds of political regime in operation in Russia ranging from quasi-democracies to 'delegative democracies'. In chapters 2 and 3 we examine the origins of Russia's ethno-territorial form of federalism and the development of constitutional and political asymmetry in the Yeltsin era. In chapter 4 we turn to a study of the ethnic make-up of the federation and the prospects for ethnic secessionism. Socio-economic asymmetry and fiscal federalism are discussed in chapter 5. In chapters 6–7 we turn to an examination of political asymmetry. Regional elections and the problems of developing a viable party system are discussed in chapter 6 and in chapter 7 we examine the struggle between executive and legislative bodies of power.

Chapter 8 provides an examination of Putin's radical reform of the federal system. Finally, in chapter 9 we examine the problems of consolidating democracy in Russia's regions and republics.

Notes

1 D. Ch. Shin, 'On the third wave of democratisation: a synthesis and evaluation of recent theory and research', *World Politics*, 47 (October, 1994), 136.
2 For excellent reviews of this literature see, A. Hadenius, *Democracy and Development* (Oxford: Oxford University Press, 1992); S. M. Lipset, 'The social requisites of democracy revisited', *American Sociological Review* (1994), 59; G. L. Munck, 'Democratic transitions in comparative perspective', Review Article, *Comparative Politics* (April 1994); K. L. Remmer, 'New theoretical perspectives on democratisation', Review Article, *Comparative Politics* (October 1995), 103–22; D. Ch. Shin, 'On the third wave of democratisation: a synthesis and evaluation of recent theory and research', *World Politics*, 47 (October 1994), 135–70; G. Sorensen, *Democracy and Democratisation* (Boulder: Westview Press, 1993).
3 D. Rueschemeyer, E. H. Stephens and J. D. Stephens, Capitalist *Development and Democracy* (Chicago: University of Chicago Press, 1992).
4 S. Huntington, *The Third Wave: Democratisation in the Late Twentieth Century* (Norman: University of Oklahoma Press, 1991); R. Putnam, *Making Democracy Work: Civic Traditions in Modern Italy* (Princeton: Princeton University Press, 1993).
5 T. A. Koelbe, 'The new institutionalism in political science and sociology', *Comparative Politics* (January 1995), 231–43; D. C. North, *Institutions, Institutional Change and Economic Performance* (Cambridge: Cambridge University Press, 1990); J. March and J. Olson, *Rediscovering Institutions: The Organisational Basis of Politics* (New York: The Free Press, 1989); S. Steinmo, K. Thelen and F. Longstreth (eds), *Structuring Politics: Historical Institutionalism in Comparative Analysis* (New York: Cambridge University Press, 1992); B. Guy Peters, *Institutional Theory in Political Science* (London: Cassell, 1999).
6 A. Lijphart, *Electoral Systems and Party Systems* (Oxford: Oxford University Press, 1994).
7 J. J. Linz, 'The perils of presidentialism', *Journal of Democracy*, 1 (Winter 1990); J. J. Linz and A. Valenzuela (eds), *The Failure of Presidential Democracy: Comparative Perspectives* (Baltimore: Johns Hopkins University Press, 1994); S. Mainwaring, 'Presidentialism, multipartism, and democracy', *Comparative Political Studies*, 26:2 (1993), 198–228; M. Shugart and J. M. Carey, *Presidents and Assemblies* (Cambridge: Cambridge University Press, 1992); A. Stepan and C. Skach 'Constitutional frameworks and democratic consolidation: parliamentarianism versus presidentialism', *World Politics*, 46 (1994), 1–22.
8 G. Sartori, *Parties and Party Systems: A Framework for Analysis* (Cambridge: Cambridge University Press, 1976); A. Ware, *Political Parties and Party Systems* (Oxford: Oxford University Press, 1996).
9 D. Rustow, 'Transitions to democracy: toward a dynamic model', *Comparative Politics*, 2:3 (1970).

10 D. Held, *Democracy and the Global Order* (Cambridge: Polity, 1995); G. Pridham, G., Herring and E., Sanford, *The International Dimension of Democratisation in Eastern Europe* (London: Leicester University Press, 1994).

11 T. L. Karl and P. C. Schmitter, 'Modes of transition in Latin America, Southern and Eastern Europe', *International Social Science Journal*, 128 (1991), 269–84; S. Mainwaring, G. O'Donnell and S. J. Valenzuela (eds), *Issues in Democratic Consolidation* (Notre Dame, Indiana: University of Notre Dame Press, 1986).

12 J. Higley and G. Lengyel, *Elites after State Socialism: Theories and Analysis* (Lanham, Boulder, New York, Oxford: Rowman and Littlefield, 2000); J. Higley and R. Gunther (eds), *Elites and Democratic Consolidation in Latin America and Southern Europe* (Cambridge: Cambridge University Press, 1992); J. Higley, J. Pakulski and W. Wesolowski, *Postcommunist Elites and Democracy in Eastern Europe* (Houndmills, Basingstoke: Macmillan, 1998); J. Kullberg, J. Higley and J. Pakulski, 'Elites, institutions and democratisation in Russia and Eastern Europe', in G. Gill (ed.), *Elites and Leadership in Russian Politics* (New York: St Martin's Press, 1988); D. Lane and C. Ross, *From Communism to Capitalism: Ruling Elites From Gorbachev to Yeltsin* (New York: St Martin's Press, 1999).

13 Higley and Gunther, *Elites and Democratic Consolidation*.

14 Lane and Ross, *From Communism to Capitalism*.

15 J. J. Linz and A. Stepan, *Problems of Democratic Transition and Consolidation* (Baltimore: Johns Hopkins University Press, 1996); J. J. Linz and A. Stepan, 'Toward consolidated democracies', *Journal of Democracy*, 7:2 (1996), 14–33; G. O'Donnell, 'Illusions about consolidation', *Journal of Democracy*, 7:2 (April 1996), 34–51; A. Schedler, 'What is democratic consolidation', *Journal of Democracy*, 9:2 (1998), 91–107.

16 D. Ch. Shin, 'On the third wave'; G. Di Palma, *To Craft Democracies: An Essay on Democratic Transitions* (Berkley: University of California Press, 1990).

17 With the notable exceptions of the excellent studies by Alfred Stepan. See, A. Stepan, 'Russian federalism in comparative perspective', *Post-Soviet Affairs*, 16:2 (2000); and also his, 'federalism and democracy: beyond the U.S. model', *Journal of Democracy*, 10:4 (October, 1999).

18 R. A. Dahl, *Polyarchy: Participation and Opposition* (New Haven: Yale University Press, 1971), p. 3. Cited in Sorenson, *Democracy and Democratisation*, p. 12.

19 L. Diamond, J. J. Linz and S. M. Lipset (eds), *Democracy in Developing Countries: Volume 4: Latin America* (Boulder: Lynne Rienner, 1989), p. xvi.

20 Sorenson, *Democracy and Democratisation*, p. 12.

21 O'Donnell, 'Illusions about consolidation', 35.

22 *Ibid.*, 36.

23 D. Beetham, *Democracy and Human Rights* (Cambridge: Polity Press, 1999), pp. 154–5.

24 *Ibid.*

25 A. Schedler, 'What is democratic consolidation?', *Journal of Democracy*, 9:2 (April 1998), 91.

26 Beetham, *Democracy and Human Rights*, pp. 69–70.

27 G. O'Donnell, 'Challenges to democratisation in Brazil', *World Policy Journal*, 5 (Spring 1998), 257. Quoted in Shin, 'On the third wave', 145.

28 Linz and Stepan, 'Toward consolidated democracies', 15.

29 *Ibid.*, 71.

30 Schedler, 'What is democratic consolidation?', 101.
31 S. J. Valenzuela in, S. Mainwaring, G. O'Donnell and S. J. Valenzuela (eds), *Issues in Democratic Consolidation* (Indiana: University of Notre Dame Press, 1992), p. 70, quoted in Shin, 'On the third wave', 145.
32 Huntington, *The Third Wave*, p. 263.
33 Linz and Stepan, 'Toward consolidated democracies', 17.
34 *Ibid.*
35 Z. Gitelman 'The democratisation of Russia in comparative perspective', in S. White, A. Pravda and Z. Gitelman (eds), *Developments in Russian Politics – 4* (Basingstoke: Macmillan, 1999).
36 D. J. Elazar, *Exploring Federalism* (Tuscaloosa and London: The University of Alabama Press, 1987), p. 6.
37 G. Smith, *Federalism: The Multiethnic Challenge* (London, New York: Longman, 1995), p. 1.
38 R. Watts, *Comparing Federal Systems* (Montreal and Kingston: McGill-Queen's University Press, 2nd edn, 1999), p. 6.
39 *Ibid.*, p. 7.
40 Watts, *Comparing Federal Systems*; A. Lijphart, *Patterns of Democracy: Government Forms and Performance in Thirty-Six Countries* (New Haven and London: Yale University Press, 1999), D. Elazar, *Exploring Federalism*; F. Requejo, 'National pluralism and federalism: four potential scenarios for Spanish plurinational democracy', *Perspectives on European Politics and Society* 2:2 (2001); D. Elazar, *Federal Systems of the World: A Handbook of Federal, Confederal and Autonomy Arrangements* (Harlow: Longman, 1991).
41 D. Kempton also adds five 'beneficial conditions for the maintenance of federalism': (1) symmetry among the components, (2) decentralised federal political parties, (3) a noncentralised bureaucracy, (4) democracy and (5) economic coordination. See, D. Kempton, 'Russian federalism: continuing myth or political salvation', *Demokratizatsiya*, 9:2 (Spring 2001), 231.
42 Elazar, *Exploring Federalism*, pp. 34, 35–7.
43 Smith, *Federalism: The Multi-Ethnic*, p. 7.
44 Elazar, *Exploring Federalism*, p. 35.
45 *Ibid.*, p. 67.
46 Watts, *Comparing Federal Systems*, p. 99.
47 *Ibid.*, p. 31.
48 G. Smith, *The Post-Soviet States: Mapping The Politics of Transition* (London, Sydney, Auckland: Arnold, 1999), p. 140.
49 A. N. Lebedev, *Status Sub'ekta Rossiiskoi Federatsii* (Moscow: Institute of State and Law, 1999), p. 24.
50 G. Marchenko, 'Nuzhno li perekraivat' Rossiyu?', in Olga Sidorovoch (ed.), *Rossiiskii Konstitutsionalism: Politicheskii Rezhim v Regional'nom Kontekste: Sbornik Dokladov* (Moscow: MONF, 2000), pp. 72–3.
51 A. Stepan, 'Russian federalism in comparative perspective', *Post-Soviet Affairs*, 16:2 (2000), 142.
52 Watts, *Comparing Federal Systems*, p. 68.
53 A. Stepan, 'Federalism and democracy: beyond the U.S. model', *Journal of Democracy*, 10:4 (October, 1999), 22–3.
54 *Ibid.*, 23.

55 *Ibid.*, 14.
56 M. Burgess and A. G. Gagnon (eds), *Comparative Federalism and Federation* (New York, London, Harvester Wheatsheaf: 1993), p. 93.
57 P. King, 'Federation and representation', in Burgess and Gagnon, *Comparative Federalism*, p. 94.
58 Smith, *Federalism: The Multi-Ethnic Challenge*, p. 8.

2

The Soviet legacy and
Russian federalism, 1991–93

Russian federalism and the Soviet legacy

According to the 1977 Constitution, 'the Union of Soviet Socialist Republics' was a 'unified, federal, multinational state formed on the principle of socialist federalism'. The federation, which was established according to the dual principles of ethnicity and territory, encompassed fifteen *ethnically* defined union republics, twenty autonomous republics, eight autonomous oblasts, ten autonomous okrugs, and 159 *territorially* based regions.

But if we adopt the definition of a federation given by Watts in chapter 1, then clearly the USSR was not an authentic federation. For whilst the Constitution proclaimed the republics' rights of sovereignty (article 76), and secession (article 72), the right to enter into treaties with foreign powers (article 80), and local control over economic developments (article 77), such rights were heavily qualified in practice, by the provisions of other articles, which made a mockery of the republic's sovereign powers.[1] And, in any case, whilst the state was supposedly based on federal principles, the party, which declared itself to be 'the leading and guiding force in society', was a unitary body. Moreover, party and state bodies operated under the principle of 'democratic centralism', whereby each administrative level was subordinate to the level above it, and centralised control from Moscow.

In 1989 Gorbachev publicly admitted that the republics' rights of sovereignty were largely formal in nature, 'Up to now', he noted, 'our state has existed as a centralized and unitary state and none of us has yet the experience of living in a federation'.[2]

This is not to say that the federal subjects in the USSR were totally powerless and subservient to the central authorities or that nationalist demands had been quelled when Gorbachev took over the reins of power in 1985. For paradoxically, the very policies which the communists had used to placate nationalism ended up giving it succour. As Bialer notes, the concept and reality of Soviet federalism contained a dangerous dualism: 'On the one hand it granted to formed nations cultural autonomy, territorial integrity, and symbols of statehood; on the other hand it insisted on the supremacy of the central state and government and strove for a state of affairs where national separateness and ethnic identity would ultimately wither away'.[3]

The USSR's adoption of an 'ethno-territorial' form of federalism was originally designed as a temporary measure, adopted to entice the non-Russian nationalities to join the union. But as Gleason notes, such a principle entailed a recognition of the 'national statehood' of the constituent republics.[4] Under Soviet federalism, 'ethnicity was institutionalised both on the individual and on group levels. On the individual level, nationality was registered on each person's internal passport . . . At the group level, the ethno-territorial basis of political organization established firm links between national groups, their territories, and their political administrations'.[5]

In addition, according to Stalin's formula 'national in form, socialist in content', the nations of the Soviet Union were supposed to develop to the point where all national groups would be equal. But as Zwick notes: 'In its attempt to neutralize tribal, ethnic and religious identifications and replace them with socialist norms, the Soviet regime awakened national feelings among its population, and then, by promising to equalize all nations, made the people acutely aware of the differences that had always existed between Russians and non-Russians'.[6]

Soviet nationality policies even promoted nation building for national communities which had 'not yet achieved ethnic awakening in the pre-revolutionary period'.[7] And far from withering away, the administrative organs of the republics gradually developed a sense of 'proprietary bureaucratic self-interest'.[8]

Federalism and nationalism under Gorbachev

Gorbachev's policies of perestroika, glasnost and democratisation opened up the nationalities and federal question to nationwide debate. Gorbachev's dilemma was how to simultaneously reform the Soviet economy and polity, whilst maintaining the unity of the communist party and the state. In the end, Gorbachev failed on all counts. His acknowledgement of the legitimate demands of the republics for greater economic and political autonomy, and his proposals for a revived 'Union of Soviet Sovereign States' came far too late to save the Union. The rise of Russian nationalism coupled with the collapse of the communist party over the period 1990 to 1991 finally propelled the Soviet Union into the abyss.

Gorbachev's reluctant acceptance of the need for an asymmetrical form of Soviet federalism, mixing confederal relations for some (the three Baltic republics, Georgia, Moldova and Armenia) with varying degrees of federal relations with the others, stemmed from a genuine belief on his part in the economic benefits to be gained in preserving the Union. Gorbachev repeatedly stressed the interdependent nature of the Soviet economic system and the fact that the republics 'rely on a division of labour in a highly institutionalised, integrated national economic complex; depend on the central authorities for resource allocations, investments, subsidies and grants-in-aid; and enjoy the diplomatic, economic and military advantages that accrue to a superpower. To cut such ties would mean to dissect a living body'.[9]

But economic decentralisation soon led to calls for political decentralisation. And once the CPSU began to fragment along political and ethnic lines there was nothing left to hold the Union together. Elections for republican parliaments in 1990 inflicted heavy defeats on the communist party candidates in the majority of the republics. In April 1990 Yeltsin gained the chair of the Russian (RSFSR) parliament and in June Russia made its historic declaration of sovereignty, whereby it proclaimed: 'full power of the RSFSR in decisions on all questions of state and public life . . . the priority of the RSFSR's Constitution and Laws on the entire territory of the RSFSR; the exclusive right of the people to ownership, use and disposal of the national riches of Russia, and the right of free exit from the USSR'.[10]

The Russian government under Yeltsin's leadership now began to champion the rights of other republics. And between 'June and October [1990], Uzbekistan, Moldova, Ukraine, Belorussia, Turkmenistan, Tajikistan and Kazakhstan declared their sovereignty, while Armenia . . . took the further step of declaring its independence'.[11] Yeltsin also entered into negotiations with these 'sovereign republics', and even signed a number of bilateral treaties with them.

Over the autumn–winter period 1990–91 Gorbachev seemed to abandon the 'democratic' camp. It appeared as if he was determined to save the Union at all costs. But after the failure of Soviet OMON troops to set up 'national salvation fronts' in the Baltics in January 1991, Gorbachev tried another tack, seeking instead to gain approval for his Union Treaty through a nationwide referendum. But the results of the referendum, held in March 1991, was inconclusive, and at best represented a pyrrhic victory for Gorbachev, for although 76.4 per cent of those participating supported 'a renewed federation of equal sovereign republics', six of the fifteen republics refused to participate in the ballot (Estonia, Latvia, Lithuania, Armenia, Georgia and Moldova).[12] As Lapidus notes:

> Faced with the choice between the hard liner's pressure to maintain the Soviet Union through force by imposing a new Union Treaty from above and the democratic demands to concede real sovereignty to the republics,

Gorbachev struck a deal with Yeltsin and the leaders of those nine republics which participated in the March 1991 referendum.[13]

According to the provisions of this so-called 9 + 1 agreement, signed on April 23, 1991, the three Baltic republics, Armenia, Georgia, and Moldova were to be allowed to secede from the USSR and a new fourth version of the Union Treaty was to be concluded in the summer. As John Miller notes, 'Implicit in this was recognition by the Union administration of the sovereignty of the Union-Republics; and that the federation inaugurated by the Union Treaty should be a very weak one in which the Centre would retain only a minimum of power'.[14]

It was the plans to sign the Union Treaty on August 20, 1991, which sparked off the attempted coup. The failure of the coup, in turn, accelerated the demise of the USSR, leading to its total collapse by December.

As we noted above, Russia's declaration of Sovereignty in June 1990 was a major catalyst in the collapse of the USSR. But the RSFSR was itself a quasi-federation comprising sixteen ethnically defined autonomous soviet socialist republics (ASSRs), ten national okrugs (districts) and five autonomous oblasts. And seven other such 'autonomies' were trapped inside a further four Soviet republics.[15] If Russia could declare its sovereignty, then why should the autonomous republics within Russia not follow suit? After all, some of these ASSRs (e.g., Tatar and Bashkir) were actually larger and more populous than some of the Soviet republics (e.g., Estonia, Latvia, Moldova). Whilst Gorbachev's polices had led to the rise of nationalism in the USSR, Yeltsin's policies were in danger of leading to a similar rise of national sentiment in the RSFSR. As, Aleksandr Tsipko warned:

> the stronger the striving of the RSFSR to free itself from the centre, the stronger will be the desire of the autonomous formations to free themselves from Yeltsin. And in their own way they are right. The relations of Russia to the autonomies is constructed on the same principle as that of the Union to the RSFSR.[16]

Over the period 1990–91 the ASSRs became embroiled in the wider struggle between Yeltsin and Gorbachev. In an attempt to weaken Russia's role in the negotiations over the Union Treaty, Gorbachev began to espouse the need to raise the status of the autonomies. In the All-Union Law, 'On the Delimitation of Powers between the USSR and the Subjects of the Federation' of April 26, 1990, the autonomous republics, were described as 'subjects of the federation' thus recognising their right to equal representation with the union republics, in the negotiations over the Union treaty.[17] In reply, Yeltsin, on a nationwide tour of the Russian Federation in August 1990, urged the ASSRs to 'take as much sovereignty as they could swallow'. Furthermore, he proclaimed, 'if this meant full independence from Russia 'your decision will be final'.[18] And it was not long before the ASSRs took Yeltsin at his word, and unilaterally declared their sovereignty. On August 30, 1990, Tatarstan declared itself the sixteenth republic of the USSR,[19] and by the end of the year almost every other autonomy had likewise declared its independence from its host union republic (see table 2.1).

On December 15, 1990 the Russian Congress of People's Deputies adopted a series of amendments to the RSFSR Constitution, which raised the status of its sixteen ASSRs to constituent republics of the Russian Federation. In addition, in July 1991, the Russian Supreme Soviet adopted a number of decrees, which, 'elevated the status of four of Russia's autonomous oblasts, Adygeya, Gornii Altai, Karachaevo-Cherkessiya and Khakasiya (with the exception of the Jewish autonomous oblast in Siberia), to constituent republics of the federation'.[20] This brought the total number of ethnic republics within Russia to twenty.

Table 2.1 Dates of declarations of sovereignty

Republic	Date of declaration of sovereignty
North Osetiya- Alaniya	July 20, 1990
Kareliya	August 9, 1990
Khakassiya	August 15, 1990
Komi	August 29, 1990
Tatarstan	August 30, 1990
Udmurtiya	September 20, 1990
Sakha (Yakutiya)	September 27, 1990
Buryatiya	October 8, 1990
Bashkortostan	October 11, 1990
Kalmykiya	October 18, 1990
Marii El	October 22, 1990
Chuvashiya	October 24, 1990
Gorno-Altai	October 25, 1990
Tuva	November 1, 1990
Karachai- Cherkessiya	November 17, 1990
Checheno- Ingushetiya	November 27, 1990
Mordova	December 8, 1990
Kabardino-Balkariya	January 31, 1991
Dagestan	May 15, 1991
Adygeya	July 2, 1991

Source: Jeff Kahn, 'The parade of sovereignties: establishing the vocabulary of the new Russian federalism', *Post-Soviet Affairs*, 16:1 (2000), 62.

After the collapse of the USSR, the number of republics within Russia increased to twenty-one, when in the summer of 1992 the Checheno-Ingush Republic was separated into Chechen and Ingush republics. Thus, the Soviet Union's hybrid ethno-territorial principal of federalism was bequeathed to Russia.

The foundations of Russia's constitutional institutions

The founding constitutional arrangements of any regime must surely be considered as one of the most important factors determining the future trajectory of the state. The tragedy for Russian federalism and Russian democracy is the fact that: (1) The collapse of communism in the USSR was at best an incomplete 'revolution' which largely witnessed the replacement of one set of Soviet leaders headed by Gorbachev, by another set of Russian elites under Yeltsin. Whilst it could be argued that a circulation of elites within the Russian state did slowly take place over the period 1991–93, only a partial circulation occurred in the regions and republics where 'nomenklatura continuity' has been the norm rather than the exception.[21] (2) A new alliance of regional political and economic elites soon took hold as Russia embarked on a massive privatisation programme in 1992–93. These groups were the first to be given access to the rich pickings of the regional 'privatisation troughs'. Both of these groups had a vested interest in demanding economic and political sovereignty for their territories, and it was not long before they took advantage of the vacuum of power in the centre to proclaim their rights of control and/or ownership over the vast natural resources and wealth of their regions. Thus, for example, in 1991 almost 80 per cent of industrial output in Tatarstan was produced by enterprises under the command of central economic bodies but by 1993, 70 per cent of these enterprises had been transferred to Tatarstan's own jurisdiction.[22]

Tragically, for Russia, the founding political and economic institutions in the regions, were forged not by newly elected democrats but rather by authoritarian leaders who emerged out of the old Soviet nomenklatura. Russia's post-communist elites, particularly in the ethnic republics, soon turned to nationalism and separatist demands, rather than democracy, to legitimate their rule. Wielding the sword of 'sovereignty' local elites were able to capture control over the major political and economic institutions in the localities. Thus, in a short space of time many of Russia's republics were headed by authoritarian regimes of one sort or another.

Over the period October 1991–October 1993 the federal authorities in Moscow were engaged in a 'civil war' which pitted the Russian presidency and government against the Russian parliament. For two years the central powers in Moscow were paralysed by this all-encompassing battle. The conflict took many forms but in essence it centred around the struggle over the ratification of a new constitution. The parliamentarians fought for a parliamentary constitution which would give them sweeping powers and relegate the president to a ceremonial figurehead. The president on the other hand sought to create a presidential constitution with a weak parliament and a powerful executive presidency. Numerous presidential and parliamentary drafts of the constitution were drawn up during this time, but it was only after the dissolution of parliament in September 1993 that Yeltsin was able to push ahead with his presidential constitution which was eventually ratified in December 1993 (see below).

During this period of weak central power the republics became especially vociferous in their demands for national autonomy. In the absence of a new federal Constitution many of the ethnic republics unilaterally granted themselves a whole series of rights and privileges. The republics and regions were also wooed by representatives of both the parliament and president, who promised the regions ever greater degrees of autonomy. Making the best of the political impasse in Moscow, regional elites scored a great victory when Yeltsin signed the 1992 Federal Treaty. The Treaty granted both the republics and regions greater powers over their own affairs, and in particular gave the ethnic republics considerable control over their natural resources; the rights of secession, citizenship and sovereignty.

Thus, the founding constitutional arrangements and concomitant political institutions, which would determine the future path of Russian federalism, were forged during a period of weak and divided federal authority (1991–93) and crucially, before the ratification of the Russian Constitution of December 1993.

The Federal Treaty

The Federal Treaty of March 31, 1992 created an 'asymmetrical federation' with the rights granted to the ethnic republics far outweighing those given to the territorially based regions.[23] For some scholars the treaty was a necessary compromise to save the Union whilst others argue that it fundamentally weakened federalism in Russia by constitutionally sanctioning an asymmetrical federal state with three types of legal subject, each possessing different rights and powers; national–state formations (sovereign republics); administrative–territorial formations (krais, oblasts, and the cities of Mocow and St Petersburg); and national–territorial formations (the autonomous oblast and autonomous okrugs). The Federal Treaty also recognised three distinct areas of competence; federal, joint federal–regional and regional.

The republics were recognized as sovereign states with rights of national self-determination territorial integrity, and by implication the right to secede from the Union. They were awarded citizenship rights and ownership of their land and natural resources. The republics were also granted their own constitutions and powers to elect their own executive heads. In addition they were free to sign bilateral treaties with foreign countries and to engage in foreign economic relations at their own discretion without the need even to consult the centre.[24] The regions were given no such rights of ownership, nor were they allowed such freedom to engage in international relations. And instead of constitutions, the regions were only permitted to draw up local charters, and their top executives were to be appointed from above.

Bashkortostan and Sakha signed the Federal Treaty only after they were granted special concessions, including special dispensions with regard to their contributions to the federal budget. Bashkortostan was also granted the additional right to create its own independent legal system.[25] Two republics, Tatarstan and Chechnya, refused to sign the treaty. Tatarstan later ratified its own republican constitution in November 1992 which (in article 61) affirmed that the republic was, 'a sovereign state and a subject of international law, *associated* with the Russian Federation'. Only Chechnya went so far as to declare its outright independence, a move which eventually led to the invasion of Russian troops into the republic in 1994, and again in 1999.

But it was not long before this two-class federal system came under attack from the regions, which demanded parity with the ethnic republics. As Lapidus and Walker note: 'Why should the inhabitants of Kareliya, where the Karelians make up only 10 per cent of the population and Russians almost 75 per cent, enjoy special economic privileges simply because they live in a region arbitrarily designated an autonomous area'?[26]

In protest, regional authorities also began to withhold their tax revenues refusing to give them up to the federal authorities. As Sakwa observes, 'In 1993, for example, Moscow collected only forty per cent of the tax revenues due to it from the regions and republics, and over two dozen refused to pay the centre their federal tax obligations'.[27] And in August 1993 the heads of a number of regions demanded that the privileges granted to the republics in the Federal Treaty be rescinded.

Indeed, a number of regions were so incensed by their second-class positions within the federation that they unilaterally elevated their status to that of republics. Thus, for example, in a referendum held in April 1993, 84 per cent of the population of Sverdlovsk Oblast supported the creation of the Urals Republic.[28] And it was not long before further regions followed suit. Thus, for example, regions in European Russia created the Pomor Republic centred in Arkhangelsk, the Central Russian Republic, made up of eleven regions with its capital in Orel, and the Leningrad Republic in St Petersburg. A Southern Urals republic was formed in Chelyabinsk, and a Siberian republic in Irkutsk. And in the Far East, the Maritime Republic was created in Vladivostok.[29] Other regions whilst not going so far as to declare themselves republics, unilaterally elevated their constitutional status. Thus, for example, Voronezh Oblast declared that the region was henceforth, an 'independent participant in international and foreign-economic relations'. Furthermore it continued, 'Federal bodies of state power of the Russian Federation may not promulgate legal acts that fall within the jurisdiction of the regional bodies of power'.[30]

Many of these issues were discussed at a special constitutional conference which Yeltsin eventually was persuaded to convene in the summer of 1993. Ostensibly the conference was devoted to the task of making peace with the parliament and the drawing up a draft constitution which would bring together elements of the rival parliamentary and presidential constitutions. However, it was clear from the start that this was not an open conference with delegates democratically elected from below, rather it was a top-down organisation whose membership was chosen from above. The proceedings were dominated by Yeltsin, who had no intention of compromising on his 'presidential version' of the constitution.

Nonetheless, during the conference Tatarstan took the lead in pushing for more autonomy for the ethnic republics insisting that Russian federalism should be 'treaty based' rather than 'constitutional'. In particular, the republics demanded:

1 the right of all of Russia's people's to self-determination,
2 recognition of themselves as sovereign states possessing full state (legislative, executive and judicial) power on their territory, except for powers that were voluntarily transferred to the jurisdiction of the Russian Federation,
3 the right to enter into direct relations with other states and to exchange diplomatic and consular missions,
4 acknowledgement that federal principles of legislation would enter into force on their territories only after they were ratified by local bodies of power, and
5 recognition of their right to secede from the Russian Federation without any restraint.[31]

The regions in return continued to press for their status to be elevated to that of the republics and for the special privileges granted to the republics to be abolished. As Vyachislav Novikov (chair of the Krasnoyarsk Krai Soviet (assembly) and head of the Association of Regional Soviets) noted, the proposed definition of republics as sovereign states was 'a bomb under Russia's future' and but the first step on the path to the creation of 'a Russian confederation'.[32]

But the president, buoyed up by the surprise show of support given to his administration in the April 1993 referendum, was in no mood for compromise with either the parliament or the ethnic republics. Indeed, the president now sought to reverse the powers which he had relinquished to the regions in the Federal Treaty. Realising which way the wind was blowing, a number of the republics walked out of the conference. But this only made it easier for Yeltsin to call for full economic and political equality to be granted to all subjects of the federation and the abolition of special rights for the ethnic subects.[33]

The work of the constitutional conference continued to operate after Yeltsin's violent dissolution of the Russian Parliament in October 1993. But it was no longer needed by the president. As Sergei Pakhomenko noted: 'The Parliament is no more – and the conference is now like the unfortunate chicken whose chopped-off head is clutched in the fist of the cook while its body continues to run around the yard in confusion for a time'.[34]

At the meeting of the Public Chamber (one of the smaller bodies set up at the conference), on October 23, it was recommended that all references to the sovereignty of the republics should be deleted from the draft constitution as should the articles which guaranteed republican citizenship. Finally, it was recommended that the Federal Treaty was to be removed from the constitution. Yeltsin's draft constitution (the fourth version) was finally published on November 10, 1993 and as discussed in chapter 3, the constitution was finally ratified on December 17, 1993.[35]

Notes

1 See, in particular, articles 73 and 134.
2 'Draft nationalities policy of the party under present conditions', adopted by the CPSU Central Committee Plenum, September 20, 1989, quoted in S. Kux, 'Soviet Federalism', *Problems of Communism* (March–April, 1990), 2.
3 S. Bialer, *Stalin's Successors: Leadership, Stability and Change in the Soviet Union* (Cambridge: Cambridge University Press: 1980), pp. 210–11.
4 G. Gleason, *Federalism and Nationalism: The Struggle for Republican Rights in the USSR* (Boulder; San Francisco; Oxford: Westview Press, 1990), p. 3.
5 P. Goldman, G. Lapidus and V. Zaslavasky, 'Introduction: Soviet federalism – its origins, evolution and demise', in G. Lapidus, V. Zaslavsky and P. Goldman (eds), *From Union to Commonwealth: Nationalism and Separatism in the Soviet Republics* (Cambridge: Cambridge University Press, 1992), p. 2.
6 P. R. Zwick, 'Soviet nationality policy: social, economic, and political aspects', in G. Smith (ed.), *Public Policy and Administration in the Soviet Union* (New York: Praeger, 1980), p. 149.
7 Lapidus, Goldman and Zaslavsky, 'Introduction', p. 2.
8 Gleason, *Federalism and Nationalism*, p. 3.
9 Kux, 'Soviet federalism', pp. 6–7.

10 See articles 5 and 7 of the Soviet Constitution.
11 A. Brown, *The Gorbachev Factor* (Oxford; New York: Oxford University Press, 1997), p. 287.
12 *Ibid.*, p. 256.
13 Goldman, Lapidus, Zaslavsky, 'Introduction', p. 15.
14 J. Miller, *Mikhail Gorbachev and the End of Soviet Power*, (New York: St Martin's Press, 1993), p. 175.
15 There were two ASSRs in Georgia and one each, in Azerbaijan and Uzbekistan. There was also one autonomous region in the republics of Azerbaijan, Georgia and Tadjikistan.
16 J. B. Dunlop, *The Rise of Russia and the Fall of the Soviet Empire* (Princeton University Press, 1993), p. 64.
17 A. Sheehy, 'Russia's republics: a threat to its territorial integrity?', *Radio Free Europe/Radio Liberty Research Report*, 2:20 (14 May 1993), 36.
18 Dunlop, *The Rise of Russia*, p. 62.
19 M. Filippov and O. Shevtsov, 'Asymmetric bilateral bargaining in the new Russian Federation: a path dependence explanation', *Communist and Post-Communist Studies*, 32 (1999), 70.
20 J. T. Ishiyama, 'The Russian proto-parties and the national republics', *Communist and Post-Communist Studies*, 29: 4 (1996), 397.
21 See D. Lane and C. Ross, *From Communism to Capitalism: Ruling Elites from Gorbachev to Yeltsin*, (New York: St Martin's Press, 1999).
22 A. Zverev, 'Qualified sovereignty: the Tatarstan model for resolving conflicting loyalities', in M. Waller, B. Coppieters and A. Malashenko (eds), *Conflicting Loyalties and the State in Post-Soviet Russia and Eurasia* (London: Frank Cass, 1998), p. 137.
23 There were actually three federal treaties, with separate agreements for the republics, the autonomies and the regions. The treaties were ratified by the Sixth Session of the Russian Congress of People's Deputies on 10 April 1992.
24 A. F. Fedorov, *Rossiiskii Federalizm: Istoricheskii Opyt i Sovremennost'* (Moscow: Nauchnya Kniga, 1997), p. 97.
25 *Ibid.*
26 G. W. Lapidus and E. W. Walker, 'Nationalism, regionalism, and federalism: center–periphery relations in post-communist Russia', in G. W. Lapidus (ed.), *The New Russia: Troubled Transformation*, (Boulder, Colorado: Westview Press, 1995), p. 96.
27 Richard Sakwa, *Russian Politics and Society* (London and New York: Routledge, 2nd edn, 1996), p. 188.
28 On October 23, 1993 Sverdlovsk Oblast adopted the Constitution of the Urals Republic. However, President Yeltsin on November 9, 1993 suspended the activities of the Soviet and declared the formation of the republic unconstitutional. See V. Shlapentokh, R. Levita and M. Loiberg, *From Submission to Rebellion: The Provinces Versus the Centre in Russia* (Boulder, Colorado: Westview Press, 1998), pp. 109–10.
29 *Ibid.*, p. 109.
30 The declaration by the oblast Soviet was made on September 3, 1993.
31 *Current Digest of the Post Soviet Press* (hereafter, *CDPSP*), 45:23 (1993), p. 12, and also Shlapentokh, Levita and Loiberg, *From Submission to Rebellion*, p. 106.

32 A. Tarasov, 'A bomb under Russia's future', *Izvestiya* (June 24, 1993), pp. 1–2, translated in *CDPSP*, 45:25 (1993), p. 4.
33 Fedorov, *Rossiiskii Federalizm*, p. 103.
34 S. Parkhomenko, *Sevodnya* (October 26, 1993), p. 1, translated in the *CDPSP*, 45:43 (1993), p. 7.
35 L. Shevtsova, *Yeltsin's Russia: Myths and Realities* (Washington, DC: Carnegie, 1999), p. 93.

3

Federalism and constitutional asymmetry

As Taras notes, 'Establishing a constitutional framework that sets out the political rules of the game and the institutions that allocate values in society is the most daunting challenge for a new regime'.[1] For Maravall and di Tella, two features of constitutionalism are particularly important. First, constitutions seek to define, 'the future substance as well as the form of politics by placing certain political, social and economic, rights beyond the reach of democratic uncertainty'. And second, 'to make such assurances credible, constitutions bind not just their drafters, but future generations'.[2]

We also need to distinguish between 'those constitutions that result from a process of extensive compromise and widespread acceptance', and those 'that are enacted by a victorious majority over the objection of minorities'.[3] In the former we are far more likely to achieve stable and long lasting constitutions, whilst in the latter case, unstable and short lived constitutions are the norm.

In Russia, as we have seen, there was little evidence of consensus and compromise in the drafting of its Constitution. Instead, the foundations of Russian constitutionalism were forged out of conflict and coercion, and the president's Constitution was largely imposed on a weak and highly divided society, still reeling from the shock of the violent dissolution of the Russian parliament. Moreover, as Stepan notes, 'the parliament never discussed the version of the constitution that was submitted to the voters for ratification, and thus the chance for constitution-making to play a focal role in building consensus for democratic state power was lost'.[4]

The Russian constitution

The 1992 victory of the republics over the federal authorities appeared to come to an end with Yeltsin's dissolution of the Russian parliament in October 1993 and the adoption of his Presidential Constitution in December 1993. The dramatic assault by Russian troops on the Russian parliament and the arrest of Khasbulatov, and the other leading parliamentarians, followed by Yeltsin's decrees abolishing the institutions of the local assemblies (soviets), frightened the regions into submission. As Zverev notes, 'tax returns hitherto withheld by the regions began pouring into Moscow and talk of separate republics in the Urals, Siberia and the Far East temporarily ceased'.[5]

The new Constitution reasserted the authority of the federal authorities, the integrity and inviolability of the Federation, the supremacy of the Constitution and federal laws throughout the territory of the country, the creation of a single unified system of executive power, and a single economic space. There was also a notable absence of the right of the 'subjects' to secede from the Federation (article 4) or to have their own republican citizenship. And to the dismay of the republics the text of the Federal Treaty was not incorporated into the Constitution, and the superiority of the Constitution over the Federal Treaty was set out in section two. Moreover, the Constitution proclaimed that all subjects of the federation were equal (article 5) thus rejecting the special privileges which had been granted to the republics in March 1992.

The distribution of powers

As we noted in chapter 1 there are wide variations in the way in which power is distributed in federations. In most federal constitutions the federal authorities and federal subjects are each granted exclusive powers over specific policy areas. However, often there is also the need for a list of 'concurrent powers' to be specified which come under the joint jurisdiction of the federal government and federal subjects. Russia's Constitution favours the federal authorities over the subjects. Thus, article 71 grants the federal government exclusive powers over a broad range of national policies (including the national economy, federal budget, federal taxes and duties; foreign and defence affairs), and article 72 lists a number of powers which are to be shared between the federal authorities and the federal subjects (see appendices 3.1 and 3.2). However, as we noted in chapter 1, unlike in the Federal Treaty, no exclusive powers were delegated to the federal subjects. Instead, the subjects are granted only 'residual powers' (article 73), that is, powers over those relatively few policy areas not provided for in articles 71 and 72.

Another important article in the Constitution is the so called 'flexibility clause' (article 78) which allows the centre to transfer `the implementation of some of its powers' to the federal subjects and vice versa.[6] As Lapidus and Walker rightly note, this left 'open the possibility of bilateral agreements between Moscow and the subjects and the further development of an asymmetrical federation', which we discuss below.[7]

Popular support for the Constitution

There was however, one major drawback to Yeltsin's supposed constitutional victory. Although the Constitution was supported by 58.4 per cent of the voters nationwide (according to official statistics), it was rejected by a majority of voters in sixteen regions, and in eight of the twenty-one republics. Additionally, in eleven regions and six republics the Constitution failed to be ratified, as turnout was below the required 50 per cent.[8] And the Constitution was boycotted altogether in Chechnya. Surely, as we have noted, an essential attribute of any democratic federation is the voluntary membership of its subjects. But in Russia the Constitution failed to be ratified in forty-two of the eighty-nine subjects. Moreover, the legitimacy of the Constitution was also weakened by doubts over the validity of the officially declared turnout of 54.8 per cent. According to some estimates the actual turnout was well below the required 50 per cent and actually lay somewhere between 38 and 43 per cent.[9]

Such doubts over the legitimacy of the Constitution has fundamentally weakened the powers and authority of the federal government in its relations with the federal subjects, particularly in those regions where the Constitution failed to be ratified. Thus, Yeltsin's victory in 1993 was like Gorbachev's before him, a pyrrhic one. Devoid of any real legitimacy, the Constitution was soon open to creative interpretation, indifference, and even outright abuse, by regional political elites, who were able to bolster their 'patrimonial' regimes with claims for economic and political sovereignty.

There was no democratic revolution or people's revolution in Russia as there had been in Eastern Europe in 1989, and 'nomenklatura continuity' was the norm in the regions, as former communist elites took power under the new banner of national sovereignty. Moreover, as scholars of federalism stress, for a democratic federation to function we need not only federal structures and institutions but a democratic political culture, an agreement by all signatories to abide by the democratic and constitutional rules of the game. In Russia all of the federal structures were put in place by the Constitution but in the absence of a federal democratic culture. Thus, as we noted in chapter 1, a federation was formed without federalism.

The formation of a bicameral national parliament

As we noted in chapter 1, one of the key structural prerequisites of federal states is the institutional representation of regions in policy making at the federal level. To this end federal states have created bicameral national parliaments with an upper chamber especially designed to accommodate regional interests. In Russia, the Constitution called for the creation of a bicameral national parliament with an upper house comprising two representatives from each of Russia's eighty-nine subjects.

There are considerable variations in the powers of upper chambers, the methods by which their member are elected, their relations with other federal and regional bodies, and the equality of representation within them. As Watts notes, members of upper chambers may be selected by the following methods: (1) direct election (e.g., USA, Austalia, Switzerland), (2) indirect election from the subject assemblies (e.g., Austria, India), (3) ex officio appointment (e.g., of Lander cabinets in Germany), (4) through direct appointment by federal bodies (e.g., the federal Prime Minister in Canada), (5) by mixed systems of indirect/direct elections and appointments (e.g., Malaysia, Belgium, Spain).[10]

According to the Russian Constitution the Federation Council consists of, 'two representatives from each component of the Russian Federation; one each from the representative and executive bodies of state power (article 95). However, the Constitution did not stipulate the precise method by which members were to be chosen. In 1993 the first Council was elected via national elections. However, the method of choosing members was changed by Yeltsin in 1995 and again by Putin in 2000 (see chapter 8). From 1996 until 2000 the heads of the legislative and executive branches of government in each region were granted ex officio membership of the Council. Thus, during this period, the Council was indirectly elected, and its composition was decided by whoever held the post of chair of a regional assembly or head of a regional administration. Members of the Council could retain their seats as long as they held their regional posts. Therefore, as Teague notes, 'Since electoral laws varied from region to region, [this] also meant that the composition of the upper chamber was effectively determined not by federal norms but by regional ones'. Thus, included in the upper chamber were a number of republican presidents who had come to power through uncontested and/or unfair elections (e.g., President Shaimiev of Tatarstan, President Rakhimov of Bashkortostan). Also by including regional executives in its ranks the upper chamber violated the democratic principle of the separation of powers.

In 2000 President Putin radically changed the method by which members of the Federation Council are 'elected', which has fundamentally weakend its authority. No longer do heads of regional administrations and chairs of regional assemblies have ex officio membership; instead each sends a deputy to represent them in the Council. We shall discuss Putin's reforms further in chapter 8.

The changes enacted in 1995 were deliberately designed to give Yeltsin control over the lower house of the parliament (the Duma). As the Federation Council has the powers to veto legislation of the lower house, Yeltsin, by controlling the membership of the upper house, was able to gain significant leverage over the work of the Duma. Thus, as Kempton notes, 'Although most republican leaders were popularly elected, the governors of most of the regions were handpicked by Yeltsin and were subject to removal by Yeltsin'.[11] The upper chamber is also charged with approving the President's nominations for the top posts in the judiciary and procuracy. Thus, by packing the Council with his appointees, Yeltsin also gained control over these bodies. Only after Yeltsin reluctantly relinquished his powers of appointment over regional governors, and gave the go ahead for nationwide gubernatorial elections (conducted over the period 1995–97) did he begin to lose control over the membership and work of the Council (see chapter 6).

Political asymmetry can be found in the over-representation of some regions in the upper chambers of federal parliaments. In Russia all eighty-nine federal subjects have equal representation in the Federation Council even although there are massive variations in the size of their populations. Thus, Moscow city and the Yevenk autonomous oktug (AO) both have two 'senators' even although Moscow's population is 443 times larger than that of Yevenk. However, as Watts observes, equality of representation in the federal second chamber (also found in the USA, and Australia), is not, in fact, the norm. In most federations representation is weighted in favour of 'smaller regional units' and/or 'significant minorities'.[12] But, as Stepan warns us, 'the greater the representation of the less populous states (and therefore the underrepresentation of the more populous states), the greater the demos-constraining potential of the upper house will be'.[13] One way of ameliorating such inequalities is to vary the number of members elected from each federal subject. Thus, for example, in Germany there are lander having between 3–6 block votes in the upper chamber depending on the size of their populations, whilst in India representation of the states varies from as much as 12 to 86.[14]

There are also considerable variations in the powers granted to upper chambers but these will usually include; 'confirmation of federal judges, approval of the federal budget, changes in tax laws affecting the components, territorial changes, education policy, language policy and cultural policy'.[15] Upper chambers also have a key role in reviewing legislation so as to ensure the interests of the regions are promoted and protected.

Stepan also argues that, 'the greater the competence of the territorial house, the more the demos – which is represented on a one person–one vote basis in the lower house – is constrained'. Thus, for example, in Brazil senators representing just 13 per cent of the total electorate have no restrictions placed on the policy areas they can vote on and indeed there are twelve areas where the upper chamber has been granted exclusive competence.[16] The 'German, Spanish and Indian systems are less demos-constraining, because their upper houses are less unrepresentative and less powerful'.[17]

From a comparative perspective the Russian Federation Council is a relatively weak federal institution, which has been dominated for much of its existence by the presidency. It is the lower house, the state Duma, which is the law-making chamber. The upper chamber has the more limited power to approve or reject the legislation of the lower house. However, a veto by the Federation Council can be overturned by a two-thirds majority in the lower house Duma. The President also has the power to veto the legislation of both houses which can only be overturned by a vote of two-thirds of the members of both chambers.

The authority of the Federation Council is also weakened by the fact that most of its members have often been too preoccupied with their duties in the regions to attend its sessions. Indeed, often it has been difficult to achieve a quorum and the Council has had to resort to postal voting. Also according to article 105, legislation of the Duma 'is deemed to have been approved by the Federation Council' if it has not been examined by the upper chamber within 14 days. Up until 2002 the Council met for only a few days each month,[18] hardly sufficient time to carry out its duties. Thus, many laws of the Duma have been approved without the scrutiny of the Council. Another sign of the weakness of the Federation Council is its failure to use its right of legislative initiative. Thus, 'only about 7 per cent of draft laws prepared by the upper chamber and its members in 1994–98 passed all stages of the legislative process and were adopted as federal laws'.[19]

Nonetheless, the Council has acted as a forum for the airing of regional interests in the centre, and regional elites have been able to defend their rights and privileges via the Council. The Council also successfully thwarted the adoption of a key law which would have tightened up centre–periphery relations and reduced the powers of the regions vis-à-vis the centre.

In the late 1990s the Council also played a more prominent role in drawing up the federal budget. And once Yeltsin lost his control over appointments to the Council his ability to influence the courts and procuracy was also weakened. Thus, for example, in 1999 the Council refused to approve Yeltsin's repeated calls for the Procurator General, Skuratov, to resign.[20]

Constititutions of the republics

Regional elites have been able to use inherent contradictions in the Russian Constitution to their own advantage. Thus, for example, whilst the Constitution declares that all subjects are equal, in fact there are three distinct classifications of 'federal subject' in the document. First, the twenty-one ethnically based republics which are classified as national–state formations. Second, krai and oblasts, which are classified as administrative–territorial formations; and third, autonomous oblasts and autonomous okrugs defined as national-territorial formations.[21] Only the republics are defined as 'states' with the right to their own constitutions, languages, flags, hymns and other trappings of statehood.

There was also a great deal of ambiguity over the status of the Federal Treaty. Thus, for example, article 11 of the Constitution states that cen-tre–periphery relations are to be determined 'by the Federal Treaty and other treaties' which suggests that the Federal Treaty and the Constitution are both still valid – a position defended by many of the republics who refused to relinquish the powers given to them in March 1992. As we discuss below, this article (alongside article 78) legitimised the creation of bilateral treaties between the national government and the federal sub-jects, increasing the levels of constitutional asymmetry in the federation.

It was not long before a number of those republics whose citizens had rejected the constitution declared that the Federal Constitution was not valid in their territories, and that their own constitutions were to take precedence. Those constitutions ratified between the signing of the Federal Treaty in March 1992 and the ratification of the Russian Constitution on December, 12 1993 (Chuvashiya, Sakha, Chechnya, Tatarstan and Tyva), were among the most radical, granting the republics rights of self-determination, sovereignty and secession. Indeed, a number of republics (Tatarstan, Bashkortostan, Sakha, Tyva, Ingushetiya and Buryatiya) went so far in their rejection of the Federal Constitution that their relations with the centre were much more typical of those in a confederation than a federation.

A majority of Russia's twenty-one republics adopted constitutions which violate the Russian Constitution (contravening articles 4 and 15 of the Russian Constitution).[22] And Constitutional asymmetry created politi-cal asymmetry. Before long there was a multitude of differing political systems operating in the Russian Federation including different types of political regime (presidential or parliamentary); electoral systems (proportional, majoritarian or mixed); and party systems. Across the federation we could soon detect a political spectrum running from partial democratisation at one end to delegative democracies and outright dicta-torships at the other. However, one universal rule could be detected – the greater the autonomy granted to a federal subject the greater the level of authoritarianism. As we discuss in chapter 9, it is in the ethnic republics, granted most autonomy by the Constitution, that we find most violations, and also the highest levels of authoritarianism.

Rights of sovereignty, self-determination and secession

In this section I analyse the constitutions as first promulgated in the early 1990s before the substantial revisions which have taken place since the inauguration of President Putin in 2000. Putin's reform of the federal system is discussed in chapter 8.

As we noted above, the Constitution unlike the Federal Treaty before it, does not grant the republics the rights of sovereignty and secession. Article 4 (1) of the Russian Constitution states that, 'The sovereignty of the Russian Federation extends to the whole of its territory', and article 4(3) declares that, 'The Russian Federation ensures the integrity and inviolability of its territory'. Nonetheless, 19 of the 21 republics (with the exception of Ingushetiya and Kalmykiya) declared their state sovereignty, and by implication the right of secession. Thus, for example, article 1 of the Constitution of Tyva stated that as a sovereign state Tyva is a member of the Russian Federation on the basis of a Federal Treaty and as such Tyva has the right to self-determination and the right to secede from the Russian Federation. Article 61 of Tatarstan's Constitution declared, 'The Republic of Tatarstan shall be a Sovereign State, a subject of international law, associated with the Russian federation on the basis of a treaty and the mutual delegation of powers'. Likewise, article 5 of Bashkortostan's Constitution noted that:

> Bashkortostan joined the Russian Federation on a voluntary and equal basis. Relations between the Republic of Bashkortostan and the Russian Federation are determined by the Treaty on the basis of intergovernmental relations between the Russian Federation and Bashkortostan, and other bilateral treaties and agreements.

The Constitution of Chechnya goes even further, failing to even note that it is actually a subject of the Russian Federation, instead it proclaims that Chechnya is an independent sovereign state and a full and equal member of the world community of states.

In the Constitution of North Osetiya-Alaniya it proclaims that the Republic is a 'state, voluntarily entering into the composition of the Russian Federation'. Other constitutions stressed that their relations with the Russian Federation were based on the free delegation of their powers to the federation (Buryatiya, Bashkortostan, Sakha). The state sovereignty of republics is also often acknowledged in their friendship treaties with other subjects of the federation. Thus, the preamble to the treaty between Bashkortostan and Chuvashiya on 24 May 1994 recognized the mutual sovereignty of each republic.[23]

Further provisions guarantee the supremacy of the Federal Constitution in the Federation. Thus, article 4(2) states that, 'the constitution of the Russian Federation and federal laws are paramount throughout the territory of the federation' and article 15(1) declares that: 'The Constitution of the Russian Federation has supreme legal force and is direct acting and applies throughout the territory of the Russian Federation. Laws and other legal enactments adopted in the Russian Federation must not contradict the Constitution'.

But these provisions are simply ignored in a number of republican constitutions which defiantly proclaimed the supremacy of their constitutions over the Federal Constitution (e.g., article 7 of the Constitution of Sakha, article 15 of Bashkortostan, article 1 of Tyva, article 1 of Dagestan, and article 7 of Komi).[24] Article 1 of Tyva's Constitution stated that at times of political or state crisis in the republic, the Republic's Constitution was to take priority over federal laws and all powers were to pass to the parliament (the Supreme Khural), president and government. Similarly, article 1 of Bashkortostan's Constitution declared that, 'The Republic of Bashkortostan has supreme authority on its territory, independently defining and conducting domestic and foreign policies, adopting the Bashkortostan Constitution and laws, which have supremacy on the entire territory'. This article went on to state, that the only federal laws that must be enforced in Bashkortostan are those that were 'voluntarily granted by Bashkortostan to the purview of the Russian Federation'. Article 59 of the Constitution of Tatarstan proclaimed that, 'the laws of the Republic of Tatarstan shall enjoy supremacy over all its territory'. In the constitutions of Sakha (articles 58 and 70), Bashkortostan (article 95) and Komi (article 73) there were further provisions granting the republic authorities the right to suspend federal laws and acts which violated their constitutions.

Unilateral expansion of powers

A number of republic constitutions have also unilaterally taken jurisdiction over policy areas which according to article 71 come under the exclusive jurisdiction of the federal government. Thus, for example, the Constitution of Tyva granted the republic the right to decide issues of war and peace. Some constitutions allowed the republics to adopt laws about military service (Bashkortostan, Sakha, Tyva) and establish procedures for declaring a state of emergency in their territory (Buryatiya, Komi, Tyva, Bashkortostan, Kalmykiya, Kareliya, North Osetiya, Ingushetiya). Others gave themselves the exclusive right to engage in foreign relations and foreign trade, and to sign international treaties (Bashkortostan (article 88), Chechnya (article 62), Dagestan, Ingushetiya (article 54), Sakha (article 69), Tatarstan (article 89)[25] Some republics (Tatarstan (article 8), Tyva (article 3), Sakha (article 6)) unilaterally declared their territories as nuclear free zones in violation of article 71, point 'm' of the Russian Constitution which states that such questions fall squarely within the competence of federal authorities.

Ownership of land and other natural resources

In the Russian Constitution, in distinction from the Federal Treaty, it clearly states that the ownership, use and disposal of land and minerals come under the joint jurisdiction of the federal authorities and federal subjects (article 72). But only two republican constitutions (Komi and Kareliya) conformed in this respect. In particular, Sakha, Tatarstan, Bashkortostan, Tyva and Buryatiya, all declared that such natural resources belong to the republics. Article 10 of Bashkortostan's Constitution stated that the, 'earth, resources, natural wealth, and other resources on the territory of Bashkortostan are the property of its people. Questions about the ownership, use, and distribution of the land, resources, natural wealth, and other resources are determined by Bashkortostan legislation'.[26] And in violation of article 67 (points 1 and 2) of the federal Constitution, Sakha's Constitution (article 5) went so far as to declare, that even the 'air space, and continental shelf of the territory is the inalienable property of the citizens of the Republic'.[27]

In a number of republic constitutions the right to private property is unconstitutionally prohibited in some areas. Thus, for example in Sakha, land and minerals may not be in private ownership. In the Constitution of Tyva it actually states that land is under state ownership. Other republics have used such provisions to try and prohibit or reverse privatisation programmes in their territories. Several republics also give themselves the right to decide questions regarding the federal budget. Thus, for example, the constitutions of Sakha and Bashkortostan noted that their legislative organs had the right to define the volume of payments to the federal budget – a provision that clearly contradicted article 71 of the Russian Constitution.

Citizenship

In the majority of republican constitutions it is stated that granting and terminating citizenship is based on republican laws. That is, such matters come under the exclusive jurisdiction of the republics.[28] Thus, for example, article 19 of the constitution of Tatarstan stated that: 'The Republic of Tatarstan shall have its own citizenship. The reasons and procedures for acquiring and renouncing the citizenship of the Republic of Tatarstan shall be established by the law on citizenship of the Republic of Tatarstan. Citizens of the Republic of Tatarstan shall be admitted to have the citizenship of the Russian Federation'. Such powers over defining citizenship rights are in clear contradiction of article 6 of the Russian Constitution which states that, 'Citizenship of the Russian Federation is acquired and terminated in accordance with federal law', and also article 71 which clearly places citizenship under federal jurisdiction.[29]

Powers over the courts

All scholars of federalism agree that a necessary prerequisite for federalism is some form of adjudication between the levels of government. To this end federal states have created supreme courts which serve as the final adjudicator in relation to all laws, and constitutional courts which specialise in constitutional interpretation.[30] Indeed, as Kempton notes, 'because of the importance that federalism gives to the judiciary it is sometimes derogatorily labelled "government by the judiciary"'.[31] And in order to ensure the independence and impartiality of the courts it is now common practice for both the federal government and the federal subjects (usually through their representation in the upper chamber of the national parliament) to be given a voice in the appointment of the court's membership. Thus, for example, in the USA members of the Supreme Court, are appointed by the President, subject to the ratification of the upper chamber. In Germany the Bundesrat representing the Lander appoints half the members of the Constitutional Court, and the Bundestag the other half. In Spain the Constitutional Court is composed of 12 members, of whom 4 are elected by Congress, 4 by the Senate, 2 are appointed on the proposal of the Government Council, and 2 are appointed on the proposal of the General Council of Judicial Power. Whilst in Belgium, the members of the Court of Adjudication are simply elected by the multi-party Federal Assembly.[32]

The Russian Constitutional Court

In Russia members of the Constitutional Court and the Supreme Court are appointed by the President subject to ratification of the Federation Council. However, the Russian Constitutional Court is organised according to federal principles. And article 72 (k) of the Russian Constitution puts personnel appointments of federal branches of the judiciary under the joint authority of the federal authorities and federal subjects. Nonetheless, in a number of regions such rights have been unilaterally transferred to the sole jurisdiction of the republics. Although fifty regional constitutions and charters outline the rights and duties of regional constitution courts only twelve regions have actually gone so far as to establish these bodies.[33] In ten regions the governor/president nominates members of the courts and these nominees are then ratified by the parliaments. In Adygeya the three branches of government (judiciary, parliament and executive) each appoint three justices. In St Petersburg, small groups of regional legislators, the Council of Judges, and the governor nominate candidates which then go before the the regional assembly for ratification.[34]

The procuracy

The procuracy in distinction to that of the Constitutional Court is not a federal body. In the Russian Constitution it states that, 'The Russian Federation Procurator's Office is a single centralised system in which the lower level procurators are subordinate to higher-level procurators and to the procurator-general of the Russian Federation' (article 129(1)). And article 129(2) notes 'the Procurator general is appointed and released from office by the Federation Council on the submission of the President'. Article 129(3) states that, 'The procurators of subjects of the Russian Federation are appointed by the procurator general of the Russian Federation by agreement with the Federation components'. However, the mechanism for reaching such an agreement is prescribed neither in the Constitution nor in other laws.[35] The constitutions of Komi (article 104), Sakha (article 110), Kalmykiya (article 40), Buryatiya (article 103), Ingushetiya (article 89) recognise the right of the procurators of the republics to be appointed by the General Procurator of the Russian Federation. However, in a number of other republican constitutions, this right of appointment is given to the republican parliaments (e.g., Bashkortostan, Chechnya, Tatarstan and Tyva).

Appointment of heads of other regional branches of federal ministries

A major weapon in the hands of regional executives has been their control over the appointment of the heads of the federal bureaucracies situated in their territory. Although article 77(2) of the Russian Constitution states that there 'is a unified system of executive power' in the Russian Federation, and article 78(1) grants federal bodies the right to appoint their own territorial bodies and 'the relevant officials', republican constitutions (and some regional charters) state that such powers of appointment come under the sole jurisdiction of the federal subjects.

There are approximately forty to fifty branches of federal bureaucracies in each region. These include: power-wielding structures (the Federal Security Service and the Ministry of Internal Affairs); economic structures (agencies of the State Property Committee, the Customs Service and the Employment Service, and enterprises under federal jurisdiction); and oversight agencies (sanitary and epidemiological supervision, the tax police, the tax inspectorate, the Ministry of Finance's Oversight and Auditing Administration).[36] And by 2000 there were currently about 450,000 members of federal bureaucracies working in the regions.[37] As we discuss in chapter 8 it is one of the main aims of the Putin regime to wrest back control of these appointments from regional executives.

Bilateral agreements and the development of an asymmetrical federation

As noted above, articles 11 and 78 of the Russian Constitution left open the door for the federal government and federal subjects to engage in bilateral treaties. Over the period 1994 to 1998, forty-six such treaties were signed which rapidly undermined the authority of the federal Constitution as the primary basis of federal relations. These bilateral accords often gave the local signatories substantial rights over the disposition of natural resources on their territory, special tax concessions and other economic and political privileges. Special and often secretive agreements attached to the bilateral treaties, have in addition, granted the republics the right to appoint federal officials in their territories, conduct their own independent relations with foreign states, set up their own national banks, and create their own political and administrative organs.[38] In many instances the bilateral treaties actually legitimised those extra-constitutional powers which the republics had unilaterally proclaimed in their republican constitutions. Most of the treaties were limited to a set period of between two and five years.[39]

In Tatarstan and Bashkortostan, bilateral agreements have led to such profitable industries as petroleum extraction, petroleum refining and power generation being removed from the centre's jurisdiction and handed over to local control and ownership. Tax concessions and increased federal subsidies are a central feature of many of the bilateral agreements. Over the period 1991 to 1993, Tatarstan, Bashkortostan and Sakha practically stopped transferring payments from taxes to the centre. Fiscal relations were of a confederative nature. There was a 'war of laws' under the slogan, 'if you do not fund us we will not send you taxes'.[40] According to Lavrov, outright tax losses to the Federation caused by just four special budgetary deals with the republics of Kareliya, Tatarstan, Bashkortostan and Sakha, totalled at least 2 trillion roubles, or 2.3 per cent of the federal budget's revenues in 1994.[41] And other funds flowed into these republics from the profits of the oil industry (Bashkortostan and Tatarstan).

In June 1995 Sakha signed a treaty with Moscow which gave the republic ownership of 26 per cent of its diamond output, 30 per cent of its gold output, and a slightly smaller percentage of its oil and gas reserves.[42] The treaty also included a section on the division of powers between the two governments and 15 other agreements dealing with a variety of issues, such as 'economic control, budget relations, the mining industry, the fuel and energy industry, the northern sea route, external relations, agriculture, communications, customs, immigration, roads, education, environment and natural resources, and federal development funds'.[43] In 1995 Sakha received the colossal sum of 1.3 milliard US dollars for the sale of its diamonds. A sum which was not less than the official budget income of the republic.[44]

In 1996 the bilateral treaties were widened to include oblasts and krais. In its bilateral treaty with the federal government, Orenburg oblast gained the status of a free economic zone, a lowering of its tax quotas, and financial control over 20 per cent of revenues accruing from oil and gas production in the region.[45] The granting of such special economic privileges to a select group of regions has done much to undermine 'fiscal federalism' in Russia (see chapter 5). Instead of reasserting fiscal control over wayward republics and regions, the federal government seemed to go out of its way to sign special treaties with them, thereby giving legal sanction to a host of unconstitutional financial and political transactions carried out by the regions.

Chronology of treaties

The first step on this path to an 'asymmetrical federation' was the land-mark treaty signed with the republic of Tatarstan on February 15, 1994. To all intents and purposes this treaty created a 'state within a state' and came as close as one could possible come to legitimising Tatarstan's own Constitution and those provisions which gave Tatarstan sovereignty over its economic and political affairs, including foreign trade and areas of foreign policy. Attached to the treaty was a package of 12 agreements signed between the governments of Russia and Tatarstan regulating relations in the spheres of trade, property, budget, finance, the banking system, the military, the military industrial complex, customs, foreign–economic ties, higher education, ecology and the coordination of the legal and security services. Undoubtedly, one of the major reasons for the treaty was to thwart the further growth of nationalist sentiment in the republic and to prevent the secession of Tatarstan from the Federation. Yeltsin admits the treaty was vitally important in that it, 'forestalled the danger of a split in the Federation' (see chapter 4).[46] Other agreements were followed up in 1994 with the republics of Kabardino-Balkariya and Bashkortostan, and in 1995 four such treaties were signed with the republics of Buryatiya, North Ossetiya, Udmurtiya and Sakha.

Political factors played a major role in determining who were to be the lucky beneficiaries. In many cases such treaties were signed on the eve of parliamentary and presidential elections and were clearly part of a package to bribe the regions into submission and win over their political support for the President. Yeltsin was also able to capitalise on the fears of regional elites who believed that if the communists or the nationalists came to power they would bring a halt to the treaties.[47]

In 1996 there were no less than nineteen such treaties, eighteen of which were signed in the run-up to the presidential elections, including the first agreement with a non-ethnic republic which was signed by Sverdlovsk oblast on January 12. Sverdlovsk benefited from the timing of the treaty. Yeltsin's popularity rating in the country was at an all time low, and there were fears in the presidential camp that the Communists would follow up their success in the 1995 Duma elections with victory in the forthcoming summer presidential elections. The bilateral treaty signed with Sverdlovsk legitimised many of the demands made by the region in 1993 when it unilaterally elevated its status to that of a republic (the Urals Republic). Thus, under the provisions of the Treaty the region was granted the right to form its own civil service and the governor was given the power to approve the appointment and dismissal of all federal posts in the region.[48] And as Stoner-Weiss notes, in article 8 of the bilateral treaty, the region was even given powers 'to suspend the normative acts of ministries and departments of the federal government'.[49] In 1997 there were a further fourteen agreements.

Those treaties that were adopted first (at a time of federal weakness), were generally more generous, granting the signatories a significant number of economic and political privileges that were denied to later signatories. Thus, for example, 'In October 1996 representatives from 6 black earth regions asked the Duma to pass a law defining the legislative and executive rights of federal subjects. Their complaint was that "those who came first earned more rights"'.[50] In February 1998 the governor of Saratov Oblast, Dmitrii Ayatskov, requested that the bilateral treaty which his region had signed with the Federal Government the year before, be renegotiated, as it was too restrictive.[51] One gets the idea of an endless cycle of negotiations and renegotiations gradually destroying any vestiges of constitutionalism leading the country inevitabily and inexorably from a 'treaty' federation to a 'contractual' federation. In total forty-six bilateral treaties were signed by the summer of 1998, the last with Moscow city, which came into operation on June 16.[52] Paradoxically, the final treaty with Moscow was signed before the adoption of a key presidential decree in June 1999 which was designed to bring the treaties into line with the Constitution and to tighten up on the procedures by which the treaties were drawn up and implemented.[53]

Legal and constitutional basis of bilateral treaties

The legal basis for the treaties is firmly stated in the Constitution in articles 11 and 78[54] and also in a Presidential Decree of March 12, 1996. In article 78 it clearly states that federal subjects of executive power may give up some of their powers to executive bodies of subjects of the federation as long as these do not conflict with the constitution and federal laws. Article 11 states that: 'the delimitation of areas of responsibility and powers – between bodies of the state power of the Russian Federation and bodies of state power of the components of the Russian Federation is effected by the present constitution, and the Federation treaty, and *other treaties* concerning the delimitation of areas of responsibility and powers'.

A special commission was set up by presidential decree on July 12, 1994 for preparing treaties, and according to the head of the commission 'all the treaties scrupulously followed uniform rules'.[55] However, it would appear that in reality there were many problems with regulating the treaties. Thus, Yeltsin was forced to enact a special decree on the regulation of the treaties in 1996.[56] According to this decree the treaties (and accompanying agreements): (1) must not violate the Russian Constitution; (2) cannot change the status of a subject of the Federation; (3) cannot add to or change what is enumerated in articles 71 and 72 of the Constitution; and (4) must respect the supremacy of the Constitution.[57]

But, as we illustrate below, these provisions have simply been ignored. As Umnova demonstrates, the treaties have significantly widened the number of areas coming under joint jurisdiction as stipulated in article 72, 'In Tatarstan there were 17 new spheres, in Bashkortostan and Sakha 11, in Kabardino-Balkariya 8, North Osetiya 14, Buryatiya 3, Sverdlovsk Oblast 8, Kaliningrad Oblast 11, and Udmurtiya 11'.[58]

Thus, for example, the following areas were transferred from the exclusive authority of the federal authorities to joint jurisdiction: state defence (Tatarstan, Bashkortostan, Kabardino-Balkariya, North Osetiya); introduction of a state of emergency (Kabardino-Balkariya); conversion of defence industries to domestic production (Tatarstan, Bashkortostan, North Osetiya, Udmurtiya, Sverdlovsk and Orenburg oblasts); coordinating of military production complex (Tatarstan and Bashkortostan); management of the defence industry (Sverdlovsk oblast, Udmurtiya); the citing of military forces (Bashkortostan); arms sales (Tatarstan); coordination of budget finance, money-credit and pricing policy and the administration of public energy, transport and communications (Tatarstan, North Osetiya, Kabardino-Balkariya).[59]

In other cases constitutional powers exclusively reserved for the Russian federation government were transferred to the sole jurisdiction of federal subjects; international relations (Tatarstan); national banks (Tatarstan, Bashkortostan); republican citizenship (Tatarstan,[60] Kabardino-Balkariya, Bashkortostan[61]); the right to appoint or approve nominations for regional representatives of federal agencies, police, procuracy, judges, treasury, tax and others (Bashkortostan, Tatarstan Sverdlovsk, and many others). Thus, for example, according to the bilateral treaty signed between Ulyanovsk and the federal government, 'the heads of the tax inspectorate, treasury, police and other offices were appointed with the agreement of the oblast authorities'.[62]

A long awaited law to regulate bilateral treaties was finally adopted by the State Duma on June 30, 1999.[63] The law 'reinforced the supremacy of federal laws and the Constitution in the legal hierarchy, categorically stated the principles of glasnost in treaty promulgation, and gave the regions three years to bring existing treaties into conformity with federal law'.[64] However, the law came too late as no more treaties were signed after June 1998. And, it would appear to have made little impact. As we discuss in chapter 8, progress in bringing bilateral treaties into line with the Constitution has been so slow that President Putin has been forced to set up yet another special commission to re-examine this whole issue.

Conclusions: bilateral treaties and the federal Constitution

As Khakimov notes, there are two basic approaches to federalism in Russia: (1) constitutional–treaty, when the centre defines the course of all the processes and delegates powers to the regions, and (2) treaty–constitutional, when relations are constructed from below up through the voluntary delegation of powers from subjects to the centre.

The supporters of the constitutional–treaty form of federalism argue that the sovereignisation of the republics on the Tatarstan model will lead to the collapse of Russia. Thus, they argue for strict controls from the centre over the subjects. Bilateral treaties according to them are simply anomalies and provincial documents which have hindered the development of a unitary state. The war with Chechnya is seen as a positive development to keep the ethnic republics in check (see chapter 4).

Those who support a treaty–constitutional federation do not consider Russia a true federation but insist on forming relations with the centre according to the model 'from below-above' through the voluntary delegation of powers with the help of bilateral treaties. Sovereignty is established on a legal basis allowing the subjects of the federation self-determination. If the first variant insists that the constitutions of the republics must correspond with that of the federal Constitution then the second variant argues the reverse, that the federal Constitution must conform to the constitutions of the republics, and that the centre must be placed under the control of the subjects. The source of power in a democracy is the people, therefore the functions of central organs must be defined by the subjects of the federation.[65] Tatarstan and Bashkortorstan have been vigorous champions of the latter model.

For other scholars the bilateral treaties have played a positive role in preventing the disintegration of the federation (see chapter 4). Thus, Hughes argues that, 'the empowerment of asymmetric federalism' in Russia, 'has been the key factor in the successful management of separatist and regionalist challenges, and is the principal factor explaining its survivability as a federation'.[66]

The treaties have also been defended on the grounds that they allow the centre to engage in a more responsive, flexible, and democratic way to the local needs of Russia's highly diverse subjects. Furthermore, as Hughes argues, 'by decentralising power over a wide range of policy domains the treaties have acted as a counterweight to the strongly centralist state tradition in Russia', engineering 'a new institutional structure for the accommodation of Russia's plural society'.[67] Supporters of such 'treaty based' federalism also often refer to the Spanish example of 'foralistic federalism' to support their case. 'Foralistic federalism' was the term given to the negotiated charters drawn up between the king and the provinces in medieval Spain. As Elazar notes, in modern day Spain, bilateral agreements are authorized and adopted 'through a complex process involving the consent of the national and regional parliaments' and the 'agreements are tailored to meet the specific constitutional needs of each federal subject'.[68] Thus, as Smith notes, developments in Russia demonstrate that federalisation may involve 'a post-constitutional process of reaching important agreements as much as it may rely on an original compact'.[69]

However, I would agree with those critics who argue that the treaties have fundamentally weakened the Constitution and the rule of law in Russia. Whilst the Constitution does allow for some flexibility, it may be argued that such treaties have fatally undermined its authority. The treaties make a mockery of article 5 of the federal Constitution which states that the relations between the centre and all the subjects are equal. Moreover, it is clear that the bilateral treaties have, in all but name, elevated a select number of oblasts to the status of de facto republics.

Furthermore, it is also important to note that the treaties were never legitimised by the national parliament (Duma or Federation Council) nor by the legislative bodies of the subjects. These were agreements between executive bodies of power – signed usually by either the President or the Prime Minister and the chief executive of the regions. In April 1997, the Federation Council vetoed legislation which would have given the Duma such powers. Also we should take note of the complete silence of the constitutional court as regards the constitutionality of the bilateral treaties. Not a single treaty was brought before the court for examination. Clearly, such sensitive areas were kept out of its purview. The court, since its reincarnation in 1995, does not have the power to initiate hearings but must have cases brought before it.

In conclusion, the bilateral treaties have led to a situation, whereby some poor regions are totally dependent on the centre and no real federal relations exist whilst a second stronger group has the trappings of federalism, and finally the most powerful autonomous entities, such as Tatarstan, coexist with Moscow as part of an exclusive club of confederative states.[70] Moreover, the treaties have increased the already high level of 'constitutional asymmetry' operating in the Federation.

Appendix 3.1   Article 71 of the December 1993 Russian Constitution

The following fall within the jurisdiction of the Russian Federation:

a) adoption and amendment of the constitution of the Russian Federation and federal laws, and the monitoring of compliance with them;

b)   the federative system and territory of the Russian Federation;
c)   the regulation and protection of human and civil rights and freedoms; citizenship of the Russian Federation; the regulation and protection of the rights of national minorities;
d)   the establishment of a system of federal bodies of legislative, executive, and judicial power, the procedure for their organization and activity; the formation of federal bodies of state power;
e)   federal state property and the management thereof;
f)   the establishment of the fundamentals of federal policy and federal programmes in the sphere of the state, economic, ecological, social, cultural and national development of the Russian Federation;
g)   the establishment of the legal foundations of the single market; financial, currency, credit and customs regulation, monetary emission and the foundations of pricing policy; federal economic services, including federal banks;
h)   the federal budget; federal taxes and duties; federal regional development funds;
i)   federal power systems, nuclear power generation, fissile materials; federal transport, railways, information and communications; activity in space;
j)   the Russian Federation's foreign policy and international relations and the Russian Federation's international treaties; issues of war and peace;
k)   the Russian Federation's foreign economic relations;
l)   defence and security; defence production; the determination of the procedure for the sale and purchase of weapons, ammunition, military hardware and other military property; the production of toxic substances, narcotic substances and the procedures for their use;
m)   the determination of the status and protection of the state border, territorial seas, airspace, the exclusive economic zone and the continental shelf of the Russian Federation;
n)   the judicial system; the procurator's office; legislation in the field of criminal, criminal-procedure and criminal-executive law; amnesty and the granting of pardons; legislation in the field of civil law, the law of civil procedure and the law of arbitration procedure; the legal regulation of intellectual property;
o)   federal law relating to the conflict of laws;
p)   the meterological service, standards and standard weights and measurements, the metric system and measurement of time; geodesy and cartography; geographic names; official statistical records and accounting;
q)   state awards and honorary titles of the Russian Federation;
r)   the federal civil service.[71]

Appendix 3.2   Article 72 of the December 1993 Russian Constitution

The following fall within the joint jurisdiction of the Russian Federation and the components of the Russian Federation:

a) the guaranteeing that the constitutions and laws of republics, and the charters, laws and other normative legal acts of krais, oblasts, cities of federal significance, the autonomous oblasts and autonomous okrugs accord with the constitution of the Russian Federation and federal laws;

b) the protection of human and civil rights and freedoms; the protection of the rights of national minorities; the guaranteeing of legality, law and order and public safety; the arrangements relating to border zones;

c) issues relating to the ownership, use and disposal of land, mineral resources, water and other natural resources;

d) the delimitation of state property;

e) the use of the natural environment; environmental protection and the guaranteeing of ecological safety; natural sites under special protection; the protection of historical and cultural monuments;

f) general issues of nurture, education and science, culture, physical fitness and sport;

g) the coordination of questions of public health; the protection of the family, mothers, fathers and children; social protection, including social security;

h) the implementation of measures for combating catastrophes, natural disasters and epidemics and the elimination of their consequences;

i) the establishment of general principles of taxation and levying of duties in the Russian Federation;

j) administrative, administrative-procedural, labour, family, housing, land, water, and forestry legislation, and legislation on mineral re-sources and on environmental protection;

k) personnel of judicial and law-enforcement bodies; attorneys and notaries;

l) protection of the primordial habitat and traditional way of life of numerically small ethnic communities;

m) the establishment of the general principles for the organization of a system of bodies of state power and local self-government;

n) the coordination of the international and foreign economic relations of components of the Russian Federation and the fulfilment of the Russian Federation's international treaties.[72]

Notes

1 R. Taras, *Consolidating Democracy in Poland* (Boulder, Colorado: Westview Press, 1995), p. 170.

2 J. M. Maravall and T. di Tella, 'Democratic institutions', in A. Prezeworski (ed.), *Sustainable Democracy* (Cambridge: Cambridge University Press, 1995), p. 50.

3 *Ibid.*

4 A. Stepan, 'Russian federalism in comparative perspective', *Post-Soviet Affairs*, 16:2 (2000), 148.

5 A. Zverev, 'Qualified sovereignty: the Tatarstan model for resolving conflict-ing loyalties', in M. Waller, B. Coppieters and A. Malashenko, *Conflicting*

Loyalties and the State in Post-Soviet Russia and Eurasia (London: Frank Cass, 1998), p. 131.

6 See, C. Ross, 'Federalism and regional politics', in M. Bowker and C. Ross (eds), *Russia after the Cold War* (Harlow: Pearson Education, 2000); C. Ross, 'The republicanisation of Russia – 2: federalism and democratisation in transition', in C. Pierson and S. Tormey (eds), *Politics at the edge* (London: Macmillan, 2000), and R. Sakwa, 'The republicanisation of Russia – 1', in the same collection.

7 G. W. Lapidus and E. W. Walker, 'Nationalism, regionalism and federalism', in G. W. Lapidus (ed.), *The New Russia: Troubled Transformation* (Boulder; San Francisco; Oxford: Westview Press, 1995), p. 102.

8 For example in the Republic of Ingushetiya turnout was just 46.0 per cent, Khakasiya (45.6), Komi (47.2), Marii-El (46.8), Tatarstan (13.4) and Udmurtiya (44.2).

9 S. White, S. Rose and M. McAllister (eds), *How Russia Votes* (New Jersey: Chatam House, 1997), p. 100.

10 R. L. Watts, *Comparing Federal Systems* (Montreal and Kingston: McGill-Queen's University Press, 2nd edn, 1999), pp. 92–5.

11 D. Kempton, 'Russian federalism: continuing myth or political salvation', *Demokratizatsiya*, 9:2 (Spring 2001), 217.

12 Watts, *Comparing Federal Systems*, pp. 95–6.

13 A. Stepan, 'Federalism and democracy: beyond the U.S. Model', *Journal of Democracy*, 10:4 (1999), 24.

14 Watts, *Comparing Federal Systems*, p. 96.

15 Kempton, 'Russian federalism', 215.

16 Stepan, 'Federalism and democracy', 27.

17 *Ibid.*

18 The upper house meets only for two days every three weeks.

19 O. Oracheva, 'Democracy and federalism in post-communist Russia', paper presented at the conference, The Fall of Communism in Europe: Ten Years On, May 14–17, 2001, The Hebrew University of Jerusalem, p. 7.

20 Kempton, 'Russian federalism', 219.

21 L. M. Karapetyan, *Federalizm i Prava Narodov* (Moscow: PRIOR, 1999), p. 49.

22 Forty-four articles of the Bashkortostan constitution contradicted the Russian Constitution.

23 I. A. Umnova, *Konstitutsionnye Osnovy Sovremennovo Rossiiskovo Federalizma* (Moscow: DELO, 1998), p. 106.

24 S. V. Alekseev, V. A. Kalamanov and A. G. Chernenko, *Ideologicheskie Orientiry Rossii, Volume 2* (Moscow: Kniga i Biznes, 1998), p. 392.

25 *Ibid.*, p. 108.

26 Rabinowich, *EWI Russian Regional Report* (December 2000).

27 Alekseev *et al.*, *Ideologicheskie Orientiry*, p. 107.

28 Karapetyan, *Federalizm i Prava*, p. 48.

29 *Ibid.*, p. 47. Article 89 also declares that the President of the Russian Federation, 'decides questions of citizenship of the Russian Federation'. The 'Law on Citizenship of the Russian Federation' which was adopted on 28 November 1991 (and was amended in 1993 and 1995) also regulates such questions. There are also republican laws on citizenship. Article 2 of the Law on Citizenship of the Russian Federation states that a citizen of the Russian Federation

permanently residing in the territory of a republic is at the same time a citizen of that republic. And article 23 further notes that termination of citizenship of the Russian Federation also means termination of such republican citizenship. For Karapetyan the fact that a citizen has both republican and Russian citizenship does not equal dual citizenship. Rather, it signifies a legal relationship with the federal state and with the republic, in the framework of a single common and indivisible citizenship. For Karapetyan, there is no provision in law for a citizen of a republic not holding at the same time citizenship of the Russian Federation (see Karapetyan, *Federalizm i Prava*, p. 48).

30 Watts, *Comparing Federal*, p. 100.
31 Kempton, 'Russian federalism', 212.
32 *Ibid.*
33 Adygeya, Bashkortostan, Buryatiya, Dagestan, Kabardino-Balkariya, Kareliya, Komi, Marii El, Sakha, Tatarstan, Sverdlovsk Oblast and the city of St Petersburg. See A. Trochev, 'The constitutional courts of Russia's regions: an overview', *IEW, Russian Regional Report*, 6:44 (December 12, 2001), 16.
34 *Ibid.*, p. 21.
35 I. Mikhailovskaya, 'The procuracy and its problems', *East-European Constitutional Review*, 8:1–2 (Winter–Spring 1999), 4.
36 M. Sergeeva, *Kommersant Daily* (26 October 1996), 1., translated in *CDPSP*, 48:43 (November 20, 1996), 1.
37 L. Smirnyagin, 'Federalizm po Putiny ili Putin po federalizmu (zheleznoi pyatoi)', *Carnegie Briefing Papers*, 3:3 (March 2001), 2.
38 See, Umnova, *Konstitutsionnye Osnovy*, pp. 108–14.
39 K. Stoner-Weiss, 'Central weakness and provincial autonomy: observations on the devolution process in Russia', *Post-Soviet Affairs*, 15:1 (1999), 91.
40 A. Lavrov, 'Asimmetriya byudzhetnovo ustroistva Rossii: problemy i resheniya', in A. Zakharov (ed.), *Asimmetrichnost' Federatsii* (Moscow: MONF, 1997), pp. 99–122, 113.
41 A. M. Lavrov, 'Russian budget federalism: first steps, first results', *Sevodnya* (June 7, 1995). Translated in *CDPSP*, 47:23 (1995), 3.
42 V. Emelyanenko, 'Russia: waiting for IOUs', *Moskovskie Novosti*, 44 (June–July 1995), 2. Translated in *CDPSP*, 47:26, 1995, pp. 14–15.
43 John F. Young, 'The republic of Sakha and republic building', in K. Matsuzato (ed.), *Regions: A Prism to View the Slavic-Eurasion World* (Sapporo, Japan: Hokkaido University, 2000), p. 186.
44 Lavrov, 'Russian budget federalism', p. 3.
45 Orenburg, December 1995, p. 116, December 10–17, 1995.
46 B. Yeltsin, 'The might of the state grows through the independence of the regions', *Rossiiskie Vesti* (November 1, 1997). Translated in *CDPSP*, 49:44 (1997), 14.
47 M. Fillipov and O. Shvetsova, 'Assymetrical bilateral bargaining in the new Russian federation: a path-dependence explanation', *Communist and Post-Communist Studies*, 32 (1999), 73.
48 EWI *Russian Regional Report*, 5:24 (June 21, 2000), 6.
49 K. Stoner-Weiss, 'Central weakness and provincial autonomy', 93.
50 Fillipov and Shvetsova, 'Asymmetric bilateral bargaining', 73.
51 *Ibid.*, 74.

52 A. Kuzmin, N. Petrov and A. Titov, 'Russian federalism: the view from the centre and from the regions', unpublished paper delivered to the Conference, Contemporary Russian Federalism: Problems and Perspectives, Carnegie Centre, Moscow, December 1997, pp. 9–10.
53 See note 63.
54 Thus article 78(2) states, 'The federal bodies of executive power, by agreement with the bodies of executive power of the components of the Russian Federation can transfer to them the implementation of some of their powers provided that this does not conflict with the constitution of the Russian Federation and federal laws'. And article 78(3) notes, 'By agreement with the federal bodies of executive power the bodies of executive power of the components of the Russian Federation can transfer to them the implementation of some of their powers'.
55 T. Sadkovskaya, *Rossiskiye vesti* (January 23, 1998), p. 3.
56 Presidential Decree Number 370, March 12, 1996 (with changes on November 25, 1996); 'Ob Utverzhdenii Polozheniia O Poriadke Raboty Po Razgranicheniyu Predmetov Vedeniya i Polnomochii Mezhdu Federal'nymi Organami Gosudarstvennoi Vlasti i Organami Gosudarsvennoi Vlasti Sub'ektov Rossiiskoi Federatsii i O Vzaimnoi Peredache Osushchestvleniya Chasti Svoikh Polnomochii Federal'nymi Organami Ispolnitel'noi Vlasti i Organami Ispolnitel'noi Vlasti Sub'ektov Rossiiskoi Federatsii', *Sobranie Zakonodatel'stva Rossiiskoi Federatsii*, 12 (1996), 1058.
57 K. Stoner Weiss, 'Central weakness and provincial', 91. Yeltsin's decree of October 5, 1995 also makes the same point and notes that subjects must remove any provisions in their laws, charters or constitutions which infringe the Russian Constitution.
58 Umnova, *Konstitutsionnye Osnovy*, p. 112.
59 *Ibid.*
60 In Tatarstan the bilateral treaty further muddies the waters by providing a number of contradictory statements on citizenship. Thus, article 4 conforms with article 71 of the Russian Constitution, stating that this is a federal matter, article 3 places citizenship under joint jurisdiction, and article 2 grants such questions to republican jurisdiction.
61 Stoner-Weiss, 'Central weakness and provincial', p. 92.
62 S. Gogin, *IEWS, Russian Regional Report*, 5:3 (January 26, 2000), 7.
63 'O Printsipakh i Poryadke Razgranicheniya Predmetov Vedeniya i Polnomochii Mezhdu Organami Gosudarstvennoi Vlasti Rossiiskoi Federatsii i Organami Gosudarstvennoi Vlasti Sub'ektov Rossiiskoi Federatsii', adopted by the State Duma, 4 June, 1999 and ratified by the President on June 24, 1999. *Rossiiskaya Gazeta* (June 30, 1999), 3.
64 J. Kahn, 'What is the new Russian federalism?', in A. Brown (ed.), *Contemporary Russian Politics: A Reader* (Oxford: Oxford University Press, 2001), p. 381.
65 R. Khakimov, 'Asimmetrichnost' Rossiiskoi Federatsii: vzglyad iz Tatarstana', 72–3.
66 'Institutional design and political stability: asymmetric federalism in Russia's state of transition', paper delivered to the ESRC Research Seminar, Regional Transformations in Russia, London School of Economics and Political Science, October 21, 1998, p. 3.

67 J. Hughes, 'From federalisation to recentralisation', in S. White, A. Pravda and Z. Gitelman (eds), *Developments in Russian Politics – 5* (Basingstoke: Palgrave, 2001), p. 145.

68 D. Elazar, *Exploring Federalism* (Tuscaloosa and London: University of Alabama Press, 1987), pp. 59, 165.

69 G. Smith, *The Post-Soviet States: Mapping the Politics of Transition* (London; Sydney; Auckland: Arnold, 1999), p. 140.

70 V. Shpak, *Kommersant Daily* (January 20, 1998), p. 4.

71 M. V. Baglai, *Konstitutsionnoe Pravo Rossiiskoi Federatsii* (Moscow: Norma, 2001), pp. 313–17.

72 *Ibid.*

4

From ethnic to legal
and economic separatism

Federalism and the 'parade of sovereignties'

With a population of 145 million citizens the Russian Federation is one of the most populous and ethnically diverse states in the world. Within its vast territory, which encompasses one-eighth of the world's land surface, reside 128 officially recognised nations and ethnic groups.[1] As we discussed in chapter 2, of the 89 republics and regions that make up the Russian Federation, 32 are based on ethnic criteria; namely, 21 republics, 10 autonomous okrugs and 1 autonomous oblast. In such large multinational states, federalism, it is argued, can be a positive or a negative phenomenon.

For those who stress the positive side, federalism functions as a form of empowerment for regional groups and protects minorities from the tyranny of the majority. According to Watts, federalism refers to the advocacy of multi-tiered government combining elements of shared rule and regional self-rule. 'It is based on the presumed values of achieving both unity and diversity by accommodating, preserving and promoting distinct identities within a larger political union'.[2]

As Kempton notes, federalism 'allows many minority groups to sustain themselves by making them the majority within a specific component of the larger state'.[3] Most importantly of all, by providing a democratic alternative to nation-statehood, federalism provides a viable alternative to regional secession and the potential disintegration of multinational states. In this regard it has been successful in quelling ethnic and religious tensions in Canada, Belgium, India, Malaysia, Nigeria, Spain and South Africa.[4]

For those who stress the negative side, federalism is the problem rather than the solution, particularly in multinational states where ethnic boundaries coincide with boundaries of the federal subjects. Federalism, according to this scenario, is much more likely to intensify the nationalist grievances it is supposed to ameliorate. As Smith notes:

Federalism provides incentives for structuring group/class conflicts along territorial lines, [and] when the territories in question are spatial surrogates of large-scale, potentially self-conscious cultural communities, most territorial conflicts become community conflicts as well. In the process, feelings of ethnicity are strengthened and new issues take on ethno-territorial significance.[5]

Federalism can also lead to the creation of new national communities, as was the case in the USSR. By granting ethnic communities virtually all of the trappings of statehood (constitutions, flags, hymns, parliaments, executive bodies, courts etc.), federalism, it is argued, simply provides such communities with the institutional and cultural building blocks to go one step further and forge separate states. In other words, the drawing of regional boundaries intrinsic to federalism acts to reify and reproduce the very group differences to which federalism is itself a response.

However, it is doubtful that the Russian state would still exist today in its current form if it were not for the federal arrangements codified in the 1992 Federal Treaty, the 1993 Constitution and the numerous bilateral treaties which were negotiated over the period 1992–98. These federal arrangements helped to quell nationalism in the republics and eventually brought an end to the 'parade of sovereignties' which dominated the political landscape in the early 1990s.

With the exception of the wars in Chechnya, and sporadic inter-ethnic conflicts and tensions in the Caucasus, even Russia's weak and imperfect form of federalism has succeeded in quelling outright demands for separation. Bilateral deals struck between the centre and the republics transformed the regions zero-sum demands for secession into more negotiable and viable demands for greater legal, economic and political sovereignty.

No doubt, Yeltsin's dissolution of the Russian parliament and the horrific events of the 'October days' in 1993, coupled with the sending of federal troops into secessionist Chechnya in 1994 and 1999, has also helped to persuade ethnic groups to change tactics and to opt for negotiation rather than conflict.[6] The rise of Russian nationalism and the calls from nationalists for the liquidation of the ethnically based federal subjects, and the 'gubernisation of Russia' may also have convinced regional elites of the need to find some urgent form of accommodation with the Yeltsin regime.

Payin argues rightly that the bilateral treaties between Moscow and the republics 'severely weakened the positions of radical nationalist forces, whose influence was based almost entirely on notions of an imperial enemy'.[7] Thus, for example, the radical nationalist movement in Tatarstan, which had been fairly strong, literally fell apart after the signing of the treaty between Moscow and Kazan in 1994.[8] And nationalist movements in other republics have so far, failed to gain support at the ballot box.[9]

However, Yeltsin's compromise with the ethnic republics was bought at a cost – at the cost of undermining the Federal Constitution and the sanctioning of authoritarianism.[10] As Furman notes: 'The federal centre agreed to grant the republics more rights than the Russian provinces, allowing them to develop into 'vassal kingdoms' in whose internal affairs Moscow did not interfere as long as they regularly paid Yeltsin their 'tribute' in the form of votes – which they did in every important federal election'.[11] We discuss these ideas further in chapter 9.

Federalism and secessionism

The outright disintegration of the Russian Federation remains highly unlikely given the ethnic makeup and geo-political status of Russia's thirty-two ethnically defined subjects. The following six demographic, geo-political and social factors have conspired to weaken or stifle the development of separatist movements. (1) Nationality based entities (including autonomous regions) occupy 53 per cent of the country's area, but only 18 per cent of the population lives in those regions.[12] (2) Furthermore, according to a micro-census carried out in 1994 Russians now make up the overwhelming majority of the population (82.95 per cent), compared to 50 per cent in the USSR.[13] (3) Of the 172 ethnic groups the largest, the Tatars, make up only 3.8 per cent of the population (followed by the Ukrainians (2.3), Chuvash with (1.2), Bashkirs (0.9), Belarussians (0.7) and Mordvinians (0.6): all the other ethnic groups comprise less than 1 per cent.[14] (4) Russians predominate not only in the Russian Federation as a whole but also in most of its regions – in 74 of the 89 members of the Federation. Indeed, forty-nine regions can be called purely Russian areas. In those regions, representatives of the ethnic majority make up 85 to 98 per cent of the population. The largest per centage of Russians in any region is now found in Tambov oblast (97.8 per cent).[15] (5) The ethnic republics make up just 28.6 per cent of the territory and only 15.7 per cent of the population.[16] Furthermore, of the twenty-one republics, the eponymous population comprises a majority in only seven; Chechnya, Chuvashiya, Dagestan,[17] Ingushetiya, Kalmykiya, North Osetiya-Alaniya, and Tyva, and a plurality in two, Kabardino-Balkariya and Tatarstan. Russians, on the other hand, have an absolute majority in nine, Adygeya, Buryatiya, Altai, Kareliya, Khakassiya, Komi, Mordoviya, Sakha (Yakutiya) and Udmurtiya; and a plurality in three, Bashkortostan, Karachai-Cherkessiya and Marii-El (see table 4.1). (6) Finally, of the eleven autonomous areas (the ten autonomous okrugs (AOs) and the autonomous oblast (AOB)) the eponymous population comprises a majority in only two, Aga-Buryatiya AO and Komi-Permyakiya AO (see table 4.2).

However, we should caution that the numbers of eponymous peoples are rising in their native regions where the rates of population growth are

Table 4.1 Ethnic composition of the republics, 1989 (%)

Republic	Eponymous population(s)	Russian population
Adygeya	22.1	68.0
Altai	31.2	60.4
Bashkortostan	21.9	39.3
Buryatiya	24.0	70.0
Chechnya-Ingushetiya	70.7	23.1
Chuvashiya	68.7	26.7
Dagestan	90.8	9.2
Kabardino-Balkariya	57.6	32.0
Kalmykiya	53.0	37.7
Karachai-Cherkessiya	40.9	42.4
Kareliya	10.0	73.6
Khakassiya	11.1	79.5
Komi	23.3	57.7
Marii-El	43.3	47.5
Mordoviya	32.5	60.8
North Ossetiya	53.0	29.9
Sakha (Yakutiya)	33.4	50.3
Tatarstan	48.5	43.3
Tyva	64.3	32.0
Udmurtiya	30.9	58.9

Source: G. W. Lapidus and E. W. Walker, Nationalism, regionalism, and federalism: centre–periphery relations in post-communist Russia', in G. W. Lapidus (ed.), *The New Russia: Troubled Transition* (Boulder, Colorado: Westview Press, 1995), pp. 88–9; E. Payin and A. Susarov, 'Line five in the mirror of demography', *Rossiiskie Vesti*, October 30, 1997, 2. Translated in *CDPSP*, 49:44 (1997), 11.

greater for the indigenous population than for the Russian population. We have also witnessed the return migration of representatives of the eponymous nationalities from other parts of Russia, the Baltic states, and the Confederation of Independent states. Whilst at the same time there has been a steady outflow of Russians from a number of regions. Thus, for example, the per centage of Kalmyki in Kalmykiya grew from 41.5 per cent in 1979 to 52.6 per cent in 1994.[18]

One would imagine that demands for secession are likely to be strongest in those republics: (1) situated in the outer rim of the Federation which border on foreign states; and (2) where a majority of the population is eponymous.[19] Of the seven republics where the eponymous population comprises a majority, Chuvashiya is an enclave with no realistic prospects for secession. This leaves only six republics where there is a majority of the eponymous population and the subjects are situated on the outer rim of the Russian state: Chechnya, Dagestan, Ingushetiya,

Table 4.2 Ethnic composition of the autonomous areas, 1989 (%)

Autonomous areas	Eponymous population(s)	Russian population
Autonomous oblast (1)		
Jewish	4.2	83.2
Autonomous okrugs (10)		
Agin-Buryat	54.9	40.8
Chukotka	7.3	66.1
Yevenk	14.0	67.5
Komi-Permyak	60.2	36.1
Koryakiya	16.5	62.0
Khanty-Mansi	0.9	66.3
Nenets	11.9	65.8
Taimyr	13.7	67.1
Ust'-Ordin Buryat	36.3	56.5
Yamala-Nenets	4.2	59.2

Source: Lapidus and Walker, *The New Russia*, p. 89.

Kalmykiya, North Osetiya-Alaniya and Tyva.[20] And indeed it is these republics, mainly to be found in the North Caucuses which have proven to be the most vociferous in their demands for autonomy. But only Chechnya has opted for secession and it has had to pay the price of two wars, the loss of thousands of its citizens, occupation by Russian troops, and the imposition of a pro-Moscow 'puppet government'. Of the other five republics, as Payin notes, North Osetiya-Alaniya can be excluded, for, 'as the only Christian autonomy in the Muslim North Caucasus, it will not want to leave Russia under any readily conceivable circumstances'.[21] Secession from the Federation is also highly unlikely in the multi-ethnic state of Dagestan, since the majority of the population realise that even the suggestion of secession from Russia would invite an explosion of demands for internal secession and of internal conflicts amongst it thirty-three ethnic groups.[22]

Another factor which has dampened down calls for independence from these states is their dire economic situation and financial dependence on the centre. Thus, for example, although we may expect nationalism to be strong in Tyva, which was nominally a sovereign state from 1921 to 1944, demands for secession have been stifled by the fact, that the Republic depends on the federal authorities for 90 per cent of its income. And Dagestan, Ingushetiya, Kalmykiya, and North Osetiya-Alaniya are also highly dependent on federal subsidies (see chapter 5).

It is interesting also in this respect to consider the point that the eponymous population in three of the most radical and confederalist republics, Bashkortostan, Sakha (Yakutiya) and Tatarstan, make up only 21.9

per cent, 33.4 per cent and 48.5 per cent of the population, respectively. Whilst the Russian population comprises a plurality of 39.3 per cent in Bashkortostan, a majority of 50.3 per cent in Sakha (Yakutiya), and a sizeable minority of 43.3 per cent in Tatarstan. And of course all three of these republics are like Chuvashiya, landlocked inside Russia with no realistic prospects for separation.

In Bashkortostan, Bashkirs are the third largest ethnic group in the Republic, some way behind Tatars, and Russians. However, in an attempt to gain an external foreign border, Bashkortostan has recently begun negotiations for an exchange of territory with the neighbouring region of Orenburg. If successful this would allow Bashkortostan to establish a direct border connection with Kazakhstan which is only fifty kilometres away. The area in question has a high per centage of Tatar and Bashkir populations.[23]

Other sources of ethnic tension can be found in the republics of Kabardino-Balkariya and Karachaevo-Cherkessiya. Here the question is not one of secession from Russia but, rather, calls for the division of each of these republics into two new entities providing separate homelands for the Kabards, Balkars, Karachais and Cherkess. In other regions there have been calls for unification rather than separation. Thus, for example, there has been strong support from citizens in Bashkortostan and Tatarstan for the idea of creating closer economic and political ties in some kind of confederacy.[24]

The autonomous formations

The ten autonomous okrugs (AOs) which are considered by the constitution to be full subjects of the federation, are in fact trapped 'matroshka doll-like', within the territories of eight other federal subjects. The Agin-Buryat AO within Chita Oblast; Chukotka (Magadan Oblast); Yevenk and Taimyr AOs (Krasnoyarsk Krai); Khanty-Mansi and Yamala-Nenets (Tyumen Oblast); Komi-Permyak (Perm Oblast); Koryakiya (Kamchatka oblast); Nenets (Arkhangelskaya Oblast); Ust'-Orda Buryat (Irkutsk Oblast).

The Constitution is rather unclear as to what their proper relationship should be with the regional authorities in whose territories they are situated. Their legal status is contradictory. On the one hand they are administratively subordinate to the regions of which they are part but on the other hand they are also constitutionally equal to them. In an attempt to solve this anomalous situation, the Constitution states that relations between the okrugs and the regions should be 'treaty based'. In 1997 the Russian Federation Constitutional Court ruled that where conflict arises and there is no treaty (as was the case in Tyumen oblast in 1997) then the autonomous okrug is equal in status to the region.[25] By this ruling the regional authorities are not allowed to interfere in the administration of the okrugs, but on the other hand, the populations of the okrugs are allowed to participate in the elections of their 'parent regions'. Such an interpretation actually appears to makes the autonomous okrugs 'more equal' than the regions in which they are situated.[26]

The special status of the autonomies becomes more questionable when we consider their ethnic makeup (see table 4.2). In only two of the eleven (Aga-Buryatiya and Komi-Permyakiya) does the eponymous population comprise a majority, whilst in the remaining nine the Russian population predominates. And in a number of the autonomous okrugs the per centage of the indigenous population is tiny. Why it may be asked are Khanty-Mansi and Yamalo-Nenets okrugs (with indigenous populations of just 0.9 and 4.2 per cent respectively) granted full membership of the federation, with the right (until January 2002, see chapter 8) to send two representatives to the upper chamber of the parliament, and to maintain their own charters and other trappings of statehood?[27] As we shall discuss below, these questions become all the more critical when they involve disputes over who should control the economic spoils of the okrugs – the okrugs, or their 'parent regions'.

Recently we have witnessed the situation of autonomous okrugs demanding independence from their 'parent' regions (e.g., Khanty-Mansi and Yamalo-Nenets from Tyumen Oblast) and paradoxically others seeking to be fully integrated into their parent oblasts (e.g., Komi-Permyak Okrug with Perm Oblast). As Paretskaya rightly stresses, the main reasons for both kinds of change of status are economic. Perm Oblast is happy to be free of the social responsibility of its impoverished okrug. By contrast, Khanty-Mansi and Yamalo-Nenents okrugs are fabulously wealthy oil and gas producers. By seceding from Tyumen Oblast the okrugs will no longer have to give up a per centage of their oil and gas revenues to the Oblast authorities. The majority of citizens in both okrugs boycotted the 1997 gubernatorial election in Tyumen Oblast.[28] Failing in their quest for seccession these two okrugs have recently adopted a new strategy – to take control of the Oblast's economy. As Arbatskaya notes: 'Effectively, the okrugs, and especially Khanty-Mansi, are buying up the largest tax-paying enterprises in the south. Over time these purchases will give the northern okrugs control of the political processes in the region, particularly local elections and elections to the oblast Duma'.[29]

A similar battle has been raging between the leaderships of Krasnoyarsk Krai and the Taimyr autonomous okrug over the profits of the Norilsk Nickel Factory which supplies 20 per cent of the world's nickel and 5 per cent of its copper. The factory provides some 70 per cent of the krai's income. The battle began when in collusion with its director, the Taimyr authorities unilaterally transferred the factory from the krai to their jurisdiction. Such a move guaranteed that the spoils of the factory would no longer go to the krai but would instead flow into the coffers of the okrug. The factory would also benefit from the move, as it would gain access to Taimyr's mineral resources and at the same time escape supervision from the krai administration. Tax evasion and corruption were also at the heart of the deal. These actions of the okrug were opposed by the mayor of Norilsk, where the factory was situated. However, after months of wrangling, federal authorities prohibited the transfer of the factory from the krai's jurisdiction. In response the okrug administration boycotted the Krasnoyarsk gubernatorial elections and it declared all laws of the krai invalid in the territory of the okrug. Finally, after years of stalemate and conflict a power sharing agreement was signed in 1997 between the krai and the okrug. The treaty granted the Okrug some of the profits generated by the plant at Norilsk. In a more recent twist to this saga, the former head of Norilsk Nickel, Aleksandr Khloponin was elected governor of Taimyr AO and he has now given his support to a proposal by deputies of the Taimyr legislative assembly to consider the exit of Taimyr from the krai.[30]

Tensions have also arisen over calls by Buryats to unite Russia's two Buryat okrugs with the Republic of Buryatiya to create a 'greater Buryatiya' republic. The Ust-Orda AO which is situated in Irkutsk Oblast and the Agin Buryat AO situated in Chita oblast have historical links with the Republic of Buryatiya, which lies between the two okrugs.[31]

New legislation is being prepared in the presidential administration to bring an end to these anomalies. The solution being suggested is simply to dissolve the okrugs and to amalgamate them with their parent regions. But for the centre to do this unilaterally would mean violating the Constitution which has strict rules for changing the borders of federal subjects.[32]

From ethnic to legal and economic separatism

For many regions a more realistic option than outright secession has been the development of 'economic' and 'legal' separatism or what Khemkin terms 'internal emigration', the process whereby a number of subjects have withdrawn themselves from the legal and economic orbit of the federation and become de facto autonomous islands within the Russian state.[33] Thus, as we noted in chapter 3, the constitutions of 19 of Russia's 21 republics (all except Kalmykiya and Kareliya) violate the Federal Constitution.[34] According to an analysis by the Ministry of Justice, of the 44,000 regional acts adopted over the period 1995–97 almost half were in violation of the Russian Constitution and federal legislation.[35] And regions and republics regularly pass legislation that infringe citizens' rights. Thus, for example, according to Voronezh Oblast Procurator,

Aleksandr Frolov, 399 regional directives of the oblast Duma which were adopted in 1998 violated human rights.[36]

What we appeared to be witnessing during the early part of the Yeltsin regime was a 'war of laws' between the federal authorities and the regions reminiscent of the struggle which existed between the Union Republics and the federal authorities during the Gorbachev period.

The ability of the regions to opt for legal separatism has been increased by the fact that the top executive and legislative bodies are now elected from below rather than appointed from above. Up until the gubernatorial elections of 1995–97 the majority of regional chief executives were appointed to their posts by the president. The fact that regional leaders now come to office through the ballot box has significantly enhanced their local powers. No longer can the Russian President simply appoint loyal supporters to rule the regions.[37] Elections for regional assemblies have also taken place throughout the country and thousands of new deputies have taken their seats in local assemblies. Regional executive heads and the chairs of regional assemblies have been until very recently exofficio members of the Federation Council and new elections in the regions led to changes in its composition weakening Yeltsin's control over the upper chamber (see chapter 6).

For Lapidus these trends gave rise during the late 1990s to fears, that, at best, Russia [was] being progressively transformed from a federation to a confederation, and at worst that it [would] be thrown backward to the period of medieval chaos and conflict known as the era of 'appanage principalities'.[38] And Sakwa argues that by the end of the Yeltsin era Russia had witnessed the development of what he calls 'segmented regionalism', a process which 'fragmented the country, juridically, economically and, implicitly, in terms of sovereignty' and which transformed the country from a multinational state into a 'multi-state state'.[39] In a similar vein, Smith speaks of the creation of 'regional states' – regions which have increasingly adopted 'many of the features usually ascribed to the modern nation-state'.[40] By the mid-1990s major economic and political powers had passed from the centre to the regions and regional politics was firmly under the control of regional elites.

Economic separatism

Regional elites have also opted for economic separatism. As Smith writes, 'seven decades of centrally directed economic coordination between the regions has given way to the anarchy of regional autarky'.[41] With the breakdown of the Soviet centrally planned system, and a massive collapse in industrial production, regions have increasingly been forced to turn inward absorbed only by their own selfish interests. One symptom has been the breakdown of inter-regional trade, exacerbated by the dramatic fall in regional production. Thus, for example, the share of inter-regional trade as a part of Russia's gross regional product fell from 22 per cent in 1990 to approximately 12–14 per cent in 2000.[42]

Benefiting from the continuing political stalemate in Moscow a number of republics have refused to implement legislation concerning the privatisation of land, and in some regions (particularly those controlled by the communists) we have witnessed a denationalisation of industry. A number of republics have also unilaterally taken control of their land and natural resources. And throughout the 1990s regions and republics continued to attempt to blackmail the federal authorities by withholding taxes from Moscow. In those regions where privatisation has gone ahead there have been fierce battles between the centre and the regions over who should benefit from the spoils of these programmes.

Federal subjects have also imposed their own import duties and sales taxes on certain goods, prohibited the export of various products from their regions and set their own prices, all in clear violation of article 74 of the Russian Constitution. For example, Omsk Oblast placed a 50 per cent duty on imported alcoholic beverages and a 10 per cent duty on the sale of all imported foods, measures which were expected to bring in additional revenue of 830 billion roubles in 1997. And Yaroslavl' Oblast introduced a 4 per cent sales tax on various goods and services to offset costs for healthcare, education, and child benefits.[43]

These early moves to create regional economic autarkies intensified after the financial crisis of August 1998, when almost every region was forced to adopt protectionist measures to survive. Such actions have continued into the Putin era threatening to turn the Russian economy into a collection of closed regional markets. Putin in his first presidential address to the Duma in July 2000, spoke out against regional protectionism:

> The federal authorities are responsible for establishing uniform conditions for economic activity throughout the country. But regional agencies . . . are creating barriers to the free circulation of capital, goods and services. This is reprehensible and disgraceful! . . . Any actions by regional authorities that are aimed at restricting economic freedom must be halted as unconstitutional.[44]

During the Yeltsin period regions were free for the first time in their history to engage in the global economy. A number of republics and regions have now set up diplomatic channels with foreign states and begun to engage in foreign economic activities. Many of the republics now have their own foreign consulates, and they are independent members of international trade organisations. Thus, according to figures published in June 1999 Russian regions had signed more than 1,200 friendship agreements with partners in 69 foreign states. And 'permanent representatives' of the regions had been created in 46 foreign countries.[45] Over the period

1991–96, the regions and republics signed more than 300 trade agreements with foreign states and in a number of cases such deals were struck without the participation or sometimes even the knowledge of the relevant ministries in Moscow. Thus, for example, the Ministry of Foreign Affairs expressed some alarm with regard to an agreement signed between Kabardino-Balkariya and the Republic of Abkhazia (Georgia). And in 1995 Moscow was forced to annul a trade treaty between Kaliningrad Oblast and Lithuania as it conflicted with Federal legislation.[46]

The inter-regional economic associations

In order to increase their leverage with Moscow all of the regions (except Chechnya) have joined one or more of the regional economic associations set up over the period 1992–94 based on Soviet-era geographical administrative divisions. As Klimanov notes: 'In conditions marked by a long-term economic crisis, an undeveloped political system, and the lack of a comprehensive federal system, interregional cooperation expands the internal potential of regions and creates conditions for a more effective resolution of local political and economic problems'.[47]

Box 4.1 lists the eight inter-regional associations, their leaders and membership. As Klimanov notes, in each association there are supra-regional institutional structures including an executive and various economic committees. The highest decision making bodies are the councils which usually meet several times a year and are attended by senior government officials, often including the Prime Minister. As a measure of their importance Prime Minister Primakov incorporated the leaders of the associations into his cabinet in 1998.[48]

The associations have played an important role in aggregating and articulating the demands of the regions. As we would expect the most powerful associations are to be found in the most powerful economic regions. In addition to the Siberian lobby, here we may include the associations of the Urals, Volga and Central Russia.[49]

However, the power of the associations to affect policy making at the highest levels has been rather disappointing. The economic interests of the regions that make up each of the associations are highly diverse and regional leaders are often too preoccupied with their own internal problems to mount a unified campaign. Thus, for example, as Klimanov notes, the Siberian agreement is undermined by the division between the regions of west Siberia, whose industries are dominated by military industrial complex, and east Siberia, whose industries are based on the extraction of natural resources.

There are also tensions between regions and ethnic republics, and between those regions which managed to sign bilateral treaties with Moscow and those which did not. As Smith notes: the 'Siberian Accord'

Box 4.1   The inter-regional associations

1 *The Far East and Baikal Association*, consists of the republics of Buryatiya and
   Sakha (Yakutia), Primorskii and Khabarovsk krais, Amur, Kamchatka,
   Magadan, Chita, and Sakhalin oblasts, the Jewish autonomous oblast, and
   Koryak and Chukotka autonomous okrugs.

2 *The Siberian Accord Association* comprises the republics of Buryatiya, Altai,
   Khakasiya, along with Altai and Kransnoyarsk krais, Irkutsk, Novosibirsk,
   Omsk, Tomsk, and Kemerovo oblasts, plus Agin-Buryat, Taimyr, Ust-Orda
   Buryat, Khanty-Mansi, Yevenk, and Yamal-Nenets autonomous okrugs.

3 *The Greater Volga Association* includes the republics of Tatarstan, Mordoviya,
   Chuvashiya, and Marii-El, as well as Astrakhan, Volgograd, Nizhnii Novgorod,
   Penza, Samara, Saratov and Ulyanovsk oblasts.

4 *The Central Russia Association* is made up of Bryansk, Vladimir, Ivanovo, Kaluga,
   Kostroma, Moscow, Ryazan, Smolensk, Tver, Tula, and Yaroslavl oblasts, along
   with the city of Moscow.

5 *The Association of Cooperation of Republics, Krais and Oblasts of the Northern
   Caucuses* has on average the lowest standard of living of the eight regional
   groupings. It includes predominantly agricultural and mountainous areas:
   the republics of Adygeya, Dagestan, Ingushetiya, Kabardino-Balkariya,
   Karachaevo-Cherkesiya, North Osetiya-Alaniya, Kalmykiya, Krasnodar and
   Stavropol Krais and Rostov oblast.

6 *The Black Earth Association* consists of Voronezh, Belgorod, Kursk, Lipetsk, Orel,
   and Tambov oblasts.

7 *The Urals Regional Association* includes the republics of Bashkortostan and
   Udmurtiya, Komi-Permyak autonomous okrug and Kurgan, Orenburg, Perm,
   Sverdlovsk and Cheliabinsk oblasts.

8 *The North-West Association* comprises the republics of Kareliya and Komi, as
   well as Arkhangelsk, Vologda, Kaliningrad, Kirov, Leningrad, Murmanask,
   Novgorod, and Pskov oblasts. Nenets Autonomous Okrug, and St Petersburg.

Source: EWI Russian Regional Report, 15 January, 1997.

---

fragmented 'in part because the larger oblasts resented the way in which
Sakha used its position to secure considerable economic and financial
autonomy from Moscow'. And Kalmykiya withdrew its membership
from the Greater Volga Association after a dispute with neighbouring
Astrakhan oblast.[50] This has allowed the federal leadership to adopt a
policy of divide and rule with the associations. Moreover, leaders of the
associations tend to use their posts to further the interests of their own
regions rather than the associations as a whole and/or as a way of
launching national careers.

Finally, Smirnyagin makes the important point that vertical relations have long dominated horizontal relations in Russia. Horizontal contacts between regions are 'partial and intermittent' and, 'Even when horizontal disputes arise between regions, the leaders of contending regions launch their appeals first to Moscow rather than to each other'.[51] Moreover, as discussed in chapter 8 the powers of the associations have significantly declined since the creation of Putin's seven federal districts in 2000.

Federalism, ethnicity and democracy

Local democracy is surely a necessary pre-requisite for democratisation at the national level. And the provision of certain basic democratic procedures should, in a democracy, be universally available to all citizens across the federation regardless of their place of residence. Clearly democracy will be that much more difficult to create and consolidate in multinational states where there are disputes over the boundaries of the state and some groups wish to secede from the federation. Russia's wars with Chechnya have not only frightened other republics into submission, they have also bolstered authoritarianism at the centre and they played a major role in bringing President Putin to power. As Rustow stresses no democracy can be consolidated until consensus has been reached over national unity and any contested boundaries of the state have been settled.[52] National unity is achieved when 'the vast majority of citizens in a democracy-to-be . . . have no doubt or mental reservations as to which political community they belong to . . . [and] the people cannot decide until someone decides who are the people'.[53]

A further problem in multinational states, as Smith notes, 'is how to counter domination by either nationalist-minded minorities or the majority national group'. One answer for those who advocate a liberal federation 'is to prioritise the individual rights of citizens regardless of their ethnic or national affiliation'.[54] For as O'Donnell rightly observes: 'Citizenship can be universally exercised only when the normative system is guided by universal criteria, when the rule of law is effectively enforced, when public powers are willing and able to protect rights, and when all individuals enjoy some social and economic prerequisites'.[55]

One of the major failings of the Russian state has been the inability or unwillingness of the federal authorities to give equal rights to its citizens and the centre's tolerance of discrimination against minority nationalities, particularly in the ethnic republics and autonomies. Article 126 of the Russian Constitution guarantees the equality of all citizens regardless of nationality – including political rights. But in Russia republican elites regularly discriminate against minority groups and give preferential political representation to their indigenous populations even when that population does not comprise a majority in the given republic. As Kahn notes, whilst republican constitutions are 'replete with declarations about the supremacy of law, open, free and fair multiparty elections, freedom of speech, assembly and conscience', in practice they, 'embed special rights and privileges' for their indigenous citizens.[56] Thus, for example, most of the constitutions begin with declarations recognising the rights of the multinational peoples of the republics, but conclude 'with the assertion of the right to self-determination of a particular national group'.[57] Thus, article 69 of Bashkortostan's constitution declared that the republic 'was formed as a result of the realisation of the right of the Bashkir nation to self-determination and to defend the interests of all multinational people of the republic', even although as we noted above ethnic Bashkirs make up only 21.9 per cent of the population.

In Adygeya where ethnic Adygeya comprise 22.1 per cent of the population, the Republican Constitution declares that the republic was formed 'as a result of the realisation of the right to self-determination of the Adygeya people and the historically formed community of people who live on its territory'.[58] Non-indigenous citizens of ethnic republics are also discriminated against when it comes to their rights to stand for elected posts (see chapter 9). Thus, for example, ten republics require that candidates, for select political offices, must possess knowledge of both Russian and the titular language. In Sakha, 'where Russians and ethnic Sakha respectively comprise 50.3 per cent and 33.4 per cent of the population, knowledge of both languages is required for candidates for the posts of President and Chairman of either house of the Parliament'. Even although only 2 per cent of Russian's know how to speak Sakha.[59] In Bashkortostan, where Bashkiri comprise just 22 per cent of the population and where Bashkir is only spoken by 15 per cent of the inhabitants (that is not even by all Bashkiry) the Bashkir language alongside Russian is mandatory for all candidates in presidential elections.[60] And furthermore this electoral law neglects the languages of the Tatar, Chuvash, Marii and other nationalities which as Khan notes, comprise 36 per cent of the population.[61]

In November 2000 President Aslan Dzharimov of Adygeya made changes to the way the electoral districts were formed in the republic in a blatant attempt to guarantee that a majority of ethnic Adygeys would gain election to the newly created upper chamber of the Republican Parliament, even although, as noted above, Adygeys make up only one-quarter of the population of the republic. In defiance of rulings by the Russian Constitutional Court and the Adygeyan prosecutors' office, which declared the elections illegal, Dzharimov pressed ahead with the elections in March 2001. As planned, ethnic Adygeys won a majority of seats.[62]

The discrimination against non-indigenous groups in the republics even when these groups comprise a larger per centage of the population than the titular nationality is graphically illustrated by their under-representation in government and parliamentary posts. Thus, for example, in the republic of Sakha (Yakutiya), Sakha make up 34 per cent of the population but 69 per cent of posts in government structures. In Tatarstan 78.1 of the governing elite are Tatar even although they comprise 48.3 per cent of the population. And Tatars make up 73.3 per cent of the members of the Tatarstan Parliament – Russians 25.1 per cent and other nationalities 1.6 per cent.[63]

In Buryatiya the Buryats comprise 24.0 per cent of the population but they held 43.1 per cent of the seats in the Republican parliament in June 1994.[64] Of the eight top politicians in Bashkortostan in 1997 (President, Prime Minister, Head of Presidential Administration, State Secretary, leaders of the State Assembly), seven were Bashkirs in 1997, and only one was Russian.[65] It is also instructive to note that the per centage of Bashkiry in the republic's elite structures has risen in the post-communist period (see tables 4.3 and 4.4).

However, factors other than the ethnic one must be considered in assessing the likelihood of secession and the prospects for democratic consolidation in the republics. The most important additional factor is the overall wealth and economic status of the federal subjects and the degree to which they are economically dependent on the centre and this is one of the topics we now turn to in chapter 5.

Table 4.3   Ethnic composition of government elite in Bashkortostan, 1990–97

Nationality	% of population	Secretaries of raikoms and gorkoms, 1990	Chairs of raion and city soviets, 1990	Chairs of executive committees of city and raion soviets, 1990	Chief administrators, cities and districts, 1997	Members of cabinet of ministers, 1997
Bashkir	21.9	44.8	44.7	32.9	58.5	65.5
Russian	39.3	31.3	32.9	21.1	15.0	19.0
Tatar	28.4	19.4	15.8	38.2	18.5	13.0
Others	10.6	4.5	6.8	7.8	8.0	2.5

Source: R. Gallyamov, 'Politicheskie elity Rossiiskikh respublik: osobennosti transformatsii v postsovetskii period', in A. Mel'vil' (ed.), *Transformatsiya Rossiiskikh regional'nykh elit v sravnitel'noi perspektive* (Moscow: MONF, 1999), p. 167.

Table 4.4   Ethnic representation of parliamentary elite, 1980–95

Nationality	Supreme Soviet, 1980	Supreme Soviet, 1985	Supreme Soviet, 1990	State assembly: chamber of representatives, 1995	State assembly: legislative chamber, 1995
Bashkir	38.6	40.3	33.5	41.1	55.8
Russian	33.2	32.8	35.7	23.3	20.5
Tatar	20.7	20.7	22.5	29.5	14.7
Other	7.5	5.7	8.2	6.1	8.8

Source: R. Gallyamov, 'Politicheskie elity Rossiiskikh respublik: osobennosti transformatsii v postsovetskii period', in A. Mel'vil' (ed.), *Transformatsiya Rossiiskikh regional'nykh elit v sravnitel'noi perspektive* (Moscow: MONF, 1999), p. 167.

Notes

1 R. Sakwa, *Russian Politics and Society* (Routledge, 2nd edn, 1996), p. 31.
2 R. L. Watts, *Comparing Federal Systems* (Montreal and Kingston: McGill-Queen's University Press, 2nd edn, 1999), p. 6.
3 D. Kempton, 'Russian federalism: continuing myth or political salvation', *Demokratizatsiya*, 9:2 (Spring 2001), 229.
4 Kempton, 'Russian federalism', 202.
5 G. Smith, *The Post-Soviet States* (London: Arnold, 1999), p. 93.
6 According to official statistics for October 1999 to October 4, 2000, 2,500 Russian troops were killed and 7,000 wounded. See E. Pain, '"Back to the USSR": new trends in Russian regional policy', *Demokratizatsiya*, 9:2 (Spring 2001), 187.
7 E. A. Payin, 'Ethnic separatism', in J. R. Azrael and E. A. Payin (eds) [in other cases transliterated as Pain], *Conflict and Consensus in Ethno-Political and Centre–Periphery Relations in Russia* (Santa Monica, California: Rand, 1998), p. 18.
8 *Ibid.*
9 However, Putin's attacks on the autonomy of regional elites and in particular the sovereignty claims of the ethnic republics may give nationalist movements new impetus and support (see chapter 6).
10 D. Furman, 'A disastrous love of symmetry – consolidation of the federation might only intensify separatism', *Obshchaya Gazeta*, 22 (June 2000), 7. Translated in the *CDPSP*, 52:22 (2000), 4.
11 *Ibid.*
12 N. Arkhangelskaya, 'The problem of separatism in Russia: elitist separatism has its price', *Kommersant Daily*, 29 (November 1996), p. 3. Translated in *CDPSP*, 48 (1996), 5.
13 E. Payin and A. Susarov, 'Line five in the mirror of demography', *Rossiiskie Vesti* (October 30, 1997), p. 2. *CDPSP*, 49:44 (1997), 10. This represents an increase of 1.42 per centage points over the last census which was compiled in

1989. The increase is largely the result of an influx of migrants from the former republics of the USSR.

14 *Ibid.*

15 *Ibid.*, 11.

16 Of the 21 republics, 7 are in the North Caucasus: (Adygeya, Chechnya, Dagestan, Ingushetiya, Kabardino-Balkariya, Karachaevo-Cherkessiya, and North Osetiya), 6 are situated in The middle reaches of the Volga River and the Urals (Bashkortostan, Chuvashiya, Marii-El, Mordoviya, Tatarstan and Udmurtiya); and 5 are located in Siberia (Buryatiya, Altai, Khakassiya, Sakha and Tuva). The remaining 3 are Kalmykiya, situated on the lower reaches of the Volga; Kareliya, on the border with Finland; and Komi, in northern European Russia. See, A. Sheehy, 'Russia's republics: a threat to its territorial integrity?', *Radio Free Europe/Radio Liberty Research Report*, 2:20 (May 14, 1993), 35.

17 In Dagestan there are 33 national groups, neither of which comprises a majority. Russians account for only 9.2 per cent of the total population of Dagestan.

18 Other ethnic groups which rose in size in their home republics were: Buryatiya (from 23 per cent of the total population in 1979 to 28.6 per cent in 1994); Adygeitsy in Adygeya from 21.4 to 25.2 per cent; Yakuty in Sakha (Yakutiya) from 36.9 to 39.6; Tuvintsy in Tyva from 60.5 to 67.2 per cent; Osetintsy in Ossetiya, from 50.5 to 59.3.

19 Fedorov singles out 13 of Russia's 89 regions where the nationalities question has led to separatist demands being made by members of the regional elites; the republics of Ingushetiya, Kalmykiya, Chechnya, Dagestan, Kabardino-Balkariya, Karachaevo-Cherkessiya, Altai, Tyva, Chuvashiya, Tatarstan and Bashkiriya; and Komi-Permyakiya and Aga-Buryatiya autonomous okrugs. However, the indigenous population comprises a majority in only six of these regions. See A. F. Fedorov, *Rossiiskii Federalizm*, p. 243.

20 One other non-ethnically based region which may eventually secede from the federation is Kaliningrad which is geographically cut off from the rest of the country nesting between the Baltic sea, bordering on Lithuania and Poland.

21 Payin, 'Ethnic separatism', p. 19.

22 This also applies to Kabardino-Balkariya and Karachaevo-Cherkessiya (see discussion below).

23 D. Treinin, *The End of Eurasia: Russia on the Border Between Geopolitics and Globalisation* (Washington, DC: Carnegie Endowment for Inernational Peace, 2001), pp. 253–4.

24 *Ibid.*, p. 258.

25 Decision of the Russian Federation Constitutional Court, no. 12, July 14, 1997.

26 S. Nysten-Haarala, *Development of Constitutionalism and federalism in Russia* (Austria: International Institute for Applied System Analysis, 2000), p. 45.

27 In the Evreiskaya autonomous oblast, the Jewish population comprises only 4.2 per cent of the overall population and the Russian population makes up 83.2 per cent.

28 A. Paretskaya, *OMRI Russian Regional Report* (1997), 5.

29 A. Arbatskaya, 'Northern okrugs strengthening political influence in Tyumen', *EWI Russian Regional Report*, 6:45 (December 19, 2001), 4. According to Arbatskaya the okrugs have agreed to invest 15 billion dollars in the southern part of Tyumen Oblast over the period 2001–6.

30 *RFE/RL Federation Report*, 3:12 (April 4, 2001).

31 *EWI Russian Regional Report*, 2 (January 1999).

32 On December 18, 2001 Putin signed a federal constitutional law 'On the order of adopting and establishing new federation subjects', *Interfax* (December 18, 2001), p. 2. As Corwin notes, according to this new law, 'if two or more federation subjects would like to combine, then the issue must first be put to a referendum for citizens within the relevant regions'. J. Corwin, 'Putin signs law on procedure for altering borders, *RFE/RL Federation Report* (December 19, 2001), 2.

33 S. Khemkin, 'Separatizm v Rossii – pozadi ili vperedi?', *Pro et Contra*, 2:2 (Spring, 1997), 18.

34 S. Parish, 'Centre continues to rail against legal separatism', *OMRI Russian Regional Report*, 11:3 (1996), 3.

35 *Izvestiya*, March 4, 1997, p. 4.

36 A. Muchnik, EWI, *Russian Regional Report*, 4:15 (1999), 8.

37 *Vybory Glav Ispolnitel'noi Vlasti Sub'ektov Rossiiskoi Federatsii 1995–97* (Moscow: Ves' Mir, 1997), p. 10.

38 G. W. Lapidus, 'Assymetrical federalism and state breakdown in Russia', *Post-Soviet Affairs*, 15:1 (1999), 77.

39 R. Sakwa, 'Federalism, sovereignty and democracy', in C. Ross (ed.), *Regional Politics in Russia* (Manchester: Manchester University Press, 2002), p. 2.

40 Smith, *The Post-Soviet States*, p. 185.

41 G. Smith, 'The ethno-politics of federation without federalism', in D. Lane (ed.), *Russia in Transition* (Harlow, Essex: Longman, 1995), p. 29.

42 A. G. Granberg, *Osnovy regional'noi Ekonomiki* (Moscow: Tacis, 2000), p. 303.

43 N. Grushina, 'Local authorities resort to unlawful means to raise money', *OMRI Russian Regional Report*, 2:10 (1997), pp. 7–8.

44 V. V. Putin, 'The kind of Russia we are building'. Annual message from the President of the Russian Federation to the Federal Assembly of the Russian Federation, *Rossiiskaya gazeta* (July 11, 2000), 1, 3. Translated in *CDPSP*, 52:28 (2000), 6.

45 A. F. Federov, *Rossiiskii Federalizm*, p. 169.

46 A. Zergunin, 'Russia's regions and foreign policy', *Internationale Politik*, 1:3 (Autumn, 2000), 27.

47 V. Klimanov, *EWI Russian Regional Report*, Part 2, 4:41 (November 4, 1999), 1.

48 *Ibid.*, 2.

49 Smith, *The Post-Soviet States*, p. 208.

50 *Ibid.*, p. 209.

51 L. Smirnyagin, 'Typologies of regional conflicts in modern Russia', in Payin and Azrael, *Conflict and Consensus*, pp. 3–4.

52 Linz and Stepan, 'Toward consolidated democracies', p. 17.

53 D. Rustow, cited in Sorenson, *Democracy and Democratisation*, p. 41.

54 Smith, *The Post-Soviet States*.

55 G. O'Donnell, 'Delegative democracy?', University of Chicago, Working Paper, 21 (1992). Cited in A. Przeworksi, *Sustainable Democracy*, p. 34.

56 J. Kahn, 'A federal façade: problems in the development of Russian federalism', D.Phil. thesis (University of Oxford, 1999), p. 211.

57 *Ibid.*, p. 213.

58 *Ibid.*
59 *Ibid.*, p. 219.
60 A. F. Fedorov, *Rossiiskii Federalizm*, p. 154.
61 Kahn, 'A federal façade', p. 219.
62 O. Tsvetkov, *EWI, Russian Regional Report* (April 5, 2001).
63 R. Gallyamov, 'Politicheskie elity Rossiiskikh respublik: osobennosti transfor-matsii v postsovetskii period', in A. Mel'vil' (ed.), *Transformatsiya Rossiiskikh Regional'nykh Elit v Sravnitel'noi Perspektive* (Moscow: MONF, 1999), p. 166.
64 Kahn, 'A federal façade', p. 254.
65 R. Gallyamov, 'Politicheskie elity Rossiiskikh respublik', p. 167.

5

Fiscal federalism and socio-economic asymmetry

He who controls the economy controls the polity. But who does control the purse strings in Russia, and how are federal funds distributed across the federation? To what degree have federal policies ameliorated the high levels of socio-economic asymmetry inherited from the USSR? To answer these questions we need to examine fiscal federalism taking into account both the formal structural aspects of the system and the more hidden informal practices.

Fiscal federalism

As Bradshaw and Hanson note, 'fiscal federalism brings together an analysis of the workings of the federal system in Russia with an assessment of the logic underlying the redistribution of federal tax revenues between regions'.[1] In addition to the formal income and expenditure flows between federal and subnational budgets which are distributed through the tax system, it is important to note that there are a wide range of other forms of fiscal transfers: subventions, net mutual payments, credits, social welfare programmes, and off-budget funds.

Ideally, fiscal federalism, it is argued, 'should promote territorial justice, economic efficiency, and political stability'.[2] According to Hanson *et al.*, fiscal federalism requires that: (1) the responsibilities of each level of government should be clearly delineated; (2) sub-national governments should have the means for primary control over economic matters within their jurisdiction; (3) the budgets of sub-national governments should be substantially independent of those at higher levels; (4) transfers between levels should be based on stable, transparent, public-domain formulae.[3] As we shall see Russia is still very far away from implementing these principles.

Fiscal centralisation or decentralisation

Two of the most commonly employed measures of fiscal decentralisation, 'are the share of the subnational budgets in consolidated revenue and expenditures, and the degree to which subnational budgets consist of revenue raised on their territories as opposed to transfers'.[4] And by both of these (aggregate) measures the Russian system especially over the period 1993–98 was 'rather decentralised'.[5] Thus, as table 5.1 clearly demonstrates, in 1992 the balance of funds between the federal and sub-national budgets was a ratio of 56.0/44.0 per cent in favour of the centre. However, over the period 1993–99 there was a steady increase in the share of revenues allocated to the regional budgets, so that by 1998 the balance of revenues was the reverse of that found in 1992, 44.0/56.0 per cent in favour of the regions. Nevertheless, by 2001 President Putin had shifted the balance back in favour of the centre (55.0/45.0 per cent).[6]

Turning to an examination of the share of federal transfers in subna-tional budgets these made up approximately 15 per cent in Russia in 1999 compared with 30 per cent in India, China and Mexico, and 25 per cent in Brazil.[7]

However, as Lavrov *et al.*, note, when we measure levels of decen-tralisation according to formal levels of 'subnational autonomy' we find that the Russian system is highly centralised. Thus, compared to federa-tions such as Canada, Switzerland and the US, where subnational gov-ernments have a great deal of fiscal autonomy, in Russia the vast majority of decisions concerning the income and expenditure of subnational budgets are decided by the Federal Government in Moscow. Indeed, in the Russian Federation 'just 15 per cent of regional revenue derives from taxes over which the regional authorities have any sort of real decision making authority, and even these taxes are usually rigidly regulated from above or subject to federal spending ceilings'.[8]

Moreover, according to changes made to the tax code that became operational in January 2001 the Federal Government has increased its

Table 5.1 Share of the income of federal and territorial (subnational) budgets (%) in total state revenue, 1992–2001

	1992	1993	1994	1995	1996	1997[a]	1998	1999	2000	2001
Federal budgets	56.0	49.0	48.0	54.0	49.0	47.0	44.0	51.0	52.0	55.0
Territorial budgets	44.0	50.0	52.0	46.0	51.0	53.2	56.0	49.0	48.0	45.0

Source: Data for 1992–97, Yu. N. Gladkii and A. I. Chistobaev, *Osnovy Regional'noi Politiki* (St Petersburg: Izdatel'stvo Mikhailova V.A., 1998), p. 430; for 2000, *EWI Russian Regional Report* 5:30 (August 2, 2000); for 2001, *EWI RRR*, 6:20 (May 30, 2001), pp. 4–5.
Note: [a] January–June 1997.

control over regional finances even further. Thus, for example, the centre now controls 100 per cent of the value-added tax whereas previously the regions controlled 15 per cent of it. The regions have also been left with a smaller percentage of turnover tax to finance housing and roads. Responding to these developments, Belgorod Governor Yevgenii Savchenko declared that the new tax regime would lead to the 'formation of a unitary state in which all regions will be dependent on the centre'.[9] And 'Moscow Mayor Yurii Luzhkov warned that the Federal Government would now control 65 per cent of the country's revenue, leaving only 35 per cent for the regions'.[10] As we shall discuss below, the vast majority of regions have had to rely on additional fiscal transfers from the federal budget to meet their expenditure obligations. However, the creation of a single 'Fund for the Financial Support of Subjects of the Federation' in 1994 has been a positive factor in channelling such extra resources to the most needy regions.[11]

In discussing fiscal federalism we need to make a distinction between 'structure' and 'process'. For whilst in formal terms the fiscal system is highly centralised, in practice it operates with a high degree of regional autonomy operating behind the scenes. As the 2000 OECD Report concludes, 'Recent years have witnessed a striking and growing contrast between a formal highly-centralised fiscal federalist system and actual practice, under which a large degree of financial authority is exercised at the subnational level through informal channels'.[12]

Non-budget' (or 'off-budget') funds are one such informal channel through which the regions are able to exercise a considerable degree of local autonomy. These funds include pensions and roads funds, income from export privileges, and hard currency allocations. As Makushkin notes, almost 50 per cent of these funds are allocated to finance social services. But, 'unlike formal budgetary issues, the spending part of these non-budgetary funds is not controlled by the federal treasury'. This opens the way for bureaucratic manipulation of these financial sources and provides grounds for corruption.[13] 'Money surrogates, particularly debt offsets, have been used as primary tools for the conduct of relatively independent fiscal policies at the subnational level'. These include the use of 'barter chains', 'creative book keeping' and 'individualised tax treatment'. Moreover, regional administrations will often have very cosy relations with the financial institutions in their territories, including direct participation in their capital, indirect participation through affiliated companies, control of utilities, control of various inspections empowered to administer penalties and fines, close ties with the courts and federal anti-trust or tax bodies, licensing, and the police.[14] As we noted in chapter 3 regional governors have also been able to capture control over the appointment of federal representatives including those from the Inspectorate of Taxes.

Turning to an examination of the expenditure side of budget relations, the OECD in its Economic Survey of Russia in 2000 noted that, 'ambiguity in expenditure assignments has plagued the development of fiscal federalist relations in Russia'.[15] In particular there has been a lack of clarity over those areas, such as education, health and social policy, which come under the joint jurisdiction of the regions and the federal government. In most cases the vast majority of such expenditures have been delegated to the subnational levels in the form of unfunded federal mandates (amounting to 600 billion roubles in 2001 or 8 per cent of the country's GDP) which most regional governments are too poor to implement. As a result, almost all regions suffer from chronic budget deficits. Thus, for example, in 1997 only Moscow city and the Nenets AO had balanced budgets.[16]

As was the case in the communist era, local administrations have also relied on local deals with the major enterprises situated on their territories for the provision of social services and maintenance of the local infrastructure.[17] In return, these enterprises can expect to be rewarded with special 'tax privileges, debt restructuring, and protection from bankruptcy or competition'.[18] Thus for example, Chelyabinsk Governor, Petr Sumin announced that he was granting political protection from possible bankruptcy to the 200 companies that were most important to the region's economy.[19] In many cases regional administrations will also own shares in local enterprises, and will have their own authorised commercial banks to conduct their financial affairs. Sverdlovsk Governor Eduard Rossel issued a decree preventing shareholders in key oblast companies from removing directors without first gaining his approval and he needled his way into bankruptcy proceedings in the region by establishing an oblast controlled management company. Privatisation of industry has also increased the opportunity for regional leaders and enterprise directors to engage in such bilateral deals, and it has put a great deal of regional economic policy out of the hands of the federal government in Moscow.

Economic and social asymmetry

There are vast differences across the Federation both in the economic status of federal subjects and the welfare provisions of their citizens. And despite the official policy, pursued for many years, of evening out the level of social, economic and cultural developments in the various regions, there are very great differences among them in terms of the level of production and consumption. According to Hanson, 'the 89 Russian provinces probably differ more widely in development level than the member states of the European Union'.[20] Indeed, the territory of the Russian Federation presents the whole spectrum of development from the 'agrarian' stage to the 'industrial' stage.[21] And economic strength leads to differentials in the political powers of regional elites. However, as we have shown in chapter 3, bilateral treaties have intensified the existing levels of socio-economic asymmetry in the Federation creating tensions both horizontally between members of the federation and vertically between subjects and the federal government.

Elites in rich and financially independent regions, such as the so called 'donor regions' will have far greater bargaining powers with the federal authorities than elites from regions which are economically dependent on the centre. As we noted in chapter 4 the economic status of federal subjects will have an important impact on their sovereignty and secessionist claims. Those subjects which are mired in poverty, and depend on federal handouts are hardly likely to pose any real ethnic or separatist challenge to Moscow.

Industrial production and gross regional product

There are tremendous variations in the volume of industrial production which ranged from a high of 228.929 million roubles in Tyumen Oblast to just 13 million in the tiny Yevenk AO, in 1998. In 1999 gross regional product varied from 362.5 billion roubles in Moscow to 1.1 billion roubles in Ingushetiya (table 5.2).

Foreign investment and exports

In 1999 the export industry in Moscow was worth 11.3 billion dollars whereas in each of the following regions the total value of exports was less than 10 million dollars; Tyva, Altai, Adygeya, Karachaevo-Cherkessiya, Kalmykiya, Komi-Permyak, Agin-Buryatiya and Ust'-Ordina Buryatiya AOs and the Yevreiskii Autonomous Oblast.[22]

There are also sharp variations in the levels of foreign investment, with the top ten regions attracting 80.4 per cent of all such investments in 1995 and 75.5 per cent in 1999. In 1995 nearly half of all foreign investments were directed to Moscow city (46.9 per cent), and in 1999 over a quarter (27.8 per cent), see table 5.3.

Tax contributions to the federal budget

These sharp variations in the level of economic development have led to a situation whereby just two-thirds of all taxes paid to the federal budget come from just 10 of Russia's 89 regions. And Moscow's contributions in 1998 and 1999 made up approximately one-third of the total tax revenues going to the federal budget (see table 5.4).[23]

Table 5.2 Top ten and bottom ten regions of Russia according to volume of gross regional product (GRP) in 1998 and industrial production (IP) in 1999

Region	GRP (billion roubles)	Region	IP (million roubles)
Top ten		*Top ten*	
Moscow city	362.5	Tyumen Oblast	228,929
Tyumen Oblast	201.2	Khanty-Mansi AO	176,787
Moscow Oblast	100.6	Moscow city	175,054
St.Petersburg	89.8	Krasnoyarsk Krai	124,498
Sverdlovsk Oblast	80.7	Sverdlovsk Oblast	114,714
Samara Oblast	72.7	Samara Oblast	108,102
Krasnoyarsk krai	71.6	St.Petersburg	104,671
Tatarstan	67.7	Tatarstan	100,534
Bashkortostan	64.2	Chelyabinsk Oblast	91,134
Perm	55.6	Bashkortostan	89,872
Bottom ten		*Bottom ten*	
Kabardino-Balkariya	6.4	Kalmykiya	910
North Osetiya-Alaniya	4.1	Chukotka	868
Adygeya	3.4	Buryatiya	609
Karachaevo-Cherkesiya	2.9	Ingushetiya	406
Chukotka	2.6	Permyak	249
Evreiskii	1.8	Altai Republic	227
Tyva	1.8	Chita Oblast	117
Kalmykiya	1.7	Taimyr	66.8
Altai Republic	1.6	Agin-Yevenk	60.6
Ingushetiya Republic	1.1	Buryatiya	13.0

Source: *Rossiya v Tsifrakh* (Moscow: Goskomstat, 2000), pp. 34–41.

Variations in the standard of living and social conditions

These sharp variations in economic development are also reflected in wide regional variations in the standard of living of the Russian population. Thus, for example, in 1999 monthly expenditure per capita in the resource-rich Yamalo-Nenets AO was twice the national average and seventeen times that of poverty stricken Ingushetiya. Average income per capita in the city of Moscow was four times the national average and fifteen times greater than in Ingushetiya (see table 5.5). In comparison, variations in the average income per capita in the German Lander vary by a factor no greater than 1.5. However, it is important to remember that such inequalities in Russia were the result of a sharp and prolonged

Table 5.3 Ten largest regions according to their share of total volume of
foreign investment in 1995 and 1999 (%)

	1995		*1999*
Moscow	46.9	Moscow	27.8
Moscow Oblast	7.4	Sakhalin Oblast	10.7
Tatarstan	5.8	Omsk Oblast	9.3
St Petersburg	5.6	St Petersburg	7.3
Tyumen Oblast	3.7	Krasnodar Krai	5.3
Samara Oblast	2.5	Moscow Oblast	4.6
Tver Oblast	2.4	Nenets AO	3.6
Nizhegorod Oblast	2.2	Leningrad Oblast	3.0
Novosibirsk Oblast	2.1	Krasnoyarsk Krai	2.1
Sakhalin Oblast	1.8	Sverdlovsk Oblast	1.8
Total	80.4	Total	75.5

Source: Leonid Vardomskii, 'Vneshneekonomicheskie svyazi regionov', in *Russian Regions
in 1999: An Annual Supplement to Russia's Political Almanac* (Moscow: Carnegie Centre, 2000),
p. 114.

economic decline in the overall growth of the Russian economy. As
Hanson and Bradshaw point out Russian GDP fell by 47 per cent over the
ten-year period 1989–99.[24]

The average monthly wage in the oil rich Khanty-Mansi AO in 2000
was four times the national average, and 10.4 times higher than in the
Republic of Dagestan.[25] In 1999 the average level of unemployment in the
Russian Federation was 13.4 per cent but there were wide variations
across the country ranging from 5.6 per cent in Moscow City to 31.2 per
cent in Dagestan, 33.4 per cent in North Osetiya-Alaniya, and 51.8 per cent
in refugee flooded Ingushetiya.[26] There are also significant variations in
the level of poverty across the Federation. In 1995 there were 51 subjects
of the Federation where a quarter of the population or higher were living
below the officially recognised subsistence level, including 5 subjects
where the figure was over 50 per cent, Kurgan (50 per cent), Buryatiya
(55), Kalmykiya (60), Chita (67), and Tyva (73 per cent).[27] In 1999 in the
aftermath of the August 1998 economic crises there was a substantial
increase in the number of subjects where poverty levels exceeded 25 per
cent (79 regions) and where over half the population were living
below the poverty line (29 regions).[28] Of these, Agin-Buryatiya AO and
Ingushetiya had staggeringly high levels of 96.8 and 95.1 per cent
respectively; Ust'-Ordin Buryatiya AO (89.4 per cent), Chita Oblast (88.8
per cent) and Tyva (78.6 per cent). In contrast, at the other end of the scale,
Yamalo-Nenets AO had a poverty level of 13.3 per cent, Khanty-Mansi

Table 5.4 Concentration of tax contributions to the federal budget, 1996–98

	1996	*1997*	*1998*	*1999*
Share of taxes of federal budget collected in Moscow	26.0	30.9	36.1	32.71
Share of taxes of federal budget collected in first 5 regions	47.3	52.7	55.1	51.53
Share of taxes of federal budget collected in first 10 regions[a]	59.6	64.3	65.4	62.74

Source: Figures for 1996–98, O.V. Kuznetsova, 'Territorial'naya struktura nalogovovo potentsiala', in A. M. Lavrov (ed.), *Federal'nyi Byudzhet i Regiony: Opyt Analiza Finansovykh Potokov* (Moscow: Instityt Vostok Zapad, MAKS Press, 1999), p. 64; figures for 1999, Olga Kuznetsova, 'Regional'nye Byudgety', in *Russia's Regions in 1999: An Annual Supplement to Russia's Political Almanac* (Moscow: Carnegie Centre, 2000), p. 77.
Note: [a] The first ten regions in 1999 were: Moscow (32.71), Khanty-Mansi AO (6.45), St Petersburg (4.54), Moscow Oblast (4.33), Samara Oblast (3.50), Yamalo-Nenets A0 (2.85), Krasnodar Krai (2.25), Krasnoyarsk Krai (2.07), Perm Oblast (2.05), and Sverdlovsk Oblast (1.99).

Table 5.5 Regional variations in per capita income and expenditure, 1999

	Monthly income (thousand roubles)		*Monthly expenditure (thousand roubles)*
Moscow City	6,002	Yamalo-Nenets AO	3,011
Yamalo-Nenets AO	5,297	Magadan Oblast	2,407
Khanty-Mansi AO	4,329	Samara Oblast	2,352
Tyumen Oblast	3,371	Tyumen Oblast	2,216
Sakha Republic	2,797	Kamchatka Oblast	2,052
Ingushetiya	390	Ingushetiya	181

Source: *Rossiya v Tsifrakh* (Moscow: Goskomstat, 2000), pp. 34–43.

AO (15.6 per cent), Tyumen Oblast (17.8 per cent), Murmansk (19.8 per cent), and Moscow city (23.3 per cent).[29]

In an excellent study of regional poverty which Smirnov conducted in 1997 each of Russia's regions was ranked according to seven key socio-economic variables:[30] (1) growth of the population in 1996 per 1000 inhabitants; (2) the balance of immigration/emigration in 1996 per 10,000 inhabitants; (3) level of unemployment as a percentage of economically active members of the population in 1997; (4) intensity of the labour market in 1997 calculated as the number of unemployed/to number of

Table 5.6   Measuring poverty in Russia's regions, 1996–97

1 Regions with favourable social conditions	Average rank	2 Regions with moderate social conditions	Average rank
Belgorod Oblast	16.3	Voronezh Oblast	34.1
Lipetsk Oblast	17.4	Ul'yanov Oblast	34.3
Moscow City	19.4	Sverdlovsk Oblast	34.7
Rep. Sakha (Yakutiya)	19.7	Nizhegorod Oblast	35.0
Orenburg Oblast	20.1	Novosibirsk Oblast	35.7
Rep. Tatarstan	20.7	Omsk Oblast	35.9
Stavropol' Krai	20.9	Astrakhan Oblast	36.1
Rep. Bashkortostan	22.9	Yevenk AO	38.0
Krasnoyarsk Krai	23.3	Kaluga Oblast	38.1
Rostov Oblast	23.7	Kamchatka Oblast	39.4
Yamalo-Nenets AO	24.0	Krasnoyarsk Krai	39.4
Khanty-Mansi AO	26.2	Volgograd Oblast	39.9
Tyumen Oblast	26.3	Tul'a Oblast	39.9
Smolensk Oblast	27.4	Tver Oblast	40.0
Vogograd Oblast	27.9	Magadan Oblast	40.9
Orel Oblast	28.7	Ryazan Oblast	40.9
St Petersburg	28.9	Kaliningrad Oblast	41.4
Kursk Oblast	29.0	Rep. Komi	42.0
Samara Oblast	29.3	Irkutsk Oblast	42.6
Moscow Oblast	30.1	Rep. Khakasiya	43.7
Kemerovo Oblast	33.6	Rep. Altai	44.1
Chelyabinsk Oblast	33.7	Amur Oblast	44.3

Source: S. N. Smirnov, *Regional'nye Aspekty Sotsial'noi Politiki* (Moscow: Gelios, 1999), pp. 63–4.

vacancies; (5) average length of time workers had been unemployed on December 31, 1996; (6) the ratio of average wages and payments from the Federal Social Fund to the minimum subsistence level of the able bodied population in December 1996; (7) housing provision in 1996, calculated as number of inhabitants per square metre.

Table 5.6 shows each region's average rank for all seven factors. The table is divided into four groups according to the aggregate rank of each region: (1) regions with relatively favourable social conditions, (2) regions with moderate conditions, (3) regions with unfavourable conditions, and finally, (4) regions in crises. Smirnov found that 44 of Russia's 89 regions were either regions in crises (22 regions) or regions with unfavourable social conditions (22 regions). And the gap between the most favourable region, Belgorod Oblast with an overall rank of 16.3, and the least favourable region, Ivanovo Oblast with a rank of 73.4, varied by a factor of 4.5.

3 Regions with unfavourable social conditions	Average rank	4 Crises regions	Average rank
Rep. Buryatiya	44.4	Sakhalin Oblast	55.4
Tomsk Oblast	45.0	Rep. Tyva	55.9
Saratov Oblast	45.7	Tambov Oblast	57.0
Ust'-Orda Buryat AO	46.5	Bryansk Oblast	58.7
Leningrad Oblast	46.9	Nenetskii AO	58.8
Novgorod Oblast	47.3	Rep Ingushetiya	59.7
Rep Kabardino-Balkariya	47.9	Yaroslavskaya Oblast	59.9
Khabarovsk Krai	48.3	Rep. Dagestan	60.4
Rep Karachaevo-Cherkesiya	48.7	Aginskii-Buryat AO	60.5
Taimyr AO	49.3	Rep. Kalmykiya	60.6
Yevreiskaya AOB	49.5	Rep. Udmurtskaya	60.6
Altai Krai.	49.7	Vladimir Oblast	60.9
Primorski Krai	50.6	Kurgan Oblast	61.0
Perm Oblast	51.6	Chita Oblast	62.0
Rep. North Osetiya-Alaniya	52.0	Pskov Oblast	63.0
Rep. Chuvashkaya	52.1	Kirov Oblast	63.1
Rep. Adygeya	52.1	Penza Oblast	63.3
Rep. Marii El	53.1	Arkhangelskaya Oblast	64.9
Rep. Kareliya	53.1	Komi-Perm Oblast	65.2
Chukotskii AO	54.0	Rep. Mordoviya	65.3
Kostroma Oblast	54.1	Koryakskii AO	66.8
Murmansk Oblast	54.3	Ivanovo Oblast	73.4

Variations in taxes maintained

There are also vast differences in the percentage of local taxes which regions are permitted to maintain for their own expenditures. Special tax concessions and increased federal subsidies have been a common occurrence in Russia and were also a central feature of many of the special agreements attached to bilateral agreements. Thus as table 5.7 demonstrates whilst the top ten regions in Russia were able to maintain between 74 and 82 per cent of the local taxes collected in their regions in 1996, those regions in the bottom ten were permitted to keep only between 9 and 54 per cent.

Federal transfers

There are also major variations in the degree to which federal subjects are dependent on federal subsidies and transfers. The number of regions

Table 5.7   % of local taxes maintained by subjects of the Federation, 1996

Top ten regions	%	Bottom ten regions	%
Vologda Oblast	74	Ingushetiya Republic	9
Komi-Permyak AO	74	Kalmykiya Republic	41
Ust'-Orda Buryat AO	74	Moscow City	42
Koryak AO	75	Khanty-Mansi AO	43
Novosibirsk Oblast	76	Yaroslavl' Oblast	49
Komi Republic	76	Omsk Oblast	51
Chukotka AO	79	Moscow Oblast	52
Khakasiya Republic	80	Orel Oblast	53
Yevenk AO	82	Samara Oblast	53
Aginsk-Buryat AO Okrug	82	Bryansk Oblast	54

Source: A. M. Laverov (ed.), *Rossiiskie Regiony Posle Vyborov-96* (Moscow: Yuridicheskaya Literatura, 1997).

receiving such financial transfers has steadily increased from 39 in 1994; 66 in 1995; 75 in 1996; 81 in 1997; to 76 in both 1998 and 1999. However, as can be seen from table 5.9 the levels of such transfers have varied from 1–90 per cent.[31]

Lavrov divides the regions into five categories depending on the level of federal transfers in their budgets; in non-subsidised regions, money coming from federal sources accounts for less than 5 per cent of budget revenues. Slightly subsidised regions are those in which, federal assistance of all types accounted for less than 10 per cent of the budget. For subsidised regions, the federal share is 10–20 per cent; for moderately subsidised areas, 20–50 per cent, and for heavily subsidised ones, more than 50 per cent.[32] Table 5.8 shows major variations in the percentage of federal transfers in the total income of two highly divergent groups of federal subjects over the period 1994–96. For example, in 1994 as much as 91.9 per cent of Dagestan's income came from federal transfers whereas in Bashkortostan the figure was only 2.6 per cent. In 1996, 79.3 per cent of Ingushetiya's income came from such subsidies, whilst for Lipetsk Oblast the figure was only 1.2 per cent. And table 5.9 shows that in 1999 wide variations in the amount of federal transfers still persisted. Thus for example, such transfers comprised between 60 and 80 per cent in the Yevreiskaya Autonomous Oblast; the Agin-Buryatiya, Komi-Permyak, Koryak, and Yevenk AOs, and the republics of Dagestan, Tyva and Kabardino-Balkariya. Whilst in the Ust'-Orda Buryatiya AO and the Republic of Ingushetiya such transfers were even higher, comprising between 80 and 90 per cent. On the other hand, thirteen regions received no federal transfers: the cities of St Petersburg and Moscow; Moscow,

Table 5.8 Federal transfers as % of total income in twelve selected regions, 1994–96

Regions	1994	1995	1996
Group A			
Aga-Buryat AO	83.3	69.4	68.6
Altai Republic	85.0	74.7	61.9
Dagestan Republic	91.9	64.4	55.5
Ingushetiya Republic	91.3	77.0	79.3
Koryak AO	81.6	81.6	68.1
Tyva Republic	86.0	78.7	68.5
Group B			
Bashkortostan Republic	2.6	0.2	2.8
Yamalo-Nenyets AO	3.7	1.2	2.0
Lipetsk Oblast	12.7	1.1	1.2
Samara Oblast	7.7	1.2	1.4
Sverdlovsk Oblast	3.4	2.1	1.9
Rep. Tatarstan	7.7	0.9	2.2

Source: A. M. Laverov (ed.), *Rossiiskie Regiony Posle Vyborov-96* (Moskva: Yuridicheskaya Literatura, 1997).

Lipetsk, Samara, Perm, and Sverdlovsk oblasts; Khanty-Mansi and Yamalo-Nenets autonomous okrugs; the republics of Komi, Tatarstan, and Bashkortostan, and Krasnoyarsk Krai; and in a further 17 regions such transfers made up less than 10 per cent.

Donor and recipient regions

For Lavrov the *donor* regions are equivalent to the non-subsidised regions which we describe above, i.e. those regions where federal transfers account for less than 5 per cent of budget revenues. In 1999, there were thirteen donors (St Petersburg and Moscow cities; Moscow, Irkutsk, Lipetsk, Samara, Perm and Sverdlovsk oblasts; republics of Bashkortostan and Tatarstan; Khanty-Mansi and Yamal-Nenets AOs, and Krasnoyarsk Krai).[33]

On the other hand, *recipient* regions, according to Kuznetsova, are those regions where the volume of taxes paid into the federal budget is less than the volume of financial assistance paid to the regions from the federal budget. In 1999 there were twenty-four recipient regions. The vast majority of which were to be found in the republics of the Northern Caucuses and the regions of Eastern Siberia and the Far East. Thus, for

Table 5.9 Typology of regions of Russia according to the share of federal budget transfers as a % of total budget income, 1999

Share of federal transfers in income of budget	*Regions (ranked according to the share of transfers coming from federal budget)*
None	Cities of St Petersburg and Moscow; Moscow, Lipetsk, Samara, Perm, and Sverdlovsk oblasts; Khanty-Mansi and Yamalo-Nenets autonomous okrugs; republics of Komi, Tatarstan, and Bashkortostan; Krasnoyarsk Krai.
Up to 10	Vologda, Chelyabinsk, Nizhegorod, Yaroslavl', Leningrad, Belgorod, Irkutsk, Orenburg, Novosibirsk, Tiumen (without okrugs), Tula, Murmansk, Volgograd, Tomsk, Omsk, Ul'yanovsk, Smolensk oblasts.
From 10–20	Kursk oblast; Udmurt republic; Tver oblast, Krasnodar krai; Kirov, Kaliningrad, Saratov, Nenets AO; republic of Khakasiya; Kemerovo oblast; Republic of Kalmykiya; Novgorod, Voronezh, Vladimir, Arkhangelsk oblasts; Stavropol' Krai; Astrakhan oblast; Republic of Kareliya; Rostov oblast.
From 20–30	Ryazan, Kaluga oblasts; Republic of Sakha (Yakutiya); Chuvash Republic; Kostroma oblast; Khabarovsk Krai; Bryansk, Magadan, Penza, Tambov oblasts; Primorsk Krai; Taimyr autonomous okrug; Kurgan, Sakhalin oblasts.
From 30–40	Ivanovo, Amur, Orel, Chita, Pskov, Kamchatka oblasts; Republic of Mordoviya.
From 40–60	Republics of Marii El, Buryatiya; Altai Krai; Republics of Altai and Adygeya; Karachaevo-Cherkessiya republic; Chutkotka AO; Republic of North Osetiya (Alaniya).
From 60–80	Evreiskaya autonomous oblast; Komi-Permyak, Koryak, and Yevenk AOs; Republic of Dagestan; Agin-Buryatiya AO; republics of Tyva and Kabardino-Balkariya.
From 80–90	Ust'-Ordin Buryatiya AO; Republic of Ingushetiya.

Source: L. I. Sergeev, *Gosudarstvennye I Territorial'nye Finansy* (Kaliningrad: Yantarnyi skaz, 2000), p. 142.

example, the volume of financial assistance from the federal budget exceeded tax payments to the federal income by almost 13 times in the Yevenk AO, approximately 10 times in Dagestan, and the Chukotka AO, from 8–9 times in Tyva and Ust-Ordin Buryatiya AO, and 4.7 times in the Yevreiskaya autonomous oblast (AOB).[34]

Political criteria for budget transfers and privileges

Until now the centre has been quite successful in its use of economic levers to dampen down nationalist demands. The centre has also been adroit at playing the game of divide and rule and capitalising on the major economic differences between the regions by playing one region off against another. As Lavrov notes, recipient regions will 'be the most staunch supporters of preserving or even increasing centralization of tax revenues', so as to benefit from tax redistribution. Donor regions on the other hand are 'interested in reducing the territorial redistribution of budget resources; decentralising control of budget expenditures, and, especially, revenues; acquiring special budget status; creating their own tax services . . . [and] removing their financial agencies from the control of the Russian Ministry of Finance.[35]

Yeltsin also sought to buy support from recalcitrant regional elites. As Tolz and Busygina note, despite the attempts undertaken since 1994 to rationalize the system of federal aid by introducing a publicised formula favouring needier regions, the system of redistribution of benefits and support apparently continues to be dependent on the political preferences of Moscow and the personal relations of governors with representatives of the federal executive.[36]

Political criteria have dominated in the distribution of budget funds and other federal transfers in both the Yeltsin and Putin regimes. Yeltsin as we have seen gave special privileges to forty-six subjects of the federation by signing bilateral treaties with them, and he has frequently used his control over budgetary transfers to quell ethnic unrest, dampen republican bids for political autonomy, purchase electoral votes, and neutralise potential regional opposition movements.

Paradoxically it is the 'oppositionist regions' and not the 'loyal subjects' which have fared best in such budget transfers. Whilst resource-rich Tatarstan, Bashkortostan and Sakha have been rewarded with special deals, and ethnically troubled Kabardino-Balkariya, North Osetiya-Alaniya and Chuvashiya were likewise privileged; impoverished but trouble-free subjects such as Tyva and Koryakiya have so far been left out. In other words loyal but poor republics and regions have been penalised whilst rich or potentially troublesome subjects have been rewarded. As Treisman concluded in his major study of budget transfers 'benefits are geographically targeted so as to appease the discontented rather than to reward the loyal'.[37] Thus Lavrov notes that: 'among the regions that supported the new Constitution in the December 12, 1993 referendum, 40 per cent made gains and 26 per cent lost out. But among the regions that rejected the Constitution, 55 per cent gained and only 18 per cent suffered losses'.[38]

There is now also a substantial amount of economic data to support the hypothesis that the ethno-national subjects of the federation have been favoured over the territorial subjects in tax concessions and federal aid. As Smith notes: 'It is the geopolitical leverage and rhetoric of nationalist politics – the threat or perceived threat of secession or withdrawal from the system of fiscal federalism – that result in the greater likelihood of a region's securing economic benefits'.[39]

As Kahn observes, over the period 1992–94, 'more than seventy presidential decrees and resolutions gave special federal dispensations and exemptions to fourteen republics in the form of export quotas, licences and special resource rights'.[40] And it was the ethnic republics which gained the most privileges from the bilateral treaties which they signed with Moscow. In 1992 one trillion roubles was allocated to the regions from the federal budget. However, an examination of those fifteen regions that received more from the federal budget than they contributed to it, showed that almost all of them (except Kamchatka) were republics or autonomous entities. As Leonid Smirnyagin observed, 'a conclusion suggests itself: the political advantages that the republics have in comparison with the provinces have ensured them economic advantages as well'.[41] And table 5.10 clearly shows that the ethnic republics and ethnic autonomies in 1996 had higher levels of expenditure per capita, retained a higher percentage of their tax revenues, and a greater portion of their income was allocated to them from federal sources.[42]

Table 5.10 Variations in the financial status of subjects of the Russian Federation with different constitutional status, 1996

	Budget expenditure per capita in (thousand roubles)	Share of federal aid in the budget as expense (%)	Share of federal taxes credited to the subject's budget (%)
Average for subjects of the Russian Federation	1,536	11.7	56.8
Republics	1,750	17.9	70.1
Krais and oblasts	1,242	12.7	61.0
Federal cities	2,635	3.9	44.0
Autonomous okrugs, oblasts	6,525	5.9	50.0
Including 'poor autonomies'[a]	2,878	42.3	74.2

Source: Aleksei M. Lavrov, 'Budgetary Federalism', in Jeremy R. Azrael and Emil A. Payin, *Conflict and Consensus in Ethno-Political and Center-Periphery Relations in Russia* (California: Rand, 1998), p. 27.
Note: [a] This refers to data for the ethnic autonomies excluding the rich Khanty-Mansi and Yamalo-Nenets AOs.

Thus, an examination of the data (in table 5.10) for the territorial krais and oblasts shows that expenditure per capita was 1,242 (thousand roubles), federal transfers 12.7 per cent, and the share of credited taxes 70.1 per cent; whereas, for the ethnic republics the figures were 1,750 thousand roubles, 17.9 per cent and 70.1 per cent; and for the poor autonomies 2,878 thousand roubles, 42.3 per cent, and 74.2 per cent, respectively.

Moreover, those ethnic republics that have been the most confederalist in their demands and which have been willing to go furthest in their claims of national sovereignty have received the most privileges from the federal government. As can be seen in table 5.11, over the period 1992–95 Tatarstan, Bashkortostan and Sakha (Yakutiya) practically stopped transferring payments from taxes to the centre. And as Lavrov notes, the total losses to the federal centre from these three republics over the first 10 months of 1996 was 3.5 trillion roubles or 2.3 per cent of the tax income of the federal budget. As Smirnyagin notes, 'In 1992 Tatarstan paid only 93 million roubles in taxes [but] the republic received 38 billion roubles from the federal treasury in the form of subventions, special dispensations and credits – more than went to a dozen central provinces with a total population several times that of Tatarstan'.[43] These provinces paid over half the taxes that were collected – almost 250 billion roubles, that is, 2,688 times more than Tatarstan.[44] And over the period 1995–98 all three republics continued to be granted much higher tax credits than the Russian Federation average.

Moreover, an examination of the draft budget for 2000 reveals that Bashkortostan, Tatarstan and Sakha continued to enjoy special privileges even although their bilateral treaties had expired.[45] For example, Tatarstan was allowed to keep all of the excise duties on the sale of spirits on its territory, whereas the norm is 50 per cent. In total, Tatarstan payed 22.4 per cent of the taxes collected in its territory to the federal budget, whereas

Table 5.11 The portion of taxes credited to the budgets of 'privileged republics' in 1992–98 as a % of total taxes collected in each republic's territory

Republics	*1992*	*1993*	*1994*	*1995*	*1996*	*1997*	*1998*
Tatarstan	99.9	100.0	83.8	77.3	80.3	75.4	88.9
Bashkortostan	99.9	100.0	87.5	73.8	71.9	73.0	82.2
Sakha	98.8	99.8	100.0	99.5	70.8	71.7	77.9
Average for subjects RF	48.3	62.9	64.8	59.1	57.3	56.3	62.9

Source: Data for 1992–96 from A. M. Lavrov, 'Asimmetriya Byudzhetnovo Ustroistva Rossii: Problemy i Resheniya' in Asimmetrichnost . . . 1997', p. 104. Data for 1997–98 from A. M. Lavarov, *Federal'nyi Byudzhet I Regiony: Opyt analiza finansovykh potokov* (Moscow: Instityt Vostok Zapad, 1999), p. 64.

the average contribution from Russian regions is 71.4 per cent.[46] And it has been calculated that if the special budget agreement with Tatarstan is rescinded, the Republic will lose 17 per cent of its income.[47]

Such politically motivated policies have done little to alleviate the sharp inequalities to be found across the federation. Putting out one fire by showering troublesome regions with extra resources has only led to the outbreak of fires in other regions. Regional inequalities have in fact increased in recent years. Whereas in 1990 the ten least developed regions were 2.3 times behind the ten most developed regions in terms of per capita industrial and agricultural output, in 1996 the gap was 4.5 times.[48] And since the August 1998 financial crises we have continued to see an increase in the gap between the rich and poor regions. Such high levels of inter-regional inequalities fuel tensions and jealousies between regional elites and intensify regional competition over the distribution of scarce federal subsidies. As Smirnyagin observes, citizens in a federation should be able to enjoy relatively equal benefits regardless of their place of residence and thus: 'It cannot be considered acceptable when some regions differ from others several times over in terms of such important indicators of social development as per capita income, production downturn, unemployment, infant mortality, or per capita support from public funds . . . citizen's rights are inevitably violated here'.[49]

However, there are signs that the special budgetary deals with the republics is finally coming to an end. President Putin has begun to recentralise the economic system. As we noted above, the balance between the federal budget and subnational budgets has now moved in the favour of the centre. Moreover, under pressure from federal authorities and the new presidential representatives ('Polpredy') from 2001 the republics have begun to transfer a far greater share of their taxes to the federal government. Thus, as Rabinowitch observes, 'in Bashkortostan, in the first quarter of 2001, the republic increased its transfers to the federal government 2.3 times in comparison with the first quarter of 2000. Of the 9.9 billion roubles in revenue collected for budgets at all levels (federal, regional, local), Bashkortostan sent more than 5 billion – more than 50 per cent to the federal budget. In the past this figure was only 18–20 per cent'.[50]

Putin's creation of seven new federal districts has also intensified the levels of socio-economic asymmetry in the federation (see table 5.12). Thus, as Slay notes, there are now two economically powerful districts – the Central and Volga districts which together account for '60 per cent of Russia's retail trade, 55 per cent of new housing contructed, 40 per cent of industrial output, and 47 per cent of its population'. In stark contrast the Southern and Far East districts 'account for only 15 per cent of Russia's industrial output, 18 per cent of housing constructed, and 13 per cent of retail trade'.[51] We discuss Putin's radical assault on the Yeltsinite federal system in chapter 8.

Table 5.12 Economic status of the seven federal districts

District	No. of subject of RF	Russian population (%)	Gross regional product (%)	Volume of industrial production (%)	Volume of agricultural production (%)	Capital investment (%)	Share of exports (%)	RF budget (%)
Central	18	25	28	20	23	30	37	37
North-Western	11	10	9	12	6	9	12	10
Southern	13	15	8	6	16	8	4	6
Volga	15	22	20	24	27	19	12	17
Ural	6	9	15	19	8	17	18	15
Siberian	16	14	14	14	17	11	13	11
Far Eastern	10	5	6	6	4	5	4	4
Total	89	100	100	100	100	100	100	100

Source: Natal'ya Zubarevich, Nikolai Petrov and Aleksei Titkov – 'Federal'nye okruga – 2000' in *Russia's Regions in 1999: An Annual Supplement to Russia's Political Almanac* (Moscow: Carnegie Centre, 2000), p. 176.

Notes

1 P. Hanson and M. Bradshaw (eds), *Regional Economic Change in Russia* (Cheltenham: Edward Elgar, 2000), p. 22.

2 K. Zhuravaskaya, 'Inter-governmental relations in Russia', *Russian Economic Trends*, 8:1 (1999), 46.

3 P. Hanson, S. Artobolevskiy, O. Kouznetsova and D. Sutherland, 'Federal government responses to regional economic change', in Hanson and Bradshaw (eds), *Regional Economic Change*, p. 113.

4 A. M. Lavrov, J. Litwack and D. Sutherland, *Fiscal Federalist Relations in Russia: A Case for Subnational Autonomy* (OECD, 2001), p. 9.

5 *Ibid.*

6 According to Emil Pain the federal share is actually 63 per cent and the regions now receive 37 per cent. See, E. Pain, '"Back to the USSR": new trends in Russian regional policy', *Demokratizatsiya*, 9:2 (Spring 2001), 186.

7 *Ibid.*, p. 10.

8 *Ibid.*

9 E. Savchenko, *Vedemosti* (27 July 2000). As cited in *EWI Russian Regional Report*, 5:30 (August 2, 2000), 3.

10 *Ibid.*

11 *Ibid.*, p. 13.

12 *Economic Surveys: Russian Federation* (OECD, 2000), p. 24.

13 A. G. Makushkin, *Federal Budget and the Regions: A Case Study of Fiscal Flows* (Moscow: Dialogue-MSU, 1999), p. 5.

14 Lavrov, *et al.*, *Fiscal Federalist*, p. 14.

15 *Economic Surveys*, p. 25.

16 Hanson *et al.*, 'Federal government responses', p. 106

17 See C. Ross, *Local Government in the Soviet Union* (New York: St Martin's Press, 1987).

18 Lavrov *et al.*, *Fiscal Federalist*, p. 14.

19 D. Lussier, *EWI Russian Regional Report* (January 2001), 23.

20 P. Hanson, 'Economic change and the Russian provinces', in J. Gibson and P. Hanson (eds), *Transition from Below: Local Power and the Political Economy of Post-Communist Transitions* (Cheltenham: Edward Elgar, 1996), p. 187.

21 E. Yasin, 'Regionalism: an evil or a boon?', *Rossiya* (December 16, 1992), 14, translated in *CDPSP*, 44: 52 (1992), 9–12.

22 L. Vardomskii, 'Vneshneekonomicheskie svyazi regionov', in *Russia's Regions in 1999* (Moscow: Camegie Centre, 2000), p. 113.

23 O. V. Kuznetsova, 'Territorial'naya struktura nalogovovo potentsiala', in A. M. Lavrov (ed.), *Federal'nyi Byudzhet i Regiony: Opyt Analiza Finansovykh Potokov* (Moscow: Instityt Vostok Zapad, MAKS Press, 1999), pp. 64–5.

24 Hanson and Bradshaw, 'Regional dynamics of economic restructuring across Russia', in Hanson and Bradshaw, *Regional Economic Change*, p. 44.

25 *PlanEcon*, Washington, DC, as reported in *Radio Free Europe/Radio Liberty, Russian Federation Report*, (March 8, 2001), pp. 11–14.

26 *Sotsial'noe Polozhenie i Uroven' Zhizn' Naseleniya Rossii 2000* (Moscow: Goskomstat Rossii, 2000), pp. 99–101.

27 L. V. Smirnyagin (ed.), *Rossiiskie Regiony Nakanyne Vyborov – 95* (Moscow: Yuridicheskaya Literatura, 1995).

28 Thirty-one subjects if we include two regions with 49.4 per cent.

29 *Sotsial'noe Polozhenie*, pp. 199–201.

30 As is usual Chechnya is not included. See S. N. Smirnov, *Regional'nye Aspekty Sotsial'noi Politiki* (Moscow, GELIOS: 1999), pp. 63–4.

31 L. I. Sergeev, *Gosudarstvennye i Territorial'nye Finansy* (Kaliningrad: Yantarnyi skaz, 2000), pp. 141–2.

32 A. M. Lavrov, 'Why subsidised regions vote for Communists – or myths about Russian budgetary federalism', *Rossiiskiye vesti*, Special Supplement, 'Political Milieu' (April 10, 1996), p. 3. Translated in *CDPSP*, 48:13 (1996), p. 7.

33 Using a different set of criteria which defines 'donors' as simply those regions where the amount of tax collected and credited to the federal budget exceeded the amount of financial aid turned over to the them, Laverov and Makushkin note that there were as many as 50 donors in 1998. See, A. M. Lavrov and A. G. Makushkin, *The Fiscal Structure of the Russian Federation: Financial Flows Between the Centre and the Regions* (Armonk, New York, London, England: M. E. Sharpe, 2001), p. xxxii. See also, A. G. Makushkin, *Federal'nyi Byudzhet i Regiony* (Moscow: Institut Vostok Zapad, Dialog-MGU, 1999).

34 3.7 times in Koryak AO; 2.1–2.8 times in Adygeya, Kabardino-Balkariya, Kamchatka and Magadan oblasts; Komi-Permyak and Koryak AOs; 1.4–1.8 times in Karachaevo-Cherkesiya, North Ossetiya, Buryatiya, Altai Krai, Amur and Chita oblasts, Agin-Buryatiya AO; 1.1 times in Marii El, Mordoviya, Ivanovo and Pskov Oblasts. O. Kuznetsova, 'Regional'nye byudgety', in *Russia's Regions in 1999*, p. 77.

35 A. Lavrov, 'Budgetary federalism', in J. R. Azrael and E. A. Payin (eds), *Conflict and Consensus in Ethno-Political and Centre–Periphery Relations in Russia* (Santa Monica, California: Rand, 1998), p. 41.

36 V. Tolz and I. Busygina, 'Regional governors and the Kremlin: the ongoing battle for power', *Communist and Post-Communist Studies*, 30:4 (1997), 423.

37 D. Treisman, 'The politics of intergovernmental transfers in post-Soviet Russia', *British Journal of Political Science*, 26 (1996), p. 329.

38 A. M. Lavrov, 'Russian budget federalism: first steps, first results', *Sevodnya* (7 June 1995), p. 5. Translated in *CDPSP*, 47:23 (July 5, 1995), p. 3.

39 Smith, *The Post-Soviet States*, p. 197.

40 Kahn, 'Federal façade', p. 203.

41 L. V. Smirnyagin, 'The distribution of subsidies to Russia's region's is unfair', *Sevodnya* (June 25, 1993), p. 2.

42 Lavrov, 'Budgetary federalism', p. 27.

43 Tambov, Ivanovo, Ryazan, Smolensk, Vladimir, Kursk, Belgorod, Yaroslavl, Orel, Bryansk, Kostroma and Kaluga Provinces.

44 Smirnyagin, 'The distribution of subsidies', p. 2.

45 Lavrov, *et al.*, *Fiscal Federalist*, p. 8.

46 Kuznetsova, 'Regional'nye byudgety', in *Russia's Regions in 1999*, p. 80.

47 L. V. Smirnyagin, 'Federalizm po Putiny ili Putin po Federalizmu (zheleznoi pyatoi)', *Carnegie Briefing Papers*, 3:3 (March 2001), 4.

48 N. Kuzina, 'The federation is bursting at the seams', *Rabochaya Tribuna* (January 17, 1998), p. 1. Translated in *Foreign Broadcast Information Service*, SOV-98-019 (January 17, 1998), 2.

49 L. V. Smirnyagin, 'Power without a strict chain of command could be weakened unless action to strengthen and develop federalism is taken', *Rossiiskiye vesti* (January 16, 1998), 1–2. *Foreign Broadcast Information Service*, SOV-98-028, January 28, 2.

50 Igor Rabinovich, *EWI Russian Regional Report*, 6:17 (2001), pp. 6–8.

51 B. Slay, *PlanEcon* (September, 2000) p. 260.

6

Federalism and political asymmetry: regional elections and political parties

Elections

As we noted in chapter 1, 'Competitive elections are one of the cornerstones of democracy. Without freely established political parties battling in honestly conducted elections, democracy by most definitions does not exist'.[1] Since the adoption of the Russian Constitution in December 1993 Russian citizens have been given the opportunity to engage in numerous rounds of national and local level election campaigns. There have now been three elections for the state Duma (1993, 1995 and 1999), two presidential elections (1996 and 2000) and two or more rounds of elections for regional level legislative and executive bodies. Thus, for example, over the period 1995–98, elections took place for more than 5,000 deputies of regional legislative assemblies in almost all subjects of the federation and a further 14,000 deputies were elected to municipal bodies.[2] In addition, during this same period citizens cast their votes for 101 republican presidents and regional governors. Average turnout for the assembly elections was 42.8 per cent and for regional governors and presidents a healthy 55.6 per cent.

To a large degree these elections marked a watershed in central–periphery relations and a recognition by the centre that the regions had to be granted a significant degree of economic and political autonomy within the federation. The higher status of the regional political bodies was also reflected in the fact that their two top leaders (chairs of assemblies and governors/presidents) were from 1996, granted ex officio membership of the Federal Council. More recently, Russian democracy has been further consolidated by a third round of regional elections conducted over the period 1999–2001.

Manipulation of the electoral system

However, the cynical nature in which President Yeltsin manipulated the election process in the regions has done much to damage the develop-

ment of a democratic political culture. Yeltsin's victory over the parliamentarians signalled a victory of executive power over legislative power
which eventually led to the development of a semi-authoritarian form of
presidential power at the federal level and more overt forms of executive
dominance at the regional level. In the wake of the dissolution of the
Russian Parliament in October 1993, Yeltsin turned his wrath on regional
officials, many of whom had sided with the parliament against the
President. Yeltsin viewed the local soviets (assemblies) as the local head-
quarters of the Communist 'intransigent opposition', and he was anxious
to see an end to their powers.[3] 'The system of Soviets', he declared, 'dis-
played complete disregard for the security of the state and its citizens',
and in so doing 'wrote the final chapter of their own political life'.[4] In
presidential decrees promulgated in October 1993, Yeltsin called for the
abolition of regional and local soviets (assemblies), which were to be
replaced in new elections by much smaller and weaker assemblies. The
decrees whilst mandatory for the regions were only recommended for the
republics.[5]

The first terms of the new assemblies were to be elected for a period of
just two years (as with the first session of the national parliament) and
elections were to be conducted over the period December 1993–March
1994. The decrees also called for a sharp reduction in the number of
deputies represented in the soviets, down from 250–300 to between 15 and
50 deputies. There was also a significant reduction in the number of
deputies permitted to work on a full-time professional basis. This was
legally restricted to two-fifths of the total number of deputies. And there
was a return to the practice of the Soviet era with the right of deputies to
combine their parliamentary duties with work in the executive bodies of
state. Members of the regional administration and lower level executives
from cities and district administrations could now also be elected deputies
to the regional assemblies. In some cases these officials were directly
appointed by the regional governors or presidents in republics (see
chapter 9).[6]

From the dissolution of the regional soviets in 1993 until the first new
elections conducted over the period 1994–96 there was an absence of legislative power in many regions. Moreover, during this period, Yeltsin personally appointed the heads of regional executives and he posted
presidential representatives to the regions (for a discussion of legislative–executive relations see chapter 7).

By May 1994 assembly elections had been successfully carried out in
seventy regions of the Federation. But, as the terms of these first regional
assemblies neared completion in 1995 and 1996, Yeltsin, fearing that the
communist opposition would sweep the board, called for the elections to
be postponed. Thus, in Presidential edicts of 17 September 1995 and 2
March 1996[7] he cynically prolonged the sessions of forty-two assemblies.

In one region, the elections were postponed until March 1997; in 31 regions until December 1997; and in four regions until as late as March 1998. Once again, this legislation did not apply to the ethnic republics which continued to elect their own presidents and to control the timing of elections to their assemblies.

A number of regional assemblies were only too happy to have their powers prolonged, whilst in others appeals against the decrees were placed before the courts (e.g. Republic of Marii El, Kemerovo, Sakhalin, and Tula oblasts). However, the Constitutional Court not surprisingly gave its support to the President. More recently, since the popular election of regional governors, the dates of elections to regional assemblies (now normally every four or five years) have been decided at the local level either by the assemblies themselves, the electoral commissions or the governors (chief executives). As we shall discuss in chapter 9, chief executives, following Yeltsin's example, have blatantly used such powers to their own advantage.

Structure and tenure of legislatures

The vast majority of regional assemblies are elected for a period of four years.[8] In three regions (Volgograd, Vologda and Sverdlovsk) there is a rotation of half of the deputies every two years. In the majority of subjects there are single chamber assemblies. Only the republics of Adygeya, Bashkortostan, Kabardino-Balkariya, Kareliya, Sakha and Sverdlovsk Oblast have bicameral legislatures. Not surprisingly with such wide variations in the size and population of federal subjects there are also considerable variations in the number of deputies elected to local assemblies. Whilst the norm is somewhere between twenty and fifty for oblast assemblies, there are less than twenty deputies in the sparsely populated autonomous okrugs of Ust-Orda Buryatiya, Aginsk Buryat, Komi-Perm, Nenetsk, Chukota, Koryak and Taimyr. In order to increase their status a number of regions have created multi-member electoral districts. In the ethnic republics, which have no restrictions placed on the size of their assemblies, we find much larger assemblies, many with 100 or more deputies. Thus for example: Bashkortostan (190); Tatarstan (130); Dagestan (121); Udmurtiya (100); and Khakasiya (100). Russia's constitutional asymmetry is reflected in the rather absurd situation whereby Moscow city with a population of over 8 million has 35 deputies in its assembly, whilst the Republic of Altai, with a population of just over 200,000, has 50 deputies.[9]

As noted above, legislation limits the number of deputies that may work full time. Only in three of the single chamber assemblies – Moscow (35 deputies), St Petersburg (50), and the Koryak autonomous okrug (with just 12 deputies) – do all the deputies work on a professional basis. This is also the case in one of the two chambers in Bashkortostan, Kabardino-Balkariya, Sakha and Sverdlovsk. In Bashkortostan, just 30 out of 144 deputies work full time. All of the full time deputies are members of the legislative chamber, whilst the Chamber of Representatives is reserved for the part time deputies. In Tatarstan just 28 of its 130 deputies are full time professional politicians. In Tatarstan there are two kinds of plenary session; those which include all deputies (full and part time) and those which are restricted to the much smaller group of full time deputies. There is also a list of key issues which can only be decided in those sessions where there is a full complement of deputies.[10] In some assemblies only a very small per centage of the deputies work full time. Thus, for example, in Kursk, of the 45 deputies only 3 are full time professional deputies, the oblast chair, deputy chair and secretary. The large number of part time deputies, many of whom are employed in district administrations (see chapter 7) has undoubtedly weakened the authority and independence of regional assemblies.

Elections for governors

Yeltsin's control over the appointment of governors lasted much longer than that over regional assemblies. Decrees adopted in November 1991, October 1994 and September 1995 placed moratoriums on gubernatorial elections. The September 1995 decree which postponed elections until 1996 was challenged in the courts by the state Duma and a number of regional assemblies. But, in April 1996 the court finally resolved that the decree was consistent with the Constitution.[11]

Gubernatorial elections finally got underway in earnest only in the period August 1995–April 1997 when there was a total of 70 elections (for which 88 million people registered). By early 1999 almost all of Russia's 89 chief executives had come to power through the ballot box.[12] The majority of executive bodies are elected for a period of four years.[13] In the 1995–97 elections there was an average of five candidates standing for each executive post, although in some ethnic republics there was a throwback to the old Soviet system with just one candidate standing unopposed (see chapter 9). In approximately one-third of these elections, candidates could win with just a plurality of the votes, whereas in two-thirds of the regions, over 50 per cent of the vote was required for victory otherwise there had to be run off elections between the two top candidates. Run-offs took place in 30 per cent of the regions.[14]

The elections armed the governors with a new democratic legitimacy and greatly enhanced their authority and status in the regions. No longer could they be appointed or dismissed on the whim of the President. The elections also brought to power new representatives of the communist and nationalist opposition, and other independents ('strong managers').

They also brought new opponents of the President to the Federation Council and weakened Yeltsin's overall control over the upper chamber. In a further round of gubernatorial elections conducted over the period 2000–1, fifty-three chief executives were elected (see below).[15]

Political parties and democracy

Whilst there is some debate about the importance of parties in contemporary industrial societies most scholars would still agree with Geoffrey Pridham that parties and party systems must remain a basic if not the central theme for examining not only the quality of the liberal democracy in question but also its progress towards and achievement of democratic consolidation.[16] As Juan J. Linz notes, 'Today, in all countries of the world, there is no alternative to political parties in the establishment of democracy. No form of non-party representation that has been advocated has ever produced democratic government'.[17] And Peter Mair adds that, 'However fragmented, weak, or undisciplined, however poorly rooted in society, however unstable and vociferous, parties are a very real and necessary part of the politics of new democracies. Democracy cannot be sustained without competing political parties'.[18]

Parties are particularly important during regime transitions and the consolidation of democracy where they play a vital role in bolstering system legitimacy at a time of political uncertainty.[19] And strong and cohesive national parties have an important integrative function in federal states binding together the diverse subjects of the federation.

According to Hague, Harrop and Breslin, parties perform four vital functions in modern democracies:

> 1) as agents of *elite recruitment* they serve as the major mechanism for preparing and recruiting candidates for public office, 2) as agents of *interest aggregation* they transform a multitude of specific demands into more manageable packages of proposals . . . 3) Parties serve as a *point of reference* for many supporters and voters, giving people a key to interpreting a complicated political world and 4) the modern party *offers direction* to government, performing the vital task of steering the ship of state.[20]

Scholars in the field have traditionally been divided over which prerequisites are necessary for the creation of a strong party system. One group stresses the external environment in which parties operate – the political culture and the strength of civil society. From this perspective, parties are seen as dependent variables and their ability to develop successfully is determined by these external cultural factors. As Karen Dawisha notes: 'a strong civil society is a necessary but not sufficient condition for a strong party and system and it is difficult to find examples where parties have been established in states with weak civil cultures'.[21]

In contrast, a second group of scholars focus on the internal structures, leadership and operational behaviour of parties. In this second approach, parties are seen as independent variables whose actions can positively or negatively shape civil society and culture. Here, institutions matter – change the institutions, change the culture. Strong cohesive parties can bring about consolidated democracies even in hostile cultural environments. Democratic parties can create democrats. But just as equally, weakly institutionalised parties and party systems can allow authoritarianism to take root. Hence, before parties can play their vital role in the process of consolidating democracy, parties themselves must be institutionalised and consolidated.

According to Scott Mainwaring, institutionalisation 'means the process by which a practice or organisation becomes well established and widely known, if not universally accepted'.[22] Strongly institutionalised parties exhibit the following characteristics: '1) high degrees of stability of inter-party competition and low electoral volatility; 2) strong roots in society; 3) they possess unassailable support and legitimacy from elites and citizenry; 4) they have strong, disciplined and territorially comprehensive organisations with well established structures and procedures; 5) significant material and human resources; and 6) an independent status not overshadowed by a personalistic leader or coterie'.[23] Mainwaring contrasts the highly institutionalised parties largely to be found in western Europe and North America with the weakly institutionalised 'inchoate' parties of the 'third wave democracies' in eastern Europe and Russia.

Party representation in regional assemblies

There has already been a significant body of work devoted to the study of parties in Russia at the national level[24] but very little has, as yet, been published on the development of parties at the regional level.[25] Here, we focus on the participation of 'national' parties[26] in elections for regional assemblies and governors. In contrast to previous studies, based on a small sample of case studies, I provide a macro-level analysis covering all eighty-nine of Russia's regions. In addition to the study of national parties in elections at the regional level we also examine the territorial comprehensiveness of national parties as indicated by their participation in the December 1999 elections to the state Duma.

Whilst there has been some progress in the consolidation and solidification of political parties at the national level, the development of parties and their participation in regional level politics, if anything, has declined since 1995. All six of Mainwaring's factors of institutionalisation are still very weak and undeveloped in Russia.

Table 6.1 Party representation in regional assemblies

Election cycle	1993–94	1995–97	2000	2001
% of candidates who stood on a party ticket	–	24.9	15.7	8.7
Party affiliation of deputies	14.0	18.6	12.7	8.4

Source: Data for 1993–94, and 1995–97, *Vybory v Zakonodatel'nye (predstavitel'nye) Organov Gosudarstvennoi Vlasti Sub'ektov Rossiiskoi Federatsii 1995–97* (Moscow: Ves' Mir, 1998). Data for 2000 and 2001, A. I. Tur and A. S. Novikov, 'O soveshchanii predstavitelei izbiratel'nykh komissii sub'ektov Rossiiskoi Federatsii', *Vestnik Tsentralnaya Izbiratel'naya Komissiya*, 6:120 (2001), 60.

There has been a proliferation of parties and political movements in Russia. Over the period 1991–97 a total of 5,000 parties and 60,000 public organisations were registered with the Ministry of Justice.[27] However, the vast majority of elections for regional assemblies and executive bodies have been, and continue to be, largely partyless. And although, some progress in party activism could be detected over the two election cycles of 1993–94 and 1995–97, it has declined precipitously in the recent round of elections which were held in 2000–1 (see table 6.1). Thus, for example, of the 3,481 deputies elected to 83 of Russia's 89 republics and regions, in post as of January 1998, only 18.4 per cent were members of national political parties, a slight improvement from 14 per cent elected in the 1993–94 elections cycle. But this figure fell to 12.7 per cent in 2000 and declined further to just 8.4 per cent in 2001. Furthermore, candidates standing for election on a party ticket in 2000 comprised 15.7 per cent and this fell dramatically in the first half of 2001 to just 8.7 per cent, a sharp drop from 24.9 per cent in 1995–97.[28]

Turning to an examination of the party affiliation of individual legislatures the data shows that party saturation of individual assemblies is very weak. Figures for January 1998 show that in 17 regional assemblies there was no party representation at all,[29] and in only 5 assemblies did party members comprise a majority of the deputies corps; Krasnoyarsk Krai (80.4 per cent), Novosibirsk Oblast (55.1 per cent), Kemerovo Oblast (57.1 per cent), Ryazan Oblast (50.0 per cent), and Sverdlovsk Oblast (69.3 per cent)[30] (see appendix 6.1). But no single party held a majority of the seats in any of Russia's 89 regional assemblies, and there were only 10 chairs of assemblies with a party affiliation.[31]

It is only in the regions of the so called 'red belt' (e.g., Stavropol' Krai, Belgorod, Vologda, Ryazan, Smolensk, Tambov, Bryansk and Penza oblasts), where we see higher levels of party saturation of assemblies. Here, the communists have been able to achieve a plurality, if not a majority of assembly seats, in coalition with other parties and blocks, such as the Agrarian Party of Russia and the National Patriotic Union of Russia. I can find no comparable data on party representation for 2001, but the situation, if anything, must be worse than in 1998. I would expect that currently there will be an even smaller number of assemblies where party members make up a plurality or a majority of the legislature.

It is also important to note that these figures for party membership refer to figures for the umbrella term 'electoral associations' which include not only parties, but a host of other 'political movements' and civic organisations, many of which should more precisely be classified as interest, or occupational groups. Thus, under this rubric we find, for example, such groups as; the 'Union of Young Jurists' (Penza oblast), the 'Capital Housing Movement', and 'Medics for the Rebirth of Health' (Moscow city), the 'Fund for the Mentally Ill' (Saratov oblast), and even the football club 'Salyut' (Saratov oblast), and what appears to be a contradiction in terms, the 'Bloc of Non-Party Independents' (Krasnoyarsk krai). Also we need to take into account the fact that, in a number of regions, party representation will most likely be higher than the officially declared results, as candidates often deliberately fail to declare their party affiliation during the elections, only to emerge as members of party factions in the first session of the newly elected assemblies. Such concealment of one's party affiliation shows that for most candidates party membership continues to be seen as more of a liability than an asset.

The political orientation of legislative assemblies in 1998

Of the 635 deputies with a party affiliation in January 1998[32] by far the largest number belonged to the Communist Party of the Russian Federation (KPRF) (279 deputies or 44.0 per cent) which won seats in 42 regions. However, overall the Communist's 279 seats made up only 8.0 per cent of the total (see table 6.2).

All of the other political parties had a minimal presence, none comprising even as much as 1 per cent of the total number of deputies. Thus, for example the Agrarian Party of Russia (APR) won a mere 28 seats in 7 assemblies, the National Patriotic Union of Russia (NPSR), 26 seats in three assemblies, Yabloko, 22 seats in 8 assemblies; Our Home is Russia (NDR), 18 seats in 12 assemblies, and the Liberal Democratic Party of Russia (LDPR), 15 seats in just 6 assemblies.

Party affiliation in gubernatorial elections

If, as we have demonstrated above, party affiliation in regional assemblies was weak, in the governors' corps it has been even more inchoate and transient. Thus, for example, of the 4,000 public associations which had the right to nominate candidates in gubernatorial elections over the

Table 6.2 Number of seats won by candidates of national parties and number of assemblies in which parties have seats, January 1998

Name of party	Total number of seats	Number of assemblies
KPRF	279	42
APR	28	7
KEDR	1	1
DVR	2	1
CO	11	4
RP	1	1
RKRP	9	5
LDPR	15	6
NPSR	26	3
DNR	18	12
YABLOKO	22	8
PST	1	1
NPR	1	1
KRO	2	1
Others	219	45

Source: 'Parties in Assemblies', special report prepared for the author by the Russian Central Electoral Commission, no author, January 1998.
Notes: KPRF = Communist Party of the Russian Federation; APR = Agrarian Party of Russia; KEDR = Ecological Party of Russia; DVR = Russia's Democratic Choice; CO = Honour and Fatherland; RP = Republican Party; RKRP = Russian Communist Workers' Party; LDPR = Liberal Democratic Party of Russia; NPSR = National Patriotic Union of Russia; NDR = Our Home is Russia; PST = Party of Independent Workers; NPR = People's Party of Russia; KRO = Congress of Russian Communities.

period 1995–97, only 100 (or 2.5 per cent) actually participated in just 48 regions.[33] And these public associations put forward just 18.8 per cent of the total number of candidates. Finally, of the 70 chief executives who were finally elected, just 10 (14.3 per cent) had a party affiliation.[34]

The majority of regional governors and republican presidents have, for the most part, rejected any party affiliation or allegiance to a particular ideology, tending to portray themselves as strong pragmatic 'economic managers' whose deep concern for the welfare of their regions transcends party politics.

As Petrov and Titov note, of the 154 candidates in the 1995–97 gubernatorial elections, two-thirds lacked any political affiliation. And of the 57 candidates which did declare a political affiliation, 36 were communists, 18 liberal reformers, and there were 3 nationalists. 36 of the 70 incumbent governors won re-election. As table 6.3 shows, leaders of parties, political movements and public organisations made up only 5.3 per cent of the candidates and they won only 2.9 per cent of the posts. Leaders of economic

Table 6.3 Comparisons of registered candidates with winners, 1995–97

Candidates	% of candidates	% of winners
Chief executives of regions	19.2	51.4
Chairs (deputy chairs) of legislative bodies of regions	4.7	13.0
Deputies of legislative bodies of subjects of RF	6.1	2.9
Deputies of the state Duma of the Federal Assembly of the RF	10.0	11.6
Assistants to Deputies of the State Duma	3.6	0.0
Leaders of economic enterprises and commercial structures	28.4	8.7
Leaders of parties, movements and public organisations	5.3	2.9
Others	22.6	10.1

Source: *Vybory glav Ispolnitel'Noi. Vlasti Sub'Ektov Rossiiskoi Federatsii 1995–97* (Moscow: Ves' Mir, 1997).

enterprises and commercial organisations fielded a much higher percentage of candidates, 28.4 per cent, and won 8.7 per cent of the posts. To a large degree the gubernatorial contests could be seen more as a struggle between representatives of executive and legislative bodies than a struggle between parties. Of the 154 candidates, 79 came from posts in the executive, 40 from representative bodies and only 35 candidates were not related to either of these two branches (for a discussion of executive–legislative relations, see chapter 7).[35]

Political affiliation of governors

Box 6.1 shows the political affiliation of governors in October 1999. However, in the wake of the success of the presidential 'party of power', Yedinstvo (Unity) in the December 1999 elections, many governors have already shifted their political allegiances and are now jumping on the political bandwagon of President Putin. The weak political affiliation of regional governors is graphically illustrated by the colourful career of Aleksandr Rutskoi, the former Russian Vice President who moved rapidly from being a staunch ally of Yeltsin in 1991 to his arch enemy by September 1993. After his release from prison for his leading role in the 'October 1993 events', Rutskoi was elected to the post of Governor of Kursk with the support of the KPRF and the National Patriotic Union of Russia (NPSR). However, it was not long before Rutskoi soon abandoned any supposed loyalty to these left-wing parties, becoming one of Yeltsin's

Box 6.1 Political affiliation of Russian governors

Unity
Adygeya President Aslan Dzharimov
Arkhangelsk Governor Anatolii Efremov
Buryatiya President Leonid Potapov
Chelyabinsk Governor Petr Sumin
Chukotka Governor Aleksandr Nazarov
Dagestan President Magomedali Magomedov
Yevenk Governor Aleksandr Bokovikov
Kaliningrad Governor Leonid Gorbenko
Kalmykiya President Kirsan Ilyumzhinov
Kamchatka Governor Vladimir Biryukov
Koryak Governor Valentin Bronevich
Kostroma Governor Viktor Shershunov

Kursk Governor Aleksandr Rutskoi
Leningrad Governor Valerii Serdyukov
Magadan Governor Valentin Tsvetkov
Nenets Governor Vladimir Butov
Omsk Governor Leonid Polezhaev
Orenburg Governor Vladimir Elagin
Primorskii Krai Governor Evgenii Nazdratenko
Rostov Governor Vladimir Chub
Sakha (Yakutiya) President Mikhail Nikolaev
Sakhalin Governor Igor Farkhutdinov
Smolensk Governor Aleksandr Prokhanov
Tver Governor Vladimir Platov

Fatherland
Kareliya Prime Minister Sergei Katanandov
Kirov Governor Vladimir Sergeenkov
Komi President Yurii Spiridonov
Mordoviya President Nikolai Merkushin
Moscow Mayor Yurii Luzhkov

Moscow Oblast Governor Anatolii Tyazhlov
Murmansk Governor Yurii Evdokimov
Nizhnii Novgorod Governor Ivan Sklyarov
Novosibirsk Governor Vitalii Mukha
Udmurtiya State Council Chairman Aleksandr Volkov

Box 6.1 *Continued*

Lebed
Krasnoyarsk Governor Aleksandr Lebed

Khakasiya Prime Minister Aleksei Lebed

Zhirinovskii
Pskov Governor Yevgenii Mikhailov

Unaffiliated with major blocs
Orel Governor Egor Stroev
Sverdlovsk Governor Eduard Rossel

Ulyanovsk Governor Yurii Goryachev
Yaroslavl' Governor Anatolii Lisitsyn

Affliation Unknown
Agin-Buriatiya Governor Bair Zhamsuev
Chita Governor Ravil Genyatulin
Khabardino-Balkariia President Valerii Kokov
Kaluga Governor Valerii Sudarenkov
Karachaevo-Cherkesiya President Vladimir Semenov

Komi-Permyak Governor Nikolai Poluyanov
Kurgan Governor Oleg Bogomolov
Lipetsk Governor Oleg Korolev
Taimyr Governor Gennadii Nedelin
Yamal-Nenets Governor Yurii Neelov

Source: Robert Orttung and Daniele Lussier, *EWI, Russian Regional Report*, October, 1999.

staunchest supporters in the Federation Council. And Rutskoi even became a member of Yedinstvo. In a similar manner, once in office, even such hard line Communists, as the President of Mordoviya (Merkushkin), and the governors of Ul'yanovsk (Gorachev), Smolensk (Glushenkov), and Lipetsk (Narolin) oblasts, quickly abandoned any pretence of party loyalty in order to curry favour with the federal government.[36]

The new governors' parties

Rather than governors joining parties in order to promote their election prospects, it is more often the case that parties are forced to turn to governors to help them bring home the regional votes. Regional presidents and governors have considerable control over electoral finances, the local media, courts and electoral commissions. There are many instances of governors resorting to outright manipulation of the electoral rules to ensure their victory in gubernatorial elections or to pack regional assemblies with their own appointed officials (we discuss these points in chapter 9).[37]

A new and worrying development is the creation of a number of governors' parties which were first created in the run-up to the 1999 Duma elections. The creation of these artificial top-down 'parties of government' have been a major blow to the development of grassroots democracy in the regions. As Slider notes, these governors' blocs were in effect, 'anti-party parties' set up specifically to preclude effective national party building in the regions.[38] These 'parties' (for example, Fatherland, All-Russia, Voice of Russia) were set up by regional governors to promote their own personal interests and the interests of their regions in the Duma. Table 6.4 shows variations in the level of governors' support for parties in 1999. However, as noted above, we must be careful to take such declarations of party allegiance with a strong pinch of salt.

Elections for chief executives, 2000–1

As Corwin notes, the results of the 2000 gubernatorial elections shows that, 'incumbency bestows best advantage, while party identification . . . means little'.[39] Thus, for example, in 60 elections which were held over the period December 1999 to January 2001, incumbents won 68 per cent of the seats. This was a much better result than in 1995–97 where just over half of the incumbents (36 of 70) were victorious. And data for the latest round of gubernatorial elections which took place from January 2000 to June 2001 show that only 1.4 per cent of electoral associations participated in 2000, and an even lower figure of just 0.74 per cent in 2001. Moreover, only 4.7 per cent of registered candidates belonged to electoral associations in 2000, and this rose slightly to 6.6 per cent in 2001. Using a

Table 6.4 Variations in the level of governors' support of parties, 1999

Bloc	No. of subjects RF	No. of electoral districts	No. of voters (millions)	Share of electorate (%)
OVR	18	74	34.6	32.0
KPRF	16	40	20.6	19.1
Yedinstvo	23	40	17.7	16.4
NDR	10	20	10.2	9.5
SPS	1	5	2.5	2.3
LDPR	1	1	0.6	0.6
Yabloko	0	0	0	0
Not stated	20	45	21.7	20.1
Total	89	225	108.0	100.0

Source: Vladimir Kozlov, Dmitrii Oreshkin, 'Bluzhdayushchie zvezdy rossiiskoi politiki (o politicheskikh migratsiiakh regional'nykh liderov)' *Golos Rossii*, no. 6, November 1, 1999, pp. 1–6, p. 4.
Notes: OVR = Fatherland–All Russia; KPRF = Communist Party of the Russian Federation; NDR = Our Home is Russia; SPS = Union of Right Forces; LDPR = Liberal Democratic Party of Russia.

different set of figures for 35 gubernatorial elections conducted over the period October 15, 2000 to January 28, 2001, Oreshkin and Kozlov show that of 300 candidates, only 9 were officially registered as 'belonging to a political party'. The KPRF had just 4 candidates, LDPR (2), Yedinstvo (1), Yabloko (1), RKRP (1). And of those who won, only 3 were party members![40]

Factors explaining Russia's weakly institutionalised party system

How can we explain the chronically low levels of party activism and representation demonstrated in the data above? I would argue that the following six factors have thwarted the institutionalisation of political parties in Russia; (1) the legacy of an authoritarian political culture, (2) the weak development of social and economic cleavages, (3) the negative impact of Russia's presidential system, (4) the choice of electoral systems, (5) Russia's weak asymmetrical form of federalism, and (6) the power of regional governors and republican presidents to thwart the development of parties in their territories and to control the electoral process.

The legacy of an authoritarian political culture
Seventy years of communist rule have left an authoritarian legacy, a very weak and inchoate civil society and massive citizen distrust in political institutions.[41] As President Putin notes, 'The roots of many of our failures

lies in the underdevelopment of civil society and the authorities' inability to communicate and work together with it . . . Only the scaffolding of a civil society has been built in Russia'.[42] A legal framework for political parties has only recently been developed and up until 2001 there was no law on parties, their judicial status, or financing. Laws on elections, as we have noted, speak of 'electoral associations' and 'blocks' among which there are 'parties', 'political movements' and 'political associations'.

Moreover, political parties still command very little trust in Russian society. In a *VTsIOM* survey of public opinion, carried out in March 1999, only 3 per cent of respondents declared full confidence in parties.[43]

The weak development of social and economic cleavages
As McFaul notes, 'Whereas most countries in transition seek to change only their system of governance, Russia had to create a new state, a new political system, and a new economic system simultaneously'.[44] But which reforms should be implemented first? Linz and Stepan have argued that political reform should come first 'because democracy legitimates the market, not the reverse'.[45] However, without comparable economic reforms accompanying political change, transitional states cannot generate the necessary social cleavages around which parties need to coalesce and compete for power. As Smolar observes, 'in state socialist societies, the typical citizen identified with only two levels of community, one was family and friends, and the other was the nation. Identification with any intermediate structures was lacking altogether. In addition, the proletarianisation of these societies made it difficult for individuals to recognize differences of interests'.[46]

In the first years of Russia's transition the implementation of political reforms far outpaced the development of economic reforms. This has led to a situation whereby we have seen the formation of a multitude of parties with very shallow roots in civil society. Thus, for example we have witnessed a proliferation of right of centre parties which were founded long before there was any sizeable property owning bourgeoisie to support them. Where sharp cleavages did emerge they were much more likely to be based on ethnic and regional conflicts rather than economics and class.

The lack of well developed social cleavages has meant that Russian parties are more often based around personalities than policies. Many parties in post-communist states are classic 'insider parties' formed from loose coalitions of deputies in the national parliament or they are top-down elite organizations with no real grassroots support (for example, the 'parties of power'). Not surprisingly, party identification is extremely low in Russia. As Stephen White notes, according to survey evidence, just 22 per cent of Russians identified to some degree with a political party, compared with 87 per cent of the electorate of the United States and more than 92 per cent in the United Kingdom.[47] And electoral volatility in Russia is, according to Matthew Wyman six times higher than in western Europe and twice as high as in eastern Europe.[48] It is estimated that just 0.5 per cent of the population are actually members of political parties compared to about 4–5 per cent in Europe.

Party cohesion is much more difficult to achieve in presidential systems than in parliamentary regimes

For Ryabov, Russia's 'super-presidential republic' with a 'legislature highly limited in power and functions' has been extremely detrimental to the development of a viable party system in Russia. In such conditions, parties do not vie for power at either the federal or regional level. With the exception of the KPRF and Yabloko, parties do not put forth their own candidates for the presidency of Russia or the governorship of the regions; in the best case they join various pre-election coalitions and backing groups, where the decisive role is played not by parties, but by other often non-institutionalised support groups.[49]

As Dawisha writes: 'Presidentialism by focusing on the election of a single individual to an all powerful post, diminishes the influence of the party system'. In contrast, 'parliamentary systems require the formation of disciplined parties and coalitions in order to keep the executive in power' (see chapter 7).[50] And as Golosov notes: 'Presidentialism has an negative impact on the development of political parties for in order to win the Presidency parties are forced to abandon any ideological orientations in order to try and win votes from as wide a constituency as possible'.[51]

Legislative stalemate and deadlock are also much more common in presidential systems. In Russia, such stalemate turned to outright hostilities between the parliament and the president, and ultimately to the forced dissolution of the White House in September 1993. Moreover, Yeltsin's claim to 'stand above party' hindered the consolidation of parties at the national level. It has clearly not been in the interest of Yeltsin or Putin to support the development of strong disciplined parties which could rise up and challenge their authority – a divided and fragmented parliament is a weak parliament.

Russia's choice of electoral system

As Lijphart observes, electoral systems are 'strong instruments for shaping party systems and (through those party systems) cabinets, executive–legislative relations'.[52] For Sartori electoral systems have two goals:

> One is representative justice that is, fair and equal representation. The other is governing capability. There is a trade-off between the advantages of proportional representation and those of majoritarian electoral laws.

Proportional-representation systems tend to maximize representation, while majoritarian ones maximize governability.[53]

In majoritarian systems we usually find two-party systems whilst in systems based on proportional representation we see multiparty systems and multiparty coalitions. Different electoral systems also benefit certain groups. Thus for example, 'First past the post systems tend to favour the incumbent powers whilst proportional representation systems allow for a more diverse set of representation'.[54]

In Russia the role of parties at the national level has matured over the three elections of 1993/95/99 helped undoubtedly by the fact that half the members of the state Duma are elected according to proportional representation using a party list system.[55] However, the maturation of parties at the regional level has been less impressive. Here the first past the post system in single-member districts is the most common system in operation.[56] However, across the federation there are various types of multi-mandate constituencies which may be formed according to territorial, administrative-territorial, national, or national-territorial criteria.[57]

The effect of the electoral system on party building in Russia's regions is borne out by the data on party saturation which is much higher in those assemblies which are elected according to some form of proportionality (data for 1995–97 election cycle); Krasnoyarsk Krai (80 per cent), Kaliningrad Oblast (34 per cent), Koryak AO (44 per cent), Ust'-Orda Buryatiya AO (21 per cent). And all of the 28 seats in the lower chamber of Sverdlovsk Oblast which are elected (half each two years) by party list. In Sverdlovsk, in contrast to most other regions the assembly is dominated by regional rather than federal parties but as we discuss below this will radically change once the new law on parties comes into operation.

The introduction of a party list system throughout the federation would undoubtedly increase party representation in the assemblies, but this change is clearly not in the interests of the incumbent governors (and economic elites) who have benefited from fragmented, weak, and party-less assemblies and the absence of a parliamentary opposition. Nonetheless, the Central Electoral Commission is currently considering new proposals to introduce party lists in the regions. If these reforms are implemented, half of the seats in regional assemblies will in the future be reserved for party members.[58]

Russian federalism has impacted negatively on the development of national parties
Russia's highly asymmetrical federalism has made it very difficult for parties to create strong unified structures, and party fragmentation has in turn intensified regional divisions within the state. Only the communist party can be said to have anything approaching a coherent national party structure and party discipline is also very low or non-existent. Through-

out the federation we can also witness a bewildering array of electoral coalitions with different regional branches of the same federal party striking up agreements with different parties in different regions and putting forward a plethora of differing party platforms.

Russia's adoption of nationally drafted party lists in a single nationwide electoral district rather than regionally drafted lists in multi-member districts (as is the case in Germany), has also worked against the development of strong nationally integrated parties. As Remington notes, the choice of one single nation-wide electoral district rather than a larger number of multimember districts, was a deliberate one, 'designed to reduce the chances that parties with a strong regional or ethnic appeal might win seats and weaken the state's unity'.[59] However, some element of federalism has now been built into the electoral system. There are two types of party list for Duma elections, an all-Union federal list with a maximum of eighteen candidates, and a second regional list of candidates.[60]

Some degree of party centralisation is also essential for parties to operate effectively in a federation. Centralised parties can help bind the members of a federation together, whilst, on the contrary, weak federalised parties can exacerbate ethnic problems in multinational federations. Thus, as Burgess argues, where there is symmetry, 'between the federal government and the constituent units we can expect the relative partisan harmony to have a binding impact upon the federation'. However, where there is asymmetry, 'the resulting differences of interest may have a centrifugal effect' which may ultimately 'lead to pressures for secession from the union'.[61]

The importance of national parties which cross ethnic and regional divisions is also vital in multinational federations. As David Laitin notes:

> National parties that seek to build alliances that crosscut cultural groups in all regions tend to modulate the demands from regionally based autonomy movements. In Nigeria, the constitutional drafters recognised this issue and required that to become accredited parties must have significant membership across a variety of regions.[62]

But, not one single party in Russia has branches in all federal subjects. And, none of the parties have been able to compete in all electoral districts. As table 6.5 shows, in the 1999 elections for the Duma even the KPRF could only field candidates in 62.2 per cent of the single member election districts. Yabloko and NDR fielded candidates in 50–60 per cent; OVR and SPS in half, and Yedinstvo ('Unity') in just 18 per cent.[63] Zhirinovsky's block failed to contest a single seat.[64] Turning to the party list elections, even here, none of the parties fielded candidates in all of the regions; NDR's candidates competed in 84 of Russia's 89 regions; the KPRF (84 regions), OVR (68), SPS (63), Yabloko (57) and Yedinstvo (53).[65]

The weak organisational base of national parties in the regions is also revealed by the stark fact that a significant number of the candidates registered for election, even in the party lists (PL), are not actually members of these parties. LDPR had the highest per centage of its own party members on its party list (92.6 per cent), followed by the KPRF (78 per cent), Yabloko (73.2 per cent), OVR (62.1 per cent), SPS (49.4 per cent). The former 'party of power' NDR, had an incredibly low figure of only 3.1 per cent[66] (see table 6.5 which also shows similar wide variations in the single member lists (SM)). And, when it comes to choosing candidates for national elections we find very poor representation of party members from the regions. Thus, for example, approximately one third of all candidates nominated by national parties for the 1999 Duma elections came from elites residing in the cities of Moscow and St Petersburg (see table 6.5).

The weak political affiliation of regional governors, and chairs of regional assemblies, is also important for party consolidation in the Federation Council where these two groups (up until January 2002 were ex officio members). In a vicious circle, weak levels of party affiliation at the regional level feed into weak party consolidation at the national level and vice versa.

The role of governors and presidents in thwarting the development
of parties in the regions
Finally, it is clearly not in the interests of most regional governors and presidents to support the development of parties in their regions. A partyless assembly is a weak assembly. As we discuss in chapter 9 many regional executives have been able to hold on to power by manipulating the electoral process, squeezing out opposition candidates, and blocking the development of parties.

The June 2001 Law on Political Parties

The new 'Law on Political Parties' which was ratified by the Duma in June 2001 does address some of the issues and problems of party building, discussed above. According to this law, which comes into operation in 2003, before a party can be registered it must have a minimum 10,000 members spread across 'more than half of the subjects of the Russian Federation' (article 3.2) with a minimum of 100 members in each regional branch. And when the law comes into force 'political blocks' and 'electoral associations' will be prohibited. Those parties which are registered will be funded by the state. Thus, any party which collects more than 3 per cent of the total vote in parliamentary elections will receive 0.2 roubles from the Federal Budget for each vote cast in its favour. The Chair of the Central Electoral Commission, Aleksandr Veshnyakov, has predicted that the law

Table 6.5 Regional distribution of parties in the December 1999
Duma elections

	SM candidates	PL candidates	% of party members		SMa reside in Moscow/St Petersburg	PLa reside in Moscow/St Petersburg
			SM	PL		
KPRF	140 62.2%	84	86.4	78.0	27.0	30.3
Yedinstvo	41 18.2%	53	–	–	46.3	41.8
OVR	118 52.4%	68	25.3	62.1	34.8	41.4
SPS	108 48.0%	63	51.4	49.4	34.2	27.8
Yabloko	135 60.0%	57	60.8	73.2	28.9	32.2
Zhir	–	–	–	92.6	–	–
NDR	118 52.4%	86	7.1	3.1	31.0	16.0

Source: 'Who is Who on the Parties' Lists?', *www.panorama.ru:8101*. (2000).
Notes: KPRF = Communist Party of the Russian Federation; OVR = Our Fatherland–All Russia; SPS = Union of Right Forces;[67] Zhir = Zhirinovsky Bloc; NDR = Our Home is Russia; SM = Single Member List; PL = Party List. aCandidates residing in Moscow and St. Petersburg oblasts and the cities, Moscow and St Petersburg.

will have the positive effect of reducing the number of parties and move-ments from the current 200 to 10–30.[68] Other politicians are not so opti-mistic. Vladimir Lysenko (head of the Republic Party) argues that the new legislation will disproportionately benefit the two largest parties, the Communist Party, and Yedinstvo, 'transforming the multi-party system into a system of only a few parties'.[69] According to Lysenko, the new law will make it impossible for any of the other parties to recruit the neces-sary number of new members in the time permitted. Furthermore, the law strikes a blow against local democracy in the regions as it bans regional parties from forming and competing in elections. As a consequence, Lysenko argues: 'The provinces will inevitably be removed from politics on all levels, and all decisions will be made in and by the centre alone. It means reverting to a unitary state, a loss of one of the major achievements of the past decade – the federal structure of the state'.[70]

Financial and other bureaucratic controls from the centre over the parties will also prohibit the development of a 'strong and constructive opposition', without which, as Lysenko argues, 'any state is doomed to stagnation and authoritarianism'.[71] Moreover, the law makes it relatively easy for the government to suspend the activity of a party or to shut it down for good. Finally, the 'law does not allow the party system to evolve naturally'. Instead, it is the state which is 'to decide what kinds of parties Russia requires and which ones it can do without, and what kind of party system Russia needs'.[72]

Conclusions

The problem of party building in Russia's regions comes not so much from what Sartori calls 'polarized pluralism' or the danger of 'anti-system parties' threatening the stability of the party system. Russia's problem is that, with the exception of the KPRF, and the transient 'parties of power' (Russia's Choice, Our Home is Russia, Yedinstvo), there are no other national parties with sufficient organisational capacity and financial resources to compete effectively in federal wide elections. Thus, one of the striking features of local politics in Russia is the almost total partyless nature of regional election campaigns and the dismal representation of political parties in regional assemblies. Politics at the regional level is highly fragmented. In the majority of cases, competition is not between disciplined nationwide parties with competing policies but rather between a host of competing individuals and personalities. If you are a communist candidate in the 'red belt' this may very well be an advantage, but in most other regions a party label is more liable to scare away potential voters.

The absence of strong institutionalised parties in the regions has intensified the clientalistic and corporatist nature of politics in Russia. As we discuss in the next chapter state officials and economic elites have benefited from the partyless nature of regional politics and the fragmented and divided nature of politics in the assemblies. As Liebert notes: 'empirical studies on Third World legislatures . . . have pointed out that legislatures are far more vulnerable to extra-constitutional attacks against their prerogatives in systems where political parties are weak; stronger parties help the legislature to generate the support it needs from mass publics to withstand challenges from bureaucratic elites'.[73] Populist regional governors have tapped into the vacuum of power in Russia's partyless regions, creating regional autocracies. As Mainwaring observes: 'The weakness of parties' social roots means that democratic political competition, rather than being channelled through parties and other democratic institutions, assumes a personalized character . . . populism and "antipolitics" are more common in countries with weak institutionalised systems'.[74]

However, fragmented and divided assemblies have also led to legislative deadlock. Governors often cannot guarantee majority support for their policies and often they are forced to enter into a 'war of laws' with the regional assemblies. Just as Yeltsin found himself caught in a deadly stalemate with the Russian parliament in 1993 so republican presidents and regional governors (mini-presidencies) have found themselves in similar predicaments (see chapter 7).

In recent years we have also seen the worrying development of governors' parties, created from above, thwarting the development of grassroots parties, from below. As the centrifugal power of the regions have expanded, the need for strong unifying parties has become more pressing. Yet as Alfred Stepan observes, 'No other federal system has a party system that to date has contributed so little to producing polity wide programmatic discipline'.[75] It is very difficult to consolidate parties in weak and fragmented federal systems, but it is even more difficult to build federal systems in the absence of strong and territorially comprehensive parties. The new law on political parties has gone some way to try and reduce the number of parties competing at the national level by demanding that in order to register they must have a minimum number of members, with representation in at least half of Russia's federal subjects. However, as we noted, the law also prohibits the development of regional parties and it has a number of other negative features. In conclusion, there can be no consolidation of democracy in Russia without a nationwide consolidation of parties and the party system. The future prospects for the development of a multi-party democracy in Russia, both at the national and local levels, looks even bleaker under Putin than it did under Yeltsin.

Appendix 6.1   Party membership of regional assemblies, January 1998

Federal subject	Total no. of deputies	No. of party members	% of party members
Krasnoyarsk Krai	41	33	80
Sverdlovsk Oblast	49	34	69
Kemerovo Oblast	21	12	57
Novosibirsk Oblast	49	27	55
Ryazan' Oblast	26	13	50
Bryansk Oblast	49	24	49
Republic of Adygeya	45	22	49
Kamchatka Oblast	43	20	47
Kaluga Oblast	40	18	45
Koryakskii Autonomous Okrug	9	4	44
Altai Krai	50	22	44
Belgorod Oblast	35	14	40
Penza Oblast	45	17	38
Udmurtskaya Republic	100	37	37
Stavropol' Krai	25	9	36
Khabarovsk Krai	23	8	35
Kaliningrad Oblast	32	11	34
Omsk Oblast	30	10	33
Smolensk Oblast	30	10	33
Kirov Oblast	54	17	31
Pskov Oblast	20	6	30
Orel Oblast	50	14	28

Federal subject	Total no. of deputies	No. of party members	% of party members
Tambov Oblast	50	14	28
Astrakhan Oblast	29	8	28
Republic of Kareliya	56	15	27
Yevreiskaya Autonomous Oblast	15	4	27
Voronezh Oblast	45	12	27
Tula Oblast	48	11	23
Moscow City	35	8	23
Rostov Oblast	45	10	22
Volgograd Oblast	47	10	21
Ust'-Ordynskii Buryatskii Autonomous Okrug	19	4	21
Karachaevo-Cherkesskaya Republic	73	15	21
Ivanovo Oblast	35	7	20
Ul'yanovsk Oblast	25	5	20
Orenburg Oblast	47	9	19
Lipetsk Oblast	38	7	18
Murmansk Oblast	24	4	17
Irkutsk Oblast	44	7	16
Chuvashskaya Republic	63	9	14
Kabardino-Balkarskaya Republic	36	5	14
Kursk Oblast	44	6	14
Vladimir Oblast	37	5	14
Aginskii-Buryatskii Autonomous Okrug	15	2	13
Moscow Oblast	50	6	12
Sakhalin Oblast	27	3	11
Republic of Marii-El	66	7	11
Republic of Tatarstan	130	13	10
Yaroslavl' Oblast	50	5	10
Republic of North Osetiya-Alaniya	73	7	10
Republic of Tyva	21	2	10
Republic of Sakha (Yakutiya)	66	6	9
Saratov Oblast	35	3	9
Republic of Komi	50	4	8
Samara Oblast	25	2	8
Tomsk Oblast	42	3	7
Vologda Oblast	30	2	7
Republic of Khakasiya	75	4	5
Republic of Altai	41	2	5
Yamalo-Nenetskii Autonomous Okrug	21	1	5
Tyumen' Oblast	25	1	4
Kurgan Oblast	33	1	3
Tver' Oblast	33	1	3
Arkhangel'sk Oblast	36	1	3

Federal subject	Total no. of deputies	No. of party members	% of party members
Nizhegorod Oblast	45	1	2
Leningrad Oblast	50	1	2
Amur Oblast	30	0	0
Republic of Bashkortostan	185	0	0
Republic of Buryatiya	64	0	0
Chelyabinsk Oblast	41	0	0
Chita Oblast	39	0	0
Chukotkskii Autonomous Okrug	13	0	0
Republic of Dagestan	121	0	0
Khanty-Mansiiskii Autonomous Okrug	23	0	0
Komi-Permyatskii Autonomous Okrug	15	0	0
Kostroma Oblast	19	0	0
Magadan Oblast	17	0	0
Nenetskii Autonomous Okrug	15	0	0
Novgorod Oblast	26	0	0
Perm' Oblast	40	0	0
Primorskii Krai	39	0	0
Taimyrskii Autonomous Okrug	11	0	0
Yevenkiiskii Autonomous Okrug	23	0	0

Source: 'Parties in Assemblies', special report prepared for the author by the Russian Central Electoral Commission, no author, January 1998.

Notes

1 J. H. Pammett, 'Elections and democracy in Russia', *Communist and Post-Communist Studies*, 32 (1999), 45.

2 A. Yashin, 'Zakonodalel'stvo sub'ektov Rossiiskoi Federatsii O vyborakh', in *Vybory i Partii v Regionakh Rossii* (Moscow, St Petersburg: IGPI, 2000), p. 44.

3 Previous elections to regional assemblies had taken place on March 4, 1990 when the assemblies were elected for five years. But the events of October 1993 brought the terms of the soviets to a sudden and early end. On October 9, President Yeltsin signed Decree 1617 – 'O reforme predstabitel'nykh organov vlasti i organov mestnovo samo-upravleniya v Rossiiskoi Federatsii', which called for the dissolution of soviets at all levels and elections for new organs of representative power.

4 'Address by the President of the Russian Federation to the citizens of Russia', *Rossiskaya gazeta* (October 7, 1993), pp. 1–2. Translated in the *CDPSP*, 45:40 (1993), pp. 21–2.

5 Decree 1617, October 9, 1993 – 'O Reforme Predstavitel'nykh Organov Vlasti i Organov Mestnovo Samo-Upravleniya v Rossiiskoi Federatsii', Decree 1723, October 23, 1993, 'Ob Osnovnykh Nachalakh Organizatsii Gosudarstvennoi Vlasti v Sub'ektakh Rossiskoi Federatsii', and Decree no. 1765, October 26,

1993, 'Ob Utverzhdenii Osnovnykh Polozhenie O Vyborakh v Predstavitel'nye Organy Gosudarstvennoi Vlasti Kraya, Oblasti, Goroda Federal'novo Znacheniya, Avtonomnoi Oblasti, Avtonomnovo Okruga'.

6 V. Gel'man, 'Regional'naya vlast' v sovremennoi Rossii: instituty, regimy i praktiki', *Polis*, 1 (1998), 97. See also, V. Gel'man, 'Subnational institutions in contemporary Russia', in Neil Robinson (ed.), *Institutions and Political Change in Russia* (Basingstoke: Macmillan, 2000), p. 95.

7 Presidential Decree no. 951, September 17, 1993, 'O Vyborakh v Organy Gosudarstvennoi Vlasti Sub'ektov Rossiiskoi Federatsii i Organy Mestnovo Samoupravleniya', and Decree no. 315, March 2, 1996, 'O Poryadke Perenosa Sroka Vyborov v Zakonodatel'nye (Predstavitel'nye) Organy Gosudarstvennoi Vlasti Sub'ektov Rossiiskoi Federatsii'.

8 In five regions the legislative term is five years.

9 Thirteen have between 50 and 75 deputies; North Osetiya (75); Karachaevo-Cherkessaya (73); Kabardino-Balkaraya (72); Sakha (Yakutiya) (70), Marii El (67); Kirov Oblast (54); Komi Republic (50); Altai Krai (50); Bryansk Oblast (50); Leningrad Oblast (50); Moscow Oblast (50); Tambov Oblast (50); Yaroslavl' Oblast (50).

10 I. Mikhailovskaya, 'Regional'nye osobennosti realizatsii printsipa razdeleniya vlastei v sovremennoi Rossii', in O. B. Sidorovich (ed.), *Rossiiskii Konstitut-sionalizm: Politicheskii Rezhim v Regional'nom Kontekste* (Moscow, MONF, 2000), p. 179.

11 V. Gel'man, 'Subnational institutions', p. 98.

12 The exceptions were Dagestan and Udmurtiya where at that time their chief executives were indirectly appointed by their parliaments. Both republics have subsequently adopted popular elections for their presidents.

13 However, in nine subjects chief executives are elected for a period of five years, and in one republic (Kalmykiya), seven years.

14 On February 15, 2001 the Duma passed new legislation requiring that hence-forth all gubernatorial elections should provide for two rounds, with run offs if no canidate wins over 50 per cent in the first round.

15 The number of candidates varied from 2 in Khabarovsk Krai to 13 in Stavropol' Krai, and turnout varied from 34 per cent in Vladimir Oblast to 75 per cent in Saratov Oblast.

16 G. Pridham, 'Southern European democracies on the road to consolidation: a comparative assessment of the role of political parties', in G. Pridham (ed.), *Securing Democracy: Political Parties and Democratic Consolidation in southern Europe* (London and New York: Routledge, 1990), p. 2.

17 Paper delivered to the conference, 'Political Parties and Democracy', November 18–19, 1996, Washington, DC, sponsored by the International Forum for Democratic Studies. See www.ned.org/pubs/reports/parties.html

18 *Ibid.*

19 G. Pridham, and P. Lewis, 'Introduction: stabilising fragile democracies and party system development', in G. Pridham and P. Lewis (eds), *Stabilising Fragile Democracies: Comparing New Party Systems in Southern and Eastern Europe* (London and New York: Routledge, 1996), p. 5.

20 R. Hague, M. Harrop and S. Breslin, *Comparative Government and Politics: An Introduction* (Macmillan, 4th edn, 1998), p. 131.

21 K. Dawisha, 'Democratisation and political participation: research concepts and methodologies', in K. Dawisha and B. Parrot (eds), *The Consolidation of Democracy in East-Central Europe* (Cambridge: Cambridge University Press, 1997), p. 55.

22 S. Mainwaring, 'Party systems in the third wave', *Journal of Democracy*, 4 (December 1999), 69.

23 *Ibid.*, 69–71.

24 J. Lowenhardt (ed.), *Party Politics in Post-Communist Russia* (London: Frank Cass, 1998); J. T. Ishiyama, 'The Russian proto-parties and the national republics', *Communist and Post-Communist Studies*, 29:4 (1996), 395–411; also by Ishiyama, 'Political parties and candidate recruitment in post-Soviet Russian politics', *Journal of Communist Studies and Transition Politics*, 15:4 (1999), 41–69; P. C. Ordeshook, 'Russia's party system: is Russian federalism viable?', *Post-Soviet Affairs*, 12:3 (1996), 195–217; Peter C. Ordeshook and Olga Shevtsova, 'Federalism and constitutional design', *Journal of Democracy* (January, 1997), 27–36; M. Makfol, S. Markov and A. Ryabov (eds), *Formirovanie Partiino-Politicheskoi Sistemy v Rossii* (Moscow, Carnegie Endowment for International Peace: 1998), G. V. Golosov, *Partiinye Sistemy Rossii i Stran Vostochnoi Evropy* (Moscow, Ves Mir: 1999).

25 See, C. Ross, 'Political parties and regional democracy in Russia', in C. Ross (ed.), *Regional Politics in Russia* (Manchester: Manchester University Press: 2002), G. V. Golosov, 'From Adygeya to Yaroslavl: factors of party development in the regions of Russia', *Europe-Asia Studies*, 51:8 (1999), 1,333–65, V. Gel'man and G. V. Golosov, 'Regional party system formation in Russia: the deviant case of Sverdlovsk Oblast', in Lowenhardt, *Party Politics*; A. Kuzmin, 'Partii v regionakh', in M. Makfola *et al.*, *Formirovanie*; D. Slider, 'National political parties in Russia's regions', paper delivered to the 31st National Convention of the AAASS, St Louis, November 20, 1999.

26 As Richard Sakwa notes, 'According to the draft Law on Political Parties adopted by the Duma on 8 December 1995, three types of political parties may be established: national, with regional organisations in at least forty-five components of the Russian Federation; interregional, with membership from at least two components; and regional'. See R. Sakwa, *Russian Politics and Society* (London: Routledge, 2nd edn, 1996), p. 90. In this study national parties are defined simply as those parties which compete for power at the national level (see my list in table 6.1). Regional parties by contrast compete for power only at the regional level. See discussion of the 2000 Federal 'Law On Parties' which we discuss below.

27 S. V. Alekseev, V. A. Kalamanov and A. G. Chernenko, *Ideologicheskie Orientiry Rossii, Volume 1* (Moscow: Kniga i Biznes, 1998), pp. 320–1.

28 A. I. Tur and A. S. Novikov, 'O soveshchanii predstavitelei izbiratel'nykh komissii sub'ektov Rossiiskoi Federatsii', *Vestnik Tsentralnaya Izbiratel'naya Komissiya*, 6:120 (2001), 60.

29 No parties were represented in the republics of Bashkortostan, Buryatiya, Dagestan; Primorskii Krai; Amur, Chelyabinsk, Chita, Kostroma, Magadan, Novgorod and Perm oblasts; Komi-Perm, Nenetsk, Taimyr, Khanty Mansi, Chukotka and Yevenk autonomous okrugs. Here we need to note that these figures refer to the party affiliation of candidates at the time of

the election campaign and do not count changes after the assemblies were formed.

30 This is the average for both chambers. The lower chamber is elected according to party lists and therefore there is 100 per cent party saturation.

31 In the regions of the so called 'red belt' (e.g., Stavropol' Krai, Belgorod, Vologda, Ryazan, Smolensk, Tambov, Bryansk, and Penza oblasts), the communists were able to achieve a plurality, if not a majority, in coalition with other parties such as the Agrarian Party of Russia and the National Patriotic Union of Russia.

32 Here we refer to affiliation of national parties and we do not include membership of regional parties.

33 *Vybory Glav Ispolnitel'noi Vlasti Sub'ektov Rossiiskoi Federatsii 1995–1997* (Moscow: 'Ves' Mir': 1997), p. 40. The largest number of such organizations were registered with the Ministry of Justice in Moscow (456), Orenburg (250), Perm (124), Sverdlovsk (120), Samara (127), Rostov (112), Kaliningrad (107), Amur (105), and Arkhangelsk (103) oblasts.

34 However, we should note here that a number of candidates whilst not actually officially nominated by parties did receive party support in their campaigns. Nonetheless, the fact that the candidates did not want to make such connections official only goes to show that a party label is still seen as more of a liability than as an asset.

35 N. Petrov and A. Titov, 'Vybory glav ispolnitel'noi vlasti regionov', in *Vybory i Partii v Regionakh*, p. 64.

36 V. N. Kozlov and D. B. Oreshkin, 'Bluzhdayushchie zvezdy rossiiskoi politiki (o politicheskikh migratsiiakh regional'nykh liderov)', *Golos Rossii*, 6 (November 1, 1999), 3.

37 See, C. Ross, 'Federalizm i demokratizatsiia v Rossii', *Polis*, 3 (1999), 16–29.

38 D. Slider, 'National political parties', p. 6.

39 J. A. Corwin, *RFE/RL Russian Federation Report* (January 4, 2001), 9–10.

40 D. B. Oreshkin and V. N. Kozlov, 'Osenne-zimnyaya seriya gubernatorskikh vyborov v zerkale statistiki', *O Vyborakh*, 1 (2001), 29. These figures refer to those candidates who officially registered as 'belonging to a political party' and not to those who were supported in the campaign by a political party or who were reputed to support a party. There are many governors who profess support for this or that party but who, as we have already noted, are happy to jump from one political bandwagon to another at the drop of a hat.

41 Dawisha, 'Democratisation and political participation', p. 55.

42 V. Putin, 'The kind of Russia we are building'. Annual message from the President of the Russian Federation to the Federal Assembly of the Russian Federation, *Rossiiskaya gazeta* (July 11, 2000), 1, 3. Translated in *CDPSP*, 52:28 (2000), 5.

43 Nationwide VTsIOM survey, March 6–21, N = 2,385, as reported at www.russiavotes.org/Duma_poll_cur.htm#109, Strathclyde University, December 1999.

44 Michael McFaul, 'Consolidating democracy in Russia', in, L. Diamond, M. F. Platter, Yun-han Chu, and Hung-mao Tien (eds), *Consolidating the Third Wave Democracies* (Baltimore and London: Johns Hopkins University Press, 1997), pp. 64–94, p. 65.

45 J. Linz and A. Stepan, *Problems of Democratic Transition and Consolidation* (Baltimore and London: Johns Hopkins University Press: 1996), p. 436. Cited by Zvi Gitelman in 'The democratisation of Russia in comparative perspective', in Stephen White, Alex Pravda and Zvi Gitelman (eds), *Developments in Russian Politics – 4* (Basingstoke: Macmillan, 1999) p. 275.

46 A. Smolar, paper delivered to the Conference, 'Political parties and democracy', 18–19 November 1996, Washington, DC sponsored by the International Forum for Democratic Studies.

47 S. White, 'Political parties', in M. Bowker and C. Ross (eds), *Russia after the Cold War* (Longman: 1999), pp. 82–3.

48 M. Wyman, 'Elections and voting behaviour', in Stephen White, Alex Pravda and Zvi Gitelman (eds), *Developments in Russian politics – 4* (Basingstoke: Macmillan, 1999) p. 119.

49 A. Ryabov, 'The outlook for the Russian multi-party system in the new political context', *Carnegie Briefing Papers*, 3:8 (August 2001), 2.

50 Dawisha, 'Democratization and political participation', p. 56.

51 G. Lyukherkhandt-Mikhaleva, 'Izbiratel'nyi protsess i partii v rossiiskikh regionakh', in *Vybory i Partii*, p. 145.

52 Lijphart comments delivered to the Conference, 'Political parties and democracy', 18–19 November 1996, Washington, DC sponsored by the International Forum for Democratic Studies.

53 G. Sartori, comments delivered to the Conference, 'Political parties and democracy'.

54 A. Lijphart, comments delivered to the Conference, 'Political parties and democracy'.

55 In the new election law – in the event that less than half of the voters were cast for lists that passed the 5 per cent threshold, the threshold was to be lowered (article 80 of Duma election law). See J. Lowenhardt and R. Verheul, 'The village votes: the December 1999 elections in Tatarstan's Pestretsy District', *Journal of Communist Studies and Transition Politics*, 16:3 (September 2000), endnote 12, p. 122.

56 On February 15, the Duma approved legislation with 305 deputies voting in favour, to establish a system of two rounds for gubernatorial elections.

57 Thus, for example, a complex system operates in Dagestan where there is a quota system with certain seats in the parliament reserved for members of ethnic groups, women, and occupational groups. As Khan notes: 'In some districts voters may be constrained to vote for a deputy that fits all three classifications (e.g. a female Avar)', J. Kahn, 'Federal façade', p. 232. In Ingushetiya, 'all parliamentary elections are conducted within a single twenty-seven seat electoral district. In other words, every voter is given a ballot to choose the entire legislature'. Kahn 'Federal façade', p. 231.

58 J. Corwin, *RFE/RL Russian Federation Report*, 3:24 (August 8, 2001), 1.

59 T. F. Remmington, *Politics in Russia* (Harlow: Longman, 1999) p. 151.

60 Article 39 of the Law, 'O Vyborakh Deputatov Gosudarstvennoi Dumy Federal'novo Sobaraniya Rossiisko Federatsii', adopted by the Duma June 24, 1999, as published in *Rossiiskaya gazeta* (July 1 and 3, 1999). However, as Lownhardt and Verheul note, the law does not give precise details as to how the regional sub-lists are drawn up. – J. Lowenhardt and R. Verheul, 'The

village votes: the December 1999 elections in Tatarstan's Pestretsy District', *Journal of Communist Studies and Transition Politics*, 16:3 (September 2000), endnote, 11, 122.

61 M. Burgess and A. G. Gagnon (eds), *Comparative federalism and Federation* (Harvester Wheatsheaf, 1993), p. 107.

62 D. Laitin, 'Transitions to democracy and territorial integrity', in A. Przeworski (ed.), *Sustainable Democracy* (Cambridge: Cambridge University Press: 1995) p. 24.

63 Data in table 6.4 is from A. Strokhanov, 'Who is who on the parties lists?', www.panorama.ru:8101. These figures refer to candidates registered by the Central Electoral Commission (August–October 1999) as eligible to stand for elections to the Duma. Interestingly, only the relatively obscure political movement, Spiritual Heritage was able to list a candidate in all 225 single mandate districts.

64 A large number of LDPR candidates were rejected by the Central Electoral Commission.

65 A. Strokanov, 'Who is who'. Here we only have figures for number of regions, rather than number of electoral districts.

66 I could find no comparable data for the party of power, 'Yedinstvo'.

67 Out of the 108 candidates on the single member list of the movement, Union of Right Forces (SPS), Democratic Choice of Russia made up 24.1 per cent (24.6 per cent of party list); New Force – 8.3 per cent (5.3 per cent of party list); Democratic Russia, 6.5 per cent (4.2 per cent of party list); Young Russia, 6.5 per cent. Other organizations belonging to the block have just one or two candidates.

68 J. Corwin, *RFE/RL Federation Report* (January 24, 2001).

69 V. Lysenko, 'From a multi-party system to a few parties', *Nezavisimaya gazeta* (May 24, 2001), translated at www.wps.ru/e_index.html. It is interesting to note of the 1,500 amendments three parties (Communists, Unity, and Fatherland-All Russia) did not propose a single amendment. Most of the amendments originated in democratic factions (the Union of Right Forces and Yabloko).

70 Lysenko, 'From a multi-party system', p. 2.

71 *Ibid.*, p. 3.

72 *Ibid.*

73 U. Liebert, 'Parliament as a central site in democratic consolidation: a preliminary exploration', in U. Liebert and M. Cotta (eds), *Parliament and Democratic Consolidation in Southern Europe* (London and New York: Pinter, 1990), p. 21.

74 Mainwaring, 'Party systems in the third wave', p. 75.

75 A. Stepan, 'Russian federalism in comparative perspective: problems of power creation and power deflation', paper delivered to the 31st National Convention of the AAASS, St Louis, Missouri, 18–21 November 1999, p. 36. See also Stepan's, 'federalism and democracy: beyond the U.S. model', *Journal of Democracy*, 10:4 (October 1999), 19–34.

7

Federalism and political asymmetry: executive versus legislative power

As we have noted, political institutions are of crucial importance during transitions to democracy, and for Mainwaring, among all the choices of institutions 'none is more important than the system of government: presidential, semipresidential, parliamentary or some hybrid'.[1] There is now a general consensus in the literature that parliamentary systems are more stable than presidential ones and that it is much easier to consolidate democracy in parliamentary regimes.[2] As Zvi Gitelman notes: 'Parliamentarism is generally more favourable to democratic consolidation than presidentialism because it gives the political system greater efficacy, the capacity to construct majorities and the ability to terminate a crisis of government without it becoming a crisis of the regime'.[3]

One of the major problems with presidential systems is that they are, 'prone to creating two opposing centres of power', and often 'legislative paralysis can set in when neither parliament nor president are strong enough to break the deadlocks which ensue'.[4] Politics quickly becomes a zero-sum game where the winner takes all. As we noted in chapter 6, presidential systems are thus often prone to chronic conflict, legislative stalemate and even complete paralysis. This is particularly the case, where, 'the executive does not have sufficient support in the congress to pass legislation but does have sufficient strength to have his or her vetoes sustained'.[5] And furthermore, as Mainwaring has shown, the deadly combination of a presidential system with a fragmented multi-party system, as in Russia, 'can have pernicious results'.[6]

In Russia, deadlock at the national level lead to outright physical violence and the dissolution of the Russian Parliament in October 1993. And this struggle between parliament and president also gravitated downwards to the local level with similar battles occurring between regional soviets (assemblies) and executive bodies of power. What followed were presidential decrees fundamentally seeking to increase the powers of the executive at the national and local levels and parliamentary (Supreme Soviet) laws which sought to enhance the powers of the national legislature and local assemblies. Soon Russia was faced with the horrifying possibility of eighty-nine battles between regional executives and assemblies.

Striking the first blow in his 'war of laws' with the Russian Parliament, Yeltsin adopted a decree on August 22, 1991[7] which granted him powers of appointment over all the chief executives (governors) in the regions.[8] Although the local assemblies were in theory supposed to approve the appointment of these executives, in many cases chief administrators were simply imposed upon them without any prior consultation. However, in March 1992 the Russian Supreme Soviet struck back adopting its own law on regional assemblies which significantly increased the powers of the soviets (regional assemblies) vis-à-vis the governors.[9] As Gel'man notes, this law instituted the dual subordination of the chief executive of a region before the regional assembly and the President, and the dual subordination of the regional administration before the assembly and the governor. The regional assemblies were also given the right to name four key members of the regional cabinets (the first deputy chief of the administration, and heads of the departments of finance, property, and social affairs).[10] Moreover, they could also declare a vote of no confidence in the governors, and appeal for the removal of governors to the President or the Constitutional Court.[11] The chief executives in their turn were given the right to veto the decisions of the assembly but their vetoes could be overturned by a simple majority of the assembly.

In December 1992 as the battle between Parliament and President intensified, the Russian Parliament adopted a further resolution which stripped Yeltsin of his 'authority to appoint regional heads of administration, and called for the abolition within one month of the presidential representatives in Russia'.[12] Yeltsin responded to this attack from the Parliament with a presidential decree which he promulgated on February 5, 1993. This decree[13] made the presidential representatives a permanent body under the direct supervision of the head of the presidential administration, and he simply ignored the parliament's moves to rescind his powers of appointment of regional governors.[14] During this period, 1991–93, Gel'man argues there was a presidential–parliamentary type system in operation in the regions.[15]

The assault on local assemblies 1993–96

Yeltsin's victory over the parliamentarians in October 1993 signalled a victory of executive power over legislative power. As Gel'man notes, from 1993 we see the development of a hierarchical chain of executive authority. Presidential decrees adopted over the period 1993–94 brought an end to the assemblies' rights of confirmation of the appointment of chief executives and members of regional administrations, and of their right to bring sanctions against the executive, or to express a vote of no confidence in the governors.[16] The right of a legislative veto over decrees of the chief executive now required the vote of two-thirds of the deputies and not as previously a simple majority. Indeed, Gel'man notes, that if you compared the competence of the regional assemblies in 1994 with the powers of the two chambers of the federal assembly, then the President had significantly less rights than the regional governors. Thus, for example, the Duma may express a vote of no confidence in the government and also may express its disagreement with this or that law. No such rights were given to regional soviets. The regional soviets were also to be part time bodies with only a small percentage of the deputies engaged in full time parliamentary work. Once again it is important to note that this legislation was aimed only at the regions, and the republics were given the go ahead to forge their own political institutions.

However, it was not long before regional assemblies fought back against executive dominance. Russia's weak and inchoate form of federalism played into the hands of the regions. Yeltsin (as we showed in chapter 3) in a search to maintain stability and to win the support of regional voters, went out of his way to grant recalcitrant regions and republics special deals and favours. Many of the bilateral treaties allowed the republics and regions to develop their own political systems.[17] Articles 72 and 77 of the Russian Constitution also grant republics and regions the right to independently structure their political institutions as long as they do not contradict the Constitution and federal laws. No such law delineating the powers of regional soviets was forthcoming until 1999.

Taking advantage of this lack of clarity in federal directives, and bolstered by new electoral mandates, a number of regional assemblies began the process of drawing up charters which, if adopted, would radically increase their powers and status, reinstating many of the rights taken away from them by presidential edicts in 1993. In some cases the assemblies drew up charters which called for the abolition of the 'presidential' systems in their regions to be substituted by fully-fledged 'parliamentary' regimes (e.g. Altai Krai, Chita, Tambov, Saratov and Kemerovo oblasts).[18] Thus, for example, in Altai Krai and Chita Oblast regional elites were able to create strong 'parliamentary charters'[19] which, 'sought to make their regional executives accountable to the regional assemblies, establish legislative control over cabinet appointments and structure, and allow for votes of no confidence in the head of the region'.[20] In many other regions there were wide variations in the specific powers which assemblies were granted vis-à-vis the executive.[21] Constitutional asymmetry soon led to political asymmetry. By 1995 there was a highly varied system of executive–legislative relations in operation in the regions (see box 7.1). In particular, the right of assemblies to ratify nominations for executive posts varied substantially across the federation. The most traditional variant was where the chief executive appointed and dismissed cabinet members and other officials of executive power. However, in other cases legislative organs of power were required to give their approval for: chairs of the government (Adygeya, Bashkortostan, Dagestan, Ingushetiya, Karachaevo-Cherkesiya, Tatarstan, Mordoviya, Sakha, North Osetiya-Alaniya), first deputy and/or deputy chiefs of executive power (Irkutsk, Saratov, Karachaevo-Cherkessiya, Kareliya, Sakha, Tyva, Tambov oblast), all members of the government, ministers, and leaders of state committees (Altai, Buryatiya, Tatarstan, Marii El, Mordoviya, Sakha (Yakutiya), Tyva), individual ministers (Adygeya, Karachaevo-Cherkessiya, Kareliya, Khakassiya, Saratov, Tambov, Perm). In some regions (e.g., Tver and Khakasiya) assemblies had the exclusive right to sign and promulgate laws (see box 7.1).

However, regional assemblies suffered yet another blow when in January 1996, the Constitutional Court declared that the 'parliamentary charters' of Altai Krai and Chita Oblast violated the constitutional principle of the 'separation of powers'.[22] In March 1996 the legislature of Altai Krai reluctantly agreed to withdraw from its charter those articles which had granted it the right to directly elect the governor and members of the regional administration. And legislators in Chita oblast were soon forced to follow suit. Armed by this constitutional precedent, governors in many other regions across the federation were able to strengthen their powers of control over the assemblies. Thus, as Gel'man notes, federal legislation over the period 1993–96 transformed politics in most regions from a 'parliamentary-presidential' system to a fully fledged 'presidential' one.[23] Nonetheless, it was still far from the case that there were uniform laws in practice throughout the federation. In some regions it was regional elites and not presidential decrees or parliamentary laws which determined the specific institutional structures that were put in place.

Elites and regional politics

In the aftermath of the collapse of the Soviet Union regional elites largely determined their own institutional structures. This was a time when institutions were in flux, and there was a power vacuum at the centre. Thus, those elites (parliamentary or presidential) which commanded the most political and economic resources and support during the period 1991–93 were largely able to impose their institutional designs on the regions. In those regions where there was a strong political affinity between the governor and the deputies compromises over the provisions of the charters were soon achieved. In others where there was no such affinity there was often a fierce and prolonged conflict. As Vladimir Lysenko observed:

Box 7.1 Variations in the powers of legislative and executive bodies of power as stipulated in regional and republican charters and constitutions

1 *Exclusive right to sign and promulgate laws:*
   • Assemblies in Tver Oblast and Republic of Khakasiya.

2 *Right to call referendums:*
   • Executive has right: Buryatiya, Ingushetiya, Marii El, Leningrad Oblast.
   • Assembly has right: Bashkortostan, Mordovya, Karachaevo-Cherkessiya, Kareliya, Khakassiya, Komi, Kostroma, Primorski Krai, Sakha, Vologda and Voronezh.
   • Both executive and legislative bodies have such a right: Kalmykiya, North Osetiya, Tatarstan and Irkutsk.

3 *Legislative agreement/consent required for appointment of key members of the executive:*
   • Chairs of government: Adygeya, Bashkortostan, Dagestan, Ingushetiya, Karachaevo-Cherkesiya, Tatarstan, Mordovya, Sakha and North Osetiya.
   • First deputy and/or deputy chiefs of executive power: Irkutsk, Tambov and Saratov oblasts; Republics of Karachaevo-Cherkessiya, Kareliya, Sakha and Tyva.
   • All members of the government/administration, ministers, and leaders of state committees: Republics of Altai, Buryatiya, Tatarstan, Marii El, Mordoviya, Sakha and Tyva.
   • Heads of specific ministries, administrations: Republics of Adygeya, Karachaevo-Cherkessiya, Kareliya, Khakassiya; Saratov, Tambov and Perm oblasts.

4 *Right to dissolve the assembly:*
   Executive has right:
   • If assembly refuses three times to ratify the governors appointment of chief of government (e.g., Irkutsk, Yaroslavl' and Sverdlovsk).
   • If there is an absence of a quorum in the assembly. Assembly: requires two-thirds of the votes of assembly members.

Source: I. Umnova, Razdelenie zakonodatel'noi i ispolnitel'noi vlasti v sub'ektov Rossiiskoi Federatsii: pravovye aspekty', in V. Gel'man, A. Kuz'min, G. Lyukhterkhandt and S. Ryzhenkov (eds), *Organy gosudarstvennoi vlasti sub'ektov Rosiiskoi Federatsii* (Moscow: IGPI, 1998), pp. 121–2.

If relations are calm and business like, the charter will be calm and relatively terse . . . But if relations have not been going well, the draft charter will resemble a blanket that each side is trying to put to its side of the bed. A great many alternative drafts will appear, and there will be struggle for every word, every letter and every comma.[24]

In some regions executive bodies dominated the process of constitution building and subsequently were able to implement strong presidential systems much as Yeltsin did at the national level. In other regions legislative bodies were able to take the upper hand and to push for strong parliamentary charters and the installation of parliamentary regimes. As Vladimir Nechaev shows in his careful study of institution building in four regions, elites in the Republic of Kareliya and Pskov Oblast were able to carve out strong and independent assemblies whilst Kursk and Astrakhan both created weak regional assemblies under the control of powerful executives. The most important determining factors in these four regions were the specific powers of the legislative and executive bodies at the time of drawing up the charters/constitutions; and the date when the charters were ratified. As Nechaev notes, in Kursk the administration controlled the process whilst in Pskov and Kareliya it was representatives of the legislative assemblies. In Astrakhan both participated. Here it was the respective powers of these bodies at the time of the formation of the charter that was crucial.[25] In Pskov work on the charter began in the first half of 1993, that is, before the dissolution of the parliament and the adoption of the 1993 federal Constitution. Those charters drawn up before the dissolution of the soviets in 1993 were more likely to see a victory of the assemblies over the executives.

In some regions there was elite stalemate and a settled political structure failed to materialise. This was most graphically seen in the conflict between executive and legislative bodies of power in Tver Oblast where conflict between the legislature and executive held up the adoption of its regional charter for a number of years. In the republic of Udmurtiya, stalemate between elites, and the realisation that in a presidential system the 'winner takes all', led elites to originally opt for a parliamentary regime.[26]

Another common source of conflict is the rivalry between the heads of regional executive bodies of power and mayors of capital cities. In Primorskii Krai the struggle between the regional governor and the mayor of Vladivostok took on epic proportions. Such tensions and conflicts were complicated and exacerbated by the dominance of independents in the majority of assemblies and an absence in all but a few of strong disciplined parties.[27]

However, the specific nature of executive–legislative relations in a region depend on a number of other factors other than the powers of the respective elites at the time the charters/constitutions were laid down. Other important factors determining this relationship are the electoral support of the chief executive, the social composition of the assembly (see section on corporatism and clientelism below) and the relationship between the governor and the federal government. In a study of executive–legislative relations in twenty-seven regions Turovskii classifies regional assemblies according to: (a) the degree of governor's control over the legislature (strong, partial, or weak), and (b) the balance of political forces in the legislature. A combination of these two criteria allows Turovskii to posit five possible 'ideal types' of legislature:[28]

1 *Nomenklatura dominated legislatures under strong governor's control*: Such legislatures (Kabardino-Balkariya, Novgorod, Samara, Saratov, Tomsk and Komi-Perm AO) are dominated by economic and administrative elites, as well as representatives of organisations funded by the regional budget. Party representation is negligent or non-existent. Here we see a fusion of executive and legislative power with the vast majority of the deputies supported by the governor in the elections, and the chair of the assembly fully in the pocket of the governor.

2 *Legislatures with sizeable party representation under strong governor's control*: (Sakha, Astrakhan, Tambov, Moscow and Yevreiskaya AOB.) For example, in Moscow city Duma a majority of party and independent deputies support the mayor.

3 *Nomenklatura under partial governor's control*: In several regions the governor's control over a nomenklatura-dominated Duma was far from complete (Leningrad, Murmansk and Perm).

4 *Party/nomenklatura legislature under partial governor's control*: This type is the most common. Several groupings compete for power but none is predominant. The governor's 'party of power' normally manages to ensure a majority, but to build it the governor has to strike alliances with various influential elite groups (Krasnoyarsk, Primorskii Krai, Stavropol', Khabarovsk, Belgorod, Kamchatka, Moscow Oblast, Novosibirsk, Penza, Smolensk and Tver').

5 *Nomenklatura legislature under weak governor's control*: In some of the legislatures the majority belongs to elite groups which do not support the governor (Altai Republic and Tyumen Oblast) (see table 7.1).

As noted above, one of the reasons why regional bodies have been able to create such varied political structures is the fact that it took until

Table 7.1 Turovskii's classification of regional legislatures, 1997

Degree of governor's control	Nomenklatura domination	Parties + nomenklatura
Strong	Kabardino-Balkariya, Novgorod, Samara, Saratov, Tomsk, Komi-Perm AO	Sakha (Yakutiya), Astrakhan, Tambov, Moscow, Jewish AO
Partial	Leningrad, Murmansk, Perm	Krasnoyarsk, Primorskii Krai, Stavropol', Khabarovsk, Belgorod, Kamchatka, Moscow Oblast, Novosibirsk, Penza, Smolensk, Tver'
Weak	Altai Republic, Tyumen	

October 1999 before the Duma adopted the long awaited federal law, 'On the general principles of organising the legislative (representative) organs of state power in the subjects of the Russian Federation'.[29] But, as Mendras notes, by the time the law was promulgated: 'all the territories had already adopted their own constitution or statute (Ustav) and had shaped their relations with federal authorities through years of daily bargaining and compromise'.[30] Moreover, as Gel'man observes, the new law was adopted just before the 1999 Duma elections at a time when the Yeltsin regime did not want to alienate the regions. Thus, Gel'man concludes, the 'law does not provide any political or legal innovations and merely served to codify the existing regional state of affairs'.[31]

Elites, clientelism and corporatism

As O'Donnell observes, when democratic institutions are weak and inchoate their place is soon taken over by informal practices, such as clientelism, patrimonialism, and corruption.[32] The chronic weakness of parties has left open the door for other groups to enter politics. Two of the most powerful are industrial executives and state bureaucrats. In a new post-communist corporatist alliance, regional economic and political elites (many of whom were formerly members of the Soviet nomenklatura) have joined forces to plunder the wealth of their regions. Politics in Russia is built upon a myriad of patron–client networks which cut across the formal administrative, rational–legal and constitutional boundaries of the state. Behind the formal façade of federalism lies a network of informal vertical and horizontal ties which have created a kind of 'pluralism of elites' which prevent any one individual, group or clan from controlling all the levers of power either at the national or regional levels.

Representation of economic elites

As Fillipov notes, 'compared to the first round of legislative elections in the regions which took place over the period 1993–94, we have witnessed a meteoric rise in the importance of financial resources'.[33] Key members of the Soviet economic and administrative elites now dominate and control the work of Russia's local assemblies.[34] Thus, for example, in the 1995–97 elections for regional assemblies there were 4,120 candidates from industry, and many of these were high ranking executives or directors of enterprises and collective farms. Of these 23.0 per cent were successful in winning seats.[35] And members of the economic elite have been able to turn their economic power into political power and victory at the ballot box. Thus for example, enterprise directors have been able to 'persuade' their employees (whom they provide with not only wages, but other vital services and goods, such as healthcare and housing) to bring home the votes.

As Lallemand notes, 'In times of uncertainty employees find they have an interest in maintaining the factory's paternalism, and they willingly vote for a member of their management'.[36]

In his 1998 study of 27 regional assemblies Turovskii concluded that by far the largest groupings in the assemblies were directors of industrial enterprises and chairs of collective farms. In ten of the assemblies entrepreneurs made up a majority or near majority of the deputies corps. Indeed, so great was the representation of business interests that the list of deputies in some assemblies read like a 'Who's Who?' of local business.[37] For example, 80 per cent of the members of the legislature of Kabardino-Balkariya represented the economic elite of factory directors and businessmen.[38] In Sakha's regional assembly, the firm Russian Diamonds was represented not only by its president but also by two vice presidents, and there were also two managers of the Sakha Gold Company. In Tyumen oblast at least five deputies, including the speaker of the assembly, belonged to the top leadership of the gas giant Gazprom.[39] Of the 130 members of the Tatarstan parliament elected in 1999, 48 were directors of enterprises and banks.[40] In 1998 representatives of large business concerns won twenty of thirty seats in the Ishevsk city Duma:

> The new members of the legislature control two of the largest banks in the city, all the private television stations, 90 per cent of private newspapers, two-thirds of the market for oil products, all three large construction companies, and the two trading companies that control produce sales in the city. Among the winners was the Chairman of 'Udmurtneft', which extracts 80 percent of the oil in the region. No political party member was elected.[41]

Members of the economic elite have also sought to win elections for governor. Thus, for example, in the elections for 70 governors conducted over the period 1995–97 there were 102 candidates from industry and commerce, of which, 6 were finally victorious. And in a recent round of gubernatorial elections conducted in 1999–2001 there was a gradual increase in the number of top businessmen among the governor's ranks. Thus, for example, the new governor of Chukotka, Roman Abramovich, is one of the heads of Russian Aluminium, a giant conglomerate which controls 70 per cent of Russia's aluminium production. Aleksandr Khloponin the new governor of Taimyr AO is the head of Norilsk Nickel. Others with backgrounds in business are Vladimir Loginov of the Koryak AO, Aleksandr Tkachev of Krasnodar, and Yurii Trutnev of Perm.[42] The former first vice president of the YUKOS oil company Viktor Kazakov was appointed first deputy governor of Samara in July 2000.[43]

Representation of members of the state

A number of republican presidents and regional governors have also been successful in creating weak ceremonial parliaments. In a flagrant violation of the democratic principle of the separation of powers they have packed legislative bodies with their subordinates from the state adminis- tration. Thus, for example, in elections conducted over the period 1995–97, 332 heads of city and district administrations won seats in 45 regional assemblies. Although federal laws prohibit deputies from combining state and municipal service there has been some confusion over the interpre- tation of what constitutes 'municipal service'. In most regions, heads of district administrations have not been considered by the courts to be 'municipal servants'. Thus, for example, in Samara oblast the regional court declared that one could combine legislative duties with a post as chief of a local administration, but in Tver this was declared illegal. In 1998 the state Duma passed a law prohibiting heads of local adminis- trations from being elected deputies but this law was vetoed by the Federation Council.[44]

Part of the explanation for allowing full time administrators to be elected deputies is explained by the fact that, as we noted in chapter 6, most deputies do not work on a full time professional basis and the major- ity combine their deputies' duties with some other kind of occupation.[45]

Representatives of executive bodies of power in regional assemblies made up 18.6 per cent of all deputies in 1997. However, in some regions this figure was much higher. The highest representation of state officials in regional parliaments were to be found in Bashkortostan (50.0 per cent), Novgorod (46.2 per cent), Sverdlovsk Oblast (35 per cent), Kabardino- Balkariya, and Komi (30 per cent, respectively).[46]

Indeed, in some cases where there are bicameral assemblies, the upper chamber was specially created to include heads of local administrations. In Bashkortostan, 73 of 74 heads of district administrations were elected members of the upper house of the parliament.[47] As Farukshin observes, in Tatarstan we find what would appear to be a contradiction in terms, a 'bureaucratic parliament' where 60 of the 130 members elected to the leg- islature (the State Council) in 1999 held full time posts in the state appa- ratus. These included, the Prime Minister, the head of the Presidential Administration, a deputy head of a branch of the Ministry of Internal Affairs, and 57 heads or deputy heads of district administrations. More- over, the majority of these state officials were directly appointed to their posts by the President.[48] And if we also consider the fact that the heads of the district administrations also hold the post of chair of district legislatures, then the idea that there is any real separation of powers in Tatarstan is patently absurd.[49]

A similar situation exists in the Komi Republic, where the 1997 law on local government contains numerous contradictions with federal law. Thus, for example according to this law President Spiridonov is granted the powers to appoint local government heads, and local legislatures are given the task of selecting the mayors on the recommendation of the president.[50] In Bashkortostan the Republic Constitution also gives President Rakhimov the power to directly appoint mayors. In Marii-El administrative territorial districts were created to allow the heads of seventeen districts to enter the Republic's Legislative Assembly. In Kursk's charter the governor has the right to name the heads of 28 district administrations, and the communist party governor Aleksandr Mikhailov has packed the administration with appointees from the communist party.[51] In Kalmykiya there is no conflict between executive and legislative bodies for the simple reason that the republic's legislative assembly (the Khural), is made up of just thirty or so unelected deputies, personally selected by the President.[52]

Elites, institutions and democracy

Whilst a great deal of the conflict between regional parliaments and executives can be explained by the political orientation of their members, as for instance, when we have a communist governor and a reformist assembly or vice versa, often there are also deeper institutional factors at work.[53] Theorists of the 'new institutionalism school' argue that democracy depends not only on economic and social conditions but also on the design of political institutions.[54] According to this school, 'Political actors are driven by institutional duties and roles as well as, or instead of, by calculated self-interest'.[55] Fundamentally, 'institutions shape politics', and they 'influence outcomes because they shape actors' identities, power and strategies'.[56]

Furthermore, institutions are not neutral, as they both incorporate and exclude certain actors, and ultimately, 'determine which agents, on the basis of which resources, claims, and procedures, are accepted as valid participants' in the decision making process. Thus, institutions matter, and they matter more the longer they are in existence. As O'Neil notes, over time institutions as 'self-replicating structures', develop their own particular characteristics – resources, values, norms, routines, and patterns – which are passed on to individuals both inside and outside the structure'.[57]

Elites and institutions

The above authors stress the primacy of institutions over individual actors. However, for other scholars who take an 'elite centred' approach, it is elites that are responsible for the creation of institutions in the first place. Institutions are created out of elite conflict and bargaining. Elites are the primary actors in crafting democracy or bolstering authoritarian regimes. Here democratic elites are necessary for democracy.

In Russia the founding charters and constitutions ('rules of the game') emerged out of elite conflict in the regions. Political elites struggled to create the rules (e.g., a presidential or parliamentary system, a unitary or federal system, a majoritarian, proportional, or mixed type of electoral system) so that they could win the game. Moreover, elites are liable to be more powerful in transitional societies such as Russia, where institutions tend to be weak and in flux. However, we should not dismiss the importance of regional institutions in Russia and their development over the last ten years. Elections, parties, constitutions and charters, assemblies, presidencies and courts, are now a normal part of the political landscape even if not all the major political actors have accepted the democratic process as the 'only game in town'. But Russia's fledgeling democracy is still far from consolidated, especially in the ethnic republics where, as we discuss in chapter 9, 'elective dictatorships' and 'delegative democracies' are the norm rather than the exception.

Notes

1 S. Mainwaring, 'Presidentialism, multipartism, and democracy', *Comparative Political Studies*, 26:2 (July 1993), 199.
2 As Lijphart notes, 'Presidentialism is said to have the advantages of stability, greater democracy and more limited government but the disadvantages of executive–legislative deadlock, temporary rigidity and less inclusive winner takes all government'. See, A. Lijphart (ed.), *Parliamentary Versus Presidential Government* (Oxford: Oxford University Press, 1992). And also his, *Patterns of Democracy: Government Forms and Performance in Thirty-Six Countries* (New Haven and London: Yale University Press, 1999), pp. 117–18.
3 Z. Gitelman, 'The democratisation of Russia in comparative perspective', in S. White, A. Pravda and Z. Gitelman (eds), *Developments is Russian Polctics: 4* (Basingstoke: Macmillan), p. 274.
4 J. M. Maravall and T. di Tella, in A. Przeworski (ed.), *Sustainable Democracy* (Cambridge: Cambridge University Press, 1995), p. 46.
5 *Ibid.*
6 Mainwaring, 'Presidentialism, multipartism', 216.
7 Decree no. 75, August 22, 1991, 'O Nekotorykh Voprosakh Deyatel'nosti Organov Ispolnitel'noi Vlasti v RSFSR'.
8 The first chief administrator appointed by the President was D'yakonov, in Krasnodar krai.
9 'O Kraevom, Oblastnom Sovete i Kraevoi, Oblastnoi Administratsii', March 5, 1992. Published in *Rossiiskaya gazeta* (20 March 1992).
10 V. Gel'man, 'Regional'naya vlast' v sovremennoi Rossii: instituty, regimy i praktiki', *Polis*, 1 (1998), 94–5.
11 *Ibid.*, 95.
12 W. A. Clark, 'Presidential prefects in the Russian provinces: Yeltsin's regional cadres policy', in G. Gill (ed.), *Elites and Leadership in Russian Politics* (Basingstoke: diacmillan, 1998), p. 41.
13 Presidential Decree no. 186, 5 February 1993, 'O predstavitele Prezidenta

Rossiiskoi Federatsii v krae, oblasti, avtonomnoi oblasti, avtomnon okruge, goradakh Moskve i Sankt-Peterburge'.

14 See, Clark, 'Presidential Prefects', p. 41.

15 Gel'man, 'Regional'naya vlast", 95.

16 Decree 1617, 9 October 1993 – 'O Reforme Predstavitel'nykh Organov Vlasti i Organov Mestnovo Samo-Upravleniya v Rossiiskoi Federatsii', Decree 1723, October 23, 1993, 'Ob Osnovnykh Nachalakh Organizatsii Gosudarstvennoi Vlasti v Sub'ektakh Rossiskoi Federatsii', and Decree no. 1765, 26 October 1993, 'Ob Utverzhdenii Osnovnykh Polozhenie O Vyborakh v Predstavitel'nye Organy Gosudarstvennoi Vlasti Kraya, Oblasti, Goroda Federal'novo Znacheniya, Avtonomnoi Oblasti, Avtonomnovo Okruga'.

17 As Lowenhardt notes, authorities in Tatarstan justified their refusal to comply with federal laws on elections 'with reference to the provision of the 1994 Bilateral Treaty which stated that Tatarstan 'establishes its own system of state organs and the way in which they are organised and operate'. J. Lowenhardt, 'The 1996 presidential elections in Tatarstan', *Journal of Communist Studies and Transition Politics*, 13:1 (March 1997), 135.

18 V. Lysenko, 'A little constitution can't be at odds with the big one', *Rossiiskiye vesti* (April 18, 1995), p. 2. Translated in *CDPSP*, 47:16 (1995), 9.

19 See, *Rossiskaya gazeta* (February 1 and 17, 1996).

20 V. Gel'man, 'Subnational institutions', in N. Robinson (ed.) *Institutions and Political Charge in Russia* (Basingstoke: Macmillan, 2000), p. 99.

21 A number of regions and republics entrench the separation of powers in their constitutions and charters. Thus according to article 7 of the Constitution of the Republic of Altai state powers is divided into legislative, executive and judicial branches. Organs of these three branches function independently and have no right to interfere in each other's areas of competence. Analogous norms are stipulated in the charters of Sverdlovsk and Nizhegorod oblasts, St Petersburg, Khanty-Mansi AO, and many other subjects of the federation. In the charter of Primorskii krai it clearly states that no organ of state power has the right to adopt decisions which infringe the rights and competence of other state bodies. See, A. S. Avtonomov, A. A. Zakharov and E. M. Orlova, *Regional'nye Parlamenty v Sovremennoi Rossii*, Nauchnaya Doklad, no. 18 (Moscow: MONF, 2000), p. 77.

22 Gel'man, 'Subnational institutions', p. 99. The rulings of the Constitutional Court are published in *Rossiiskaya gazeta* (February 1 and 17, 1996). For a discussion of the ruling on Altai Krai, see O. Barabanov, 'Altaiskii Krai kak syb'ekt Rossiiskoi federatsii: konstitutsionno pravova kharakteristika', *KPVO*, 3–4 (1997).

23 See Gel'man, 'Regional'naya vlast".

24 V. Lysenko, 'A little constitution', 8.

25 V. Nechaev, 'Regional'nye politicheskie sistemy v postsovetskoi Rossii', *Pro et Contra*, 5 (Winter, 2000), internet version, 3.
    http:/pubs.carnegie.ru/p@c/Vol5–2000/1/04nechaev.asp

26 For a discussion of regional elites and democratisation see V. Gel'man, 'Regime transition, uncertainty and prospects for democratisation: the politics of Russia's regions in a comparative perspective', *Europe–Asia Studies*, 51:6 (1999), 939–56; V. Gel'man, 'Democratisation, structural pluralism and fragile

bi-centrism: the case of Volgograd Oblast', in C. Ross (ed.), *Regional Politics in Russia* (Manchester: Manchester University Press, 2002), 154–77; V. Gel'man, *Transformatsiya v Rossiiskikh Regional'nykh Elit v Sravenitel'noi Perspektive* (Moscow: MONF, 1999).

27 For a discussion of democratisation in Primorskii Krai, see J. W. Hahn, 'The development of political institutions in three regions of the Russian far east', in C. Ross (ed.), *Regional Politics in Russia* (Manchester: Manchester University Press, 2002).

28 R. F. Turovskii, 'Gubernatory nachinayut i vyigryvayut?', in I. M. Bunin and B. I. Makarenko (eds), *Politicheskie Protsessy v Regionakh Rossii* (Moscow: Tsentr Politicheskikh Tekhnologii, 1998), p. 232.

29 See, the Federal Law, no. 184–F3, 'Ob Obshchikh Printsipakh Organizatsii Zakonodatel'nykh (Predstavitel'nykh) i Ispolnitel'nykh Organov Gosudarstvennoi Vlasti Sub'ektov Rossiiskoi Federatstii', which was ratified by the president on October 6, 1999 and was published in *Rossiskaya gazeta* (October 19, 1999).

30 Marie Mendras, 'How regional elites preserve their power', *Post-Soviet Affairs*, 15:4 (1999), 301–2.

31 Vladimir Gel'man, 'New law on regional institutions preserves status quo', *EWI Russian Regional Report*, 4:42 (November 11, 1999), 12.

32 G. O'Donnell, 'Delegative democracy', *Journal of Democracy*, 5:1 (January 1994), 59.

33 A. Filippov, 'Vybory zakonodatelnykh (predstavitel'nykh) organov gosu-darstvennoi vlasti', in G. Lyukhterkhandt-Mikhaleva and S. Ryzhenkov (eds), *Vybory i Partii v Regionakh Rossii* (Moscow: IGPI, 2000), p. 126.

34 See, D. Lane and C. Ross, *The Transformation from communism to Capitalism: Ruling Elites From Gorbachev to Yeltsin* (New York: St Martin's Press, 1999).

35 *Vybory v Zakonodatel'nye Predstavitel'nye Organy*.

36 J. C. Lallemand, 'Politics for the few: elites in Bryansk and Smolensk', *Post-Soviet Affairs*, 15:4 (1999), p. 332.

37 R. F. Turovskii, 'Gubernatory nachinaiut i vyigryvaiut?', in R. F. Turovskii (ed.), *Politicheskie Protsessy v Regionakh Rossii* (Moscow: Tsentr Politicheskikh Tekhnologii, 1998), p. 203.

38 R. Orttung, 'Directors, businessmen dominate Kabardino-Balkariya returns', *EWI Russian Regional Report*, 2:44 (December 18, 1997), 13.

39 Turovskii, 'Gubernatory nachinaiut', p. 204.

40 M. Farukshin, 'Izbiratel'noe zakonodatel'stvo i vybory v Tatarstane: opyt regional'novo pravovovo separatizma', in V. V. Mikhailov, V. A. Bazhanov, and M. Kh. Farukshin (eds), *Osobaya Zona: Vybory v Tatarstane* (Ul'yanovsk: Mezhdunarodnoi Pravozashchitnoi Assamblei, 2000), p. 12.

41 'Mayor, businessmen win local elections in Izhevsk', *EWI Russian Regional Report*, 3:6 (April 23, 1998), 382.

42 M. Weinstein, *EWI Russian Regional Report*, 6:20 (May 30, 2001), 14–17.

43 *RFE/RL Russian Federation Report*, 2:26 (July 19, 2000), 9.

44 Federal Law, 8 January, 1998, no. 9–F3, 'Ob Osnovakh Munitsipal'noi sluzhby v Rossiiskoi Federatsii', *Rossiiskaya gazeta* (January 14, 1998).

45 A. Fillipov, 'Vybory zakonodatel'nykh (predstavitel'nykh) organov gosu-darstvennoi vlasti sub'ektov Rossiiskoi Federatsii (1990–98)', in *Vybory i Partii,*

p. 118. See also I. Mikhailovskaya, 'Regional'nye osobennosti realizatsii printsipa razdeleniya vlastei v sovremennoi Rossii', in O. B. Sidorovich (ed.), *Rossiiskii Konstitutsionalizm: Politicheskii Rezhim v Regional'nom Kontekste* (Moscow, MONF, 2000), pp. 178–80.

46 *Vybory v Zakonodatel'nye Predstavitel'nye Organy*, p. 636.

47 Kahn, 'Federal façade', p. 253.

48 Farukshin, 'Izbiratel'noe zakonodatel'stvo', p. 12.

49 Also elected was 1 deputy chair of Kazan City Soviet, 3 chief doctors, 1 deputy head of a department in a hospital, 1 chief editor of a journal, 1 trades union boss, 1 professor, 1 head of a scientific-research institute, 1 deputy head of a department of the Ministry of Internal Affairs, 1 chair of the Union of Writers', and 48 directors of enterprises and banks. See, Farukshin, *ibid*.

50 Yu. Shabaev, *EWI Russian Regional Report*, 6:13 (April 11, 2001), 8–9.

51 S. Sarychev, *EWI Russian Regional Report*, 6:20 (May 30, 2001), p. 11.

52 Ye. Tregubova, 'Kirsan Iliumzhinov dreams of a stable and peaceful Kalmyk Khanate within Russia', *Sevodnya* (October 17, 1995), 3. Translated in *CDPSP*, 48:42 (1995), 16.

53 By institutions here we refer to constitutions, elections, parties, parliaments, executives, judicial and other such bodies.

54 J. G. March and J. P. Olsen, *Discovering Institutions: The Organizational Basis of Politics* (The Free Press: 1989), p. 17.

55 *Ibid.*, p. 159.

56 R. Putnam, *Making Democracy Work: Civic Traditions in Modern Italy* (Princeton: Princeton University Press, 1993).

57 P. H. O'Neil, 'Revolution from within, institutional analysis, transitions from authoritarianism, and the case of Hungary', *World Politics* 48 (July 1996), 581.

Federalism under Putin

In August 1991 Yeltsin created two new administrative bodies to keep the regions in check: presidential representatives and regional governors. Between 1991 and 1996 Yeltsin was able to maintain control over the governors through his powers of appointment. However, once Yeltsin relinquished these powers and governors were able to come to power via the ballot box (see chapter 6), he was forced to turn to his presidential representatives to win back control of the regions.

As we noted in chapter 3 one of the major powers of the governors was their control over the appointment of the heads of federal bodies situated in their territories. By controlling the appointment of such powerful officials (e.g., heads of the tax inspectorate, financial oversight bodies, and customs officers, the judiciary, procuracy, central electoral commissions and others), regional executives were able to undermine the authority of the federal government and to thwart the implementation of federal policies. In some regions (for example Stavropol') governors were even able to appoint their own regional security councils thus giving them a significant degree of leverage over the 'power ministries' (security, internal affairs) in their territories.

According to Yeltsin's Presidential Decree of August 24, 1991, 'On Representatives of the President of the RSFSR in Krais and Oblasts of the RSFSR', the presidential representatives were charged with overseeing the work of the governors and federal agencies. However, three further presidential decrees followed in a largely unsuccessful attempt to raise the profile of the representatives.[1] In the last of these decrees promulgated in July 1997 the presidential representatives were given increased powers to monitor the implementation of federal programmes and to coordinate the activities of the myriad of federal bureaucracies situated in the regions.

However, these decrees failed to give the representatives sufficient powers and resources to challenge the authority of the popularly elected governors. Many of the envoys appointed by Yeltsin had strong ties with their regions, and they soon turned 'native' taking on the interests of those whom they were supposed to be controlling. Moreover, governors in many regions captured control over the appointment of the representatives. In some cases bilateral treaties actually gave the governors the right to appoint their own presidential representatives or to approve presidential nominees. Indeed, in some cases presidential representatives were actually high ranking members of regional elites. Thus, for example, in Stavropol' Krai we had the absurd sitation whereby the presidential representative simultaneously held the post of deputy governor of the region. In 1994 Yeltsin bowed to the will of the Primorskii krai regional administration and sacked his presidential representative.[2]

Other more loyal lieutenants of the President simply did not have sufficient authority, or the resources, to stand up to the governors. The representatives relied on the regional administrations to supply them with housing, office space, transportation and other administrative supports. The governors also controlled access to the best schools and hospitals, and other local services for the families of the envoys. As Hyde notes, by the mid-1990s, 'Some representatives came to fulfill a function better described as representative of the regions to the centre'.[3] Indeed, in 1997 the situation was so bad that the Kremlin was forced to replace 60 per cent of its representatives because of fears that 'their loyalty had been co-opted by the regional power elites'.[4] We should also note that the legislation setting up the presidential representatives was aimed at the regions and not the ethnic republics, many of which were able to escape the imposition of Yeltsin's envoys.

Putin's radical assault on federalism

It was Putin's election victories in 1999 and 2000 which paved the way for his audacious assault on the powers of the regional governors and his radical reform of the federal system. Armed with a democratic mandate from his impressive victory in the 2000 presidential elections, coupled with the surprise success of his presidential party Yedinstvo (Unity) in the December 1999 Duma elections, Putin was able to persuade a now 'tame parliament' that a radical overhaul of the federal system was essential if Russia was not to collapse into anarchy and ethnic turmoil. Moreover, Putin was able to win over key oligarchs to his view that the only way to bolster Russia's flagging economy was to reduce the anarchic powers of the governors, and to strengthen, 'the power-vertical'. As Putin stated in his message to the Federal Assembly: 'It's a scandalous thing when a fifth of the legal acts adopted in the regions contradict the country's Basic Law, when republic constitutions and province charters are at odds with the Russian Constitution, and when trade barriers, or even worse, border demarcation posts are set up between Russia's territories and provinces'.[5] In order, to 'restore an effective vertical chain of authority' and to implement a uniform policy, Putin called for a 'dictatorship of law', in order to ensure that every citizen whether in Moscow or 'the most remote backwoods of Russia', would be guaranteed the same rights, and federal legislation would be 'understood and enforced' in a uniform manner throughout the federation.[6]

Putin's primary objectives are to create a unified economic, legal and security space in the federation and to tighten the federal government's controls over the regions. There are six major strands to Putin's federal reforms: (1) The creation of seven new federal super-districts, (2) a reform of the Federation Council, (3) the creation of a new State Council, (4) the granting of new powers to the President to dismiss regional governors and dissolve regional assemblies, (5) new rights for regional governors to dismiss municipal officials, and (6) a major campaign to bring regional charters and republican constitutions into line with the Russian Constitution. Below we examine each one of these reforms in turn.

By stressing the need to strengthen what he called the 'power vertical', Putin's reform agenda was very much in tune with many of the ideas which had recently been put forward by political parties in the run up to the 1999 Duma elections. Indeed, many of the same issues had already been raised by former Prime Minister Yevegenii Primakov. On coming to power in the autumn of 1998 Primakov had warned the country that the federation was in danger of splitting up into separate parts. And in January 1999 he called for a 'restoration of the vertical state power structure', demanding that separatist trends 'must be quelled, liquidated, and uprooted'.[7] Primakov also sought to bring the governors under federal control by coopting them into the cabinet and government presidium.[8] Thus for example, eight of the most powerful governors, each heading a regional economic association, were made members of the Presidium.[9] After the anarchy of the Yeltsin years when the regions had almost turned into the 'personal fiefdoms' of the governors there was a general consensus that something had to be done to reinstate a single legal space in Russia.

The creation of federal districts

If Putin's major aim was to reassert federal authority over the regions then something had to be done to improve the work of the presidential representatives and to remove them from the clutches of the regional governors. And, even more importantly Putin had to recapture control over the work of the myriad of federal agencies which were situated in the regions and which had also fallen under the sway of the regional executives. Thus, on the May 13, 2000 Putin adopted what was to be the first of a package of decrees whose key aim was to rein in the power of the governors and to 'strengthen the unity of the state'.[10]

In this first major reform of the federal system, Putin divided the country into seven super-districts, each of which contained a dozen or more federal subjects, and he appointed a plenipotentiary representative (Polpredy – 'Polnomochnyi Predstavitel' Prezidenta') to each district (see box 8.1). Putin deftly sidestepped calls to format the new districts to conform to the contours of Russia's eight inter-regional associations or eleven socio-economic regions. Instead, the new federal districts were drawn up to closely match Russia's military districts, thus giving the envoys (most of whom had a background in the military or security organs, direct access to the command and control networks of the military garrisons in their districts. And in a blow against the sovereignty claims of the ethnic republics, Putin drew up the boundaries of the new federal districts in such a way that each district would include a mixture of ethnic republics and territorially defined regions. None of the capital cities of the federal districts are situated in an ethnic republic. This has led some commentators to speculate that the creation of the federal districs is but the first step in Putin's programme of levelling down the status of the republics to that of the regions. For a list of the districts and 'polpredy' see box 8.1.

However, many of the regions are not too happy with their new federal districts. Thus, for example, Astrakhan and Volgograd currently part of the Southern district would rather be in the Volga federal district. Perm, which is placed in the Volga district would rather be in the Urals, while Tyumen which is in the Urals wants to be part of the Siberian district, and Bashkortostan would like to be moved from the Volga District to the Urals.[11]

Putin's creation of the seven federal districts and the instigation of the 'polpredy' fully comply with article 83 of the Russian Constitution which simply states that the President, 'appoints and removes plenipotentiary representatives of the President of the Russian Federation'. As Oracheva notes, 'the Constitution does not specify in what particular form this institution exists, what functions presidential representatives perform, how many representatives may be appointed'.[12] Thus, Putin can argue that the changes brought about by the May 13 decree were simply changes to his presidential administration, and not constitutional changes to the federation itself which would have been required to go through (and certainly failed to pass) complex and protracted amendement procedures provided for by the Constitution. However, as discussed below, Putin's federal reforms taken together undoubtedly are an assault on the federal idea and they certainly violate the spirit of the Constitution if not the actual Constitution itself.

The administrations of the federal districts
Five of the seven polpredy have a background in the army or security services. Of the two civilians, only one (Kirienko the former Prime Minister)

Box 8.1 The seven federal districts

Central District
Presidential Representative: Lieutenant-General Georgii Poltavchenko.
District capital: Moscow. Belgorod, Bryansk, Ivanovo, Kaluga, Kostroma, Kursk,
Lipetsk, Moscow, Orel, Ryazan, Smolensk, Tambov, Tver, Tula, Vladimir, Voronezh
and Yaroslavl oblasts; and the city of Moscow.

Far Eastern District
Presidential Representative: Lieutenant General Konstantin Pulikovskii (retired).
District capital: Khabarovsk. Republic of Sakha; Khabarovsk and Primorsky Krais;
Amur, Kamchatka, Magadan and Sakhalin oblasts; the Jewish autonomous oblast;
and the Koryak and Chukchi autonomous okrugs.

North-western District
Presidential Representative: Goneral Viktor Cherkesov.
District capital: St Petersburg.
Republics of Karelia and Komi; Arkhangelsk, Kaliningrad, Leningrad, Murmansk,
Novgorod, Pskov and Vologda oblasts; the Nenets autonomous okrug; and the
city of St Petersburg.

Siberian District
Presidential Representative: Leonid Drachevskii (April 5, 1942).
District capital: Novosibirsk.
Republics of Altai, Buryatia, Khakassia and Tyva; Altai and Krasnoyarsk Krais;
Chita, Irkutsk, Kemerovo, Novosibirsk, Omsk and Tomsk oblasts; and the Evenk,
Taimyr and Ust-Orda Buryat autonomous okrugs.

Southern District
Presidential Representative: Army General Viktor Kazantsev.
District capital: Rostov-on-Don.
Republics of Adygeya, Chechnya, Dagestan, Ingushetia, Kabardino-Balkaria,
Kalmykia, Karachaevo-Cherkessia and North Ossetia; Krasnodar and Stavropol
Krais; and Astrakhan, Rostov and Volgograd oblasts.

Urals District
Presidential Representative: Colonel-General (Police) Peter Latyshev.
District capital: Yekaterinburg.
Chelyabinsk, Kurgan, Sverdlovsk and Tyumen oblasts; and the Khanty-Mansii
and Yamal-Nenets autonomous okrugs.

Volga District
Presidential Representative: Sergei Kirienko.
District capital: Nizhnii Novgorod.
Republics of Bashkortostan, Chuvashia, Marii El, Mordovia, Tatarstan and
Udmurtiya; Kirov, Nizhnii Novgorod, Orenburg, Penza, Perm, Samara, Saratov
and Ulyanovsk oblasts; and the Komi-Permyak autonomous okrug.

Source: *RFE/RL Russian Federation Report*, nos 18 and 19, 2000, compiled by Julie Corwin.

has experience of working in politics at the national level, and the other is a former diplomat. In terms of responsibilities, their rank is somewhere between deputy chief of staff of the presidential administration and Deputy Prime Minister.[13] The high status of the polpredy is also reflected in their membership of the Russian Security Council, and their right to attend cabinet meetings of the federal government. In fact, the decree setting up the federal districts was drafted by the Security Council. The status of the polpredy is also reflected in their regular meetings with the President. To prevent the polpredy going native the presidential administration will fund them directly.

The polpredy also have a not inconsiderable backup bureaucracy to assist them in their duties. In each of the seven federal districts there are approximately 100 members of staff. In addition, in each district there are also five 'deputy polpredy', a chief federal inspector, and a federal inspector appointed to each region within the federal districts.

Many of the major ministries have begun to restructure their administrations bringing them into line with the new federal districts. Thus, each of the federal districts now has a deputy prosecutor general and each district has a department for combating organised crime under the dual subordination of the polpredy and the Russian Minister of Internal Affairs. In addition, the Ministry of Justice also recently created branches in each of the seven districts and the Ministry of Finance, and the Tax Inspectorate have likewise begun to restructure their administrations in line with the reforms. Other federal bodies such as the Ministry of Health are in the process of following suit.

Power and responsibilities of the polpredy
The powers and responsibilities of the polpredy, at least on paper, are very impressive. Their key tasks are: (1) to monitor the regions' compliance with the Russian Constitution, federal laws and presidential decrees, (2) to oversee the selection and placement of personnel in the regional branches of the federal bureaucracy, (3) to protect the national security interests of the regions, and (4) to set up and coordinate within their districts inter-regional economic programmes.[14] They also have the power to recommend to the President that he suspend specific local laws or decrees when they contradict federal laws and to call for the dismissal of governors and the dissolution of regional assemblies if they adopt decrees or laws which violate federal laws (see below).

Putin has been at pains to stress that the primary role of the polpredy are not to supplant the role of the elected governors but rather to coordinate the work of the federal agencies in the their districts. Putin noted: 'The authorised representatives, needless to say, will help in effectively solving the problems in their regions. But they do not have the right to interfere in areas under the jurisdiction of the electoral heads of the regions'.[15] This statement reminds one of pronouncements made during the Soviet era about the proper role of the party and state bodies. The party was charged with 'leading and guiding' the work of state bodies, but not 'supplanting' them. Of course, what happened in practice was quite the opposite, party bodies did meddle in the affairs of state bodies, often hindering, rather than helping them to carry out their administrative functions. It would appear that the polpredy may face a similar dilemma in their relations with the governors and federal bureaucracies.

One of the most important and controversial powers of the polpredy is that of the selection and placement of personnel. As presidential representative to the Volga district, Kirienko notes: 'In essence, the presidential representatives will oversee personnel policy for the president and will approve all appointments and promotions. The representatives will also maintain a reserve of personnel for all federal agencies'.[16] These powers will bring the polpredy into direct conflict with the governors who can cite article 72 of the Russian constitution to defend their right to be consulted over such appointments especially with regard to the judiciary and law enforcement bodies.

There is also some confusion over what controls the polpredy will be given in the economic sphere. Whilst they will not have direct control over the purse strings they are nonetheless charged with monitoring all the federal funds which come into their districts and overseeing the collection and transfer of taxes to the federal budget. Kirienko has stated that the districts will not have their own budgets. However, he did confirm that they will have their own socio-economic development plans, and thus, the ability to exercise some influence over economic policy making in the regions.

Thus, Putin's unelected polpredy have ostensibly been granted considerable powers over the internal politics of federal subjects and their democratically elected representatives. And it is difficult to imagine how these new federal representatives will be able to carry out their functions without infringing the constitutionally guaranteed rights of the federal subjects.

The creation of seven quasi-states
Whilst the powers of the polpredy seem impressive, it remains to be seen how effective they will be in practice. Given the fact that each presidential envoy will have to take charge of a dozen or so regions (whose administrative centres may be hundreds of miles apart), and the fact that every region has between forty and fifty federal agencies operating on its territory, this means that each presidential envoy will have to coordinate and

control the work of approximately 400–600 agencies. In some of the very large districts it is difficult to see how the envoys will be able to exercise control over such vast territories and/or populations. Moreover, as we noted in chapter 5 the formation of the new federal districts has made the Federation even more asymmetrical. Thus, for example, almost half of the Russian population is situated in just two of the federal districts: the Central district and the Volga district.

Putin's reforms may simply have created seven powerful quasi-regional states. Already the polpredy have begun to create the institutions necessary to turn their districts into mini-regional states. Thus, for example, we are beginning to see the development in the federal districts of councils of the heads of regional legislative and executive bodies (mini-federal councils), councils of regional governors (mini-state councils). Councils for local self-government, and expert consultative and scientific research councils.[17] Thus, for example Poltavchenko has created a council in his federal district which includes all the chief executives of the eighteen regions under his jurisdiction.[18] The council will deal with all aspects of economic development. The new council would also appear to usurp the role of the Black Earth and Central Russian inter-regional economic associations.

In the Volga district, Kirienko has created a coordinating council for regional legislative chairmen. The aim of the council is to develop a united approach for drafting regional legislation and bringing regional laws into line with federal norms. These new mini-councils will soon co-exist next to a series of new district-level banks and financial bodies.[19]

Emboldened by their new powers to appoint leaders of the regional branches of the All Union Television and Radio Company the polpredy have also been actively promoting the development of a 'single information space' in each of their federal districts. To this end they have also set up district-wide mass media councils. Now the press will not only come under the control of the governors but the polpredy, hardly a recipe for the creation of a vibrant and open 'civil society' in Russia.

The capital cities of the seven federal districts are also rapidly becoming the home to new branches of the federal bureaucracy. Thus, for example, in addition to the district offices of the law-enforcement and justice departments, the following agencies have been established in Rostov region: the inter-regional Tax Inspectorate, the Federal Tax Police Service's Chief Administration for the Southern Federal District, the Southern Customs Administration, the Southern District Inspectorate of the President's Oversight Administration; the Russian Finance Ministry's Oversight and Auditing Administration for the Southern Federal District, the District Administration of the Federal Service for Financial and Bankruptcy, and others. There are twenty-eight district government agencies in all.[20] These developments have further undermined the constitutional equality of the federal subjects and intensified the levels of asymmetry between members of the federation.

Also regional clientelism is already working against the creation of a new intermediate level of bureaucracy beholden to Putin. Each of the seven polpredy have begun to build up their staffs based on patron–client relations, much as the President himself has appointed to his administration many of his former associates from St Petersburg and the security services. As Badovskii notes in some regions the polpredy have acted as a powerful force limiting the powers of the regional governors. But, in many regions, the apparatus of the polpredy is created from the governor's people, is quickly integrated and absorbed by the local elites, and we see the merging or joining of federal and regional bureaucracies – eventually creating a highly effective system of regional lobbying.[21] The relations between governors, presidential representatives, and federal bureaucrats is still unclear and will undoubtedly vary from district to district. As Orttung and Reddaway note: 'Rather then creating a stronger vertical hierarchy of authority leading from the central government to the regions, Putin has created a triangle, with the ministries, the presidential representatives, and the regions making up the triangle's three points'.[22] It is also becoming apparent that such power relations will be worked out on the ground and cannot be planned and mapped out by Putin at the centre.

Reform of the Federation Council

In a second major initiative Putin stripped the governors and chairs of regional assemblies of their ex officio right to sit in the upper chamber of the parliament.[23] These were to be replaced (from January 2002), with 'delegates' chosen by the regional assemblies and chief executives. More specifically, the governors have the right to appoint and dismiss their delegates as long as their choice of candidate is not vetoed by a vote of two-thirds of the members of their regional parliaments. And the regional assemblies appoint and dismiss their representatives according to their own voting procedures.

For a number of commentators, such changes will inevitably lead to a decline in the powers of the upper chamber and perhaps even in the long run to a situation whereby the upper house may be dispensed with altogether. As Kostyukov argues, the Federation Council will soon be filled with nonentities, 'bureaucrats beholden to their regions and without any political clout in Moscow's corridors of power'.[24]

On the other hand, as Putin himself has stressed, the new body will now meet full time, and not as in the past just for a few days a month. This will give the new members, who are totally reliant on their masters in the regions, far greater opportunities to scrutinise legislation coming from the Duma and presidency. And we will no longer have the spectacle of members of the executive sitting in a legislative chamber thus making a mockery of the principle of the separation of executive and legislative powers.

And, it is by no means the case, that the representatives of the governors and assemblies are as Kostyukov argues, 'non-entities'. Indeed, an examination of those selected shows this to be far from true. Indeed in a surely unforeseen scenario we have witnessed the selection of outgoing governors to represent incoming governors,[25] or the choice of deputy governors as representatives. Legislative chairs have also selected high ranking members of their assemblies as their representatives.[26] And in other cases, regions have chosen Moscow insiders or high ranking entrepreneurs.[27] However, it must also be noted that these changes undermine King's stress on the 'legislative entrenchment' of the regions in central decision making (see chapter 1) as many of the new appointees to the upper chamber have only very tenuous links with their regions, or in some cases, none at all.

More worrying for the governors is the fact that when they are denied membership of the upper chamber they will automatically lose their right to immunity from criminal prosecution. And they will no longer have a direct say in the ratification of top posts to the judiciary and procuracy (although this will fall to their delegates). Putin will now be able to use the threat of prosecution to keep the chief executives in line.

The State Council

To sweeten the pill and to partially compensate the regional elite for their loss of membership in the upper chamber, Putin on September 1, 2000 created a new presidential advisory body – the State Council.[28] The new body which is made up of all of the chief executives from the regions meets once every three months and is chaired by the President. There is also an inner presidium made up of seven governors (one from each of the federal districts), whose membership rotates each six months. The members of the presidium meet with the President once every month.

However, neither the State Council nor its presidium is likely to have real powers. The new body is purely consultative and has no law making functions. Moreover, as it was drawn up by presidential decree, it may similarly be dissolved by the President if it is not to his liking. The magazine *Itogy* has called the new council 'the factory of governor's dreams'.[29] Its main aim at present is to give the regional leaders a direct channel to the President and some limited input into policy making. However, as Teague notes, there may be a more sinister motive behind the creation of the new Council. Putin may be planning in the future to replace the Federation Council with this much weaker rubber stamping body.[30]

Dismissal of governors and dissolution of regional legislatures

The third major reform strikes at the very heart of the regions' power structures – a new law giving Putin powers to dismiss popularly elected governors and to dissolve regional assemblies.[31] As Putin explains such legislation now makes it possible for federal intervention 'in situations in which government bodies at the local level [have flouted] the Russian Constitution and federal laws, violating the uniform rights and freedoms of Russian citizens'.[32] The new law gives both chambers of the legislature, the general procurator and the regional legislatures the right to recommend that a governor be removed. However, as Corwin notes, the process is so long and involved that regional leaders would have to demonstrate 'unprecedented obstinacy, audacity, and even stupidity' before they could be fired. For a regional head to be dismissed: 'One, he must on two different occasions ignore presidential decrees, two, allow the passage of two bills with provisions that violate federal laws, or three, make use on two different occasions of regional acts previously denounced by the president or the courts. And, in each of these cases, a court verdict is required ruling that these actions constitute violations of federal law'.[33]

The president can also temporarily remove a governor while criminal charges that have been filed against him are being studied. If the president removes a governor from office he appoints a temporary governor to replace him. However, it is interesting to note that Putin did not use his new powers against the Governor of Primorskii krai, Yevgenii Nazdratenko. Instead Putin simply dismissed Nazdratenko and to keep him quiet, rewarded him with a ministerial post in Moscow. Moreover, as Orttung and Reddaway note: 'even if the president does force a governor out of office, the region will hold new elections within six months, and there is no guarantee that the new governor will be any more pleasing to the federal government than the old one'.[34]

The law also calls for the dissolution of regional assemblies if they violate federal legislation. According to this legislation regional assemblies have three months to amend any legislation that violates federal laws or legal proceedings may be enacted against them. However, the president must gain the approval of the State Duma before an assembly can be dissolved. Whilst it is certainly the case that regional assemblies do pass legislation that infringes the constitution, it is highly questionable that Putin's right to dissolve democratically elected assemblies is itself constitutional.

The governors' rights to dismiss lower level officials

Putin also steered passage of a law through the Duma which gives the governors the right to dismiss lower level administrative heads (with the exception of the mayors of capital cities) within their regions. As Putin explained: 'if under certain conditions, the head of a region can be removed from office by the country's president, then the regional leader should have a similar right with respect to lower-ranking authorities'.[35]

Also to win over the governors' support Putin promoted the so-called third-term law in the Duma. Under this law, the leaders of 69 Federation members will now be able to run for a third term and some even for a fourth even although such extensions to their tenure violate regional charters and republican constitutions (see chapter 9).[36]

Bringing regional legislation into line with federal laws

One of the main aims of the Putin's reforms is to create a unified legal space in the Russian Federation. To this end therefore, the polpredy have been charged with overseeing the complex process of bringing republic constitutions and regional charters (and other local laws and decrees) into line with the federal constitution and federal laws. By 2001 the number of normative legal acts adopted by the regions and republics exceeded 300,000, and of these, just under a quarter (70,000) contradicted the federal constitution and federal laws.[37]

Within a matter of just a few months after his election to the Russian Presidency in March 2000, Putin issued decrees demanding that the republics of Adygeya, Altai, Bashkortostan and Ingushetiya; and Amur, Smolensk and Tver oblasts, bring their regional laws into accordance with the Russian Constitution and federal legislation. Putin's decrees were backed up by two landmark decisions of the Constitutional Court (adopted on June 7 and June 27, 2000) which ruled that the republics' declarations of sovereignty were incompatible with the sovereignty of the Russian Federation.[38]

In its ruling of June 7 the court declared that several clauses in the Altai Constitution were illegal. In particular the court ruled against Altai's declarations of sovereignty, stating that 'the subjects of the Russian Federation do not possess any state sovereignty, which belongs to the Russian Federation alone'. And on June 27 the court declared that similar clauses in the constitutions of Adygeya, Ingushetiya, Bashkortostan, Komi, North Osetiya, and Tatarstan were also illegal.[39]

In August 2000 the Chief Procurator of the Russian Federation called for all regional laws to be brought into line with federal laws by January 1, 2001. And reporting back, in January 2001, the deputy head of the Presidential Administration, Dmitrii Kozak, boasted that about 80 per cent of the regional laws checked by the administration had either already been brought into compliance with federal law, or were being considered in the courts.[40] In the same month Putin declared that sixty constitutions and regional charters, as well as over 2,000 regional laws had been brought into compliance with the constitution.[41] However, there would appear to be as many different figures about the number of laws which have been brought into line as there are members of the presidential administration, and as Orttung notes there are good reasons to believe, 'that the numbers they cite are probably about as meaningful as Soviet era crop statistics'. In April 2001 the Justice Ministry reported that 23 regions continued to adopt laws which contradicted federal legislation. According to Interfax these regions included the republics of Adygeya, Altai, Ingushetiya, Bashkortostan, Komi, Tatarstan, Sakha and Tyva in addition to Arkhangelsk, Voronezh, Novgorod, Pskov, Ryazan, Moscow, Kamchatka, Irkutsk, Novosibirsk, Chita, Sverdlovsk and Chelyabinsk regions; Krasnoyarsk Krai, and the cities of Moscow and St Petersburg.[42] And in his April 2001 address to the Russian Parliament, Putin declared that over 3,500 normative acts adopted in the regions contradicted the Russian Constitution and federal laws.[43]

Indeed, it is possible that the number of laws violating federal norms may actually have grown in number! As I demonstrate below we are still very far away from the creation of a 'unified legal space' in the Russian Federation.

Putin's efforts efforts to rein in the regions has elicited a range of reactions from reluctant acquiescence to outright defiance. Many republics and regions have dragged their feet in implementing the reforms and/or they have steadfastly refused to renounce their sovereignty and their control over natural resources. And just as quickly as old legislation is being revised to conform to federal norms, regional and republican parliaments have been able to adopt new laws with new infringements. For example, more than two dozen amendments made to the constitution of Khakasiya (in its revised edition of November 21, 2000) are in violation of federal laws.[44] And only under considerable pressure from the presidential representative in the Siberian district and threats that federal subsidies would be cut off, did Tyva finally adopt a new version of its constitution on May 6, 2001. The previous version of the constitution gave the republic the right to secede from Russia and declared that only republican laws would be in effect during crises (see chapter 3). However, there have been so many legal violations in the process of writing the new constitution that its legitimacy is now being challenged in the courts.[45]

In Bashkortostan the new Constitution which was adopted in November 2000 is reported to contain almost as many violations as the old one! And whilst the new version, places limits on the republic's sovereignty, no longer declares its laws above Russian laws, removes claims that the republic is a subject of international law, and introduces procedures for appointing judges and procurators in line with federal norms, it still includes the full text of the Republic's power-sharing treaty.[46] The Bashkortostan authorities have refused to recognise the rulings of the

Russian Constitutional Court and continue to adopt legislation that violates federal laws.[47] In December 2001, 72 per cent of Bashkortostan's laws still violated federal norms, a figure which was actually higher than it was in May 2000 at the beginning of Putin's reforms.[48]

The Tatarstan leadership has also steadfastly refused to renounce the Republic's sovereignty, and a Bilateral Commission set up to examine the Republic's Constitution also agreed to uphold the 1994 bilateral treaty, 'even though it contradicts both the federal and republican constitutions in several places'. Moreover, President Shaimiev has repeatedly called for the Russian Constitution to be brought into line with republican constitutions rather than vice versa. As Graney observes, Tatarstan's strategy of defiance includes, 'a legal defense of the republic's sovereignty . . . appeals to international bodies for help in protecting Tatarstan's sovereignty, political maneuvering aimed at forcing the centre to take a more moderate position on re-centralisation, attempts to co-opt various agents of federal re-centralisation',[49] or simply ignoring federal laws and decrees.

It is also informative to note that the presidential representative in Tatatarstan, General Marsel Galimardanov, is not only an ethnic Tatar, but he is from the same rural district as President Shaimiev, which surely must lead us to question where his real loyalties lie – to his master in the Volga Federal District (Kirienko) or Tatarstan?[50]

Likewise in Sakha there has been strong opposition to Putin's reforms. Thus, for example, on January 16, 2001 the Sakha Republican Legislature rejected a law proposed by the Republican Procurator that would have renounced the Republic's sovereignty. Nineteen of the legislature's thirty-two members voted against it. And in March 2001, the legislators (in the lower house of the republican parliament) refused to make amendments to article 5 of the Republic's Constitution which gives it ownership over its land and natural resources. The Sakha government had signed a 25-year agreement with the Alrosa diamond company on January 11, 2001, and it was in no mood to give up its control over such a lucrative source of income. Diamond production in the republic makes up 77 per cent of the government's revenue.[51] However, the legislators did agree to remove from the Republic's constitution ten of the most egregious violations of federal law, including a provision which allowed the republic to have its own army.[52] However, little progress had been made in amending Sakha's constitution by the summer of 2001. Thus, for example, on May 3, 2001, the Sakha (Yakutiya) Supreme Court declared that about half of the 144 articles in the republican constitution were unconstitutional.[53]

And it is not only in the republics that such infringments of federal legislation have taken place. Thus, Latyshev, the presidential representative to the Urals Federal District, in an examination of 1,544 regional laws found that 306 violated the Russian constitution and federal legislation. The study also revealed that 92 per cent of municipal charters and 48 of the 67 agreements signed between federal agencies and regional executive branch agencies in the federal district also violated federal laws.[54] Within the Urals Federal District, the governor of Sverdlovsk Oblast, Rossel, has been particularly defiant. An analysis of 157 regional laws in his region uncovered federal violations in eighty one. And by January 2001 the regional Duma had only amended 22 of these.[55]. The head of the Constitutional Court, Marat Baglai, who visited Sverdlovsk in January 2001, called for the region to speed up its programme for bringing its legislation into line. Baglai justified his demands by declaring that it 'was impermissible for citizens of Russia to have different rights in different regions'.

In the summer of 2001 Putin, realising that his reforms were being bogged down, announced a new initiative – the setting up of a commission to examine Russia's bilateral treaties. Addressing the first session of the commission, which took place on July 17, 2001, Putin admitted that adding yet another layer of bureaucracy to deal with the governors had been a failure. Regional leaders, he noted, had responded by building 'a Great Wall of China' between themselves and the centre.[56] The commission called for regions to unilaterally rescind their bilateral treaties. However, to date only six regions have withdrawn from the power-sharing agreements (Marii El Republic, and Perm, Nizhnii Novgorod, Ulyanovsk, Omsk and Novosibirsk oblasts).[57] It remains to be seen how many others will follow.

Putin's federal reforms and democracy

There is a paradox at the heart of Putin's reforms – that is, they can be read as both promoting and restricting democracy. Bringing regional legislation into line with the Russian Constitution is absolutely essential for the consolidation of democracy, particularly in those ethnic republics which have deprived their citizens of universal democratic norms and human rights (see chapter 9). Thus for example recent moves to bring Bashkortostan's law enforcement bodies into line has undoubtedly improved the human rights of citizens in the Republic. In May 2001 under pressure from federal authorities Bashkortostan Prosecutor Yavdat Turumtaev admitted that republican law enforcement agencies 'grossly violated criminal procedure law' and that 50 per cent of all arrests and detentions in the republic were illegal. A total of 2,545 individuals have recently filed suits claiming that they were arrested and detained illegally. By reasserting the rule of law and due process, Putin's reforms in Bashkortostan and many other republics are positive steps in creating equal rights for all citizens across the federation. However, Putin's new powers to sack democratically elected governors and to dissolve regional legislatures is a setback for the consolidation of democracy.

Whilst most students of Russian federalism support Putin in his quest to discipline unruly regional bosses, many have argued that the President's radical reform of the federal system may have ended up, throwing the baby out with the bath water. Putin, it is argued, could have simply called for a more vigorous enforcement of existing executive powers.

There are real worries that Putin's quest for law and order will be bought at the expense of civil liberties and the consolidation of democracy. For Boris Berezovskii, Putin's reforms, 'will destroy the system of the balance of power, which is necessary for the normal functioning of any democratic government and market economy, significantly increase the authority of the executive branch of power at the expense of the legislative and limit citizens' participation in the representative management of government'.[58]

Moreover, Putin's reforms also put into doubt his adherence to the principles of federalism as enshrined in the Russian Constitution. In his book, *First Person*, Putin states that, 'from the very beginning, Russia was created as a super centralised state. That's practically laid down in its genetic code, its traditions, and the mentality of its people'.[59] Putin's reorganisation of the Federation Council, his usurpation of unilateral powers to dismiss regional assemblies and chief executives, combined with his creation of the seven federal districts, make a mockery of federalism and democracy. 'What kind of federation is it', asked President Ruslan Aushev of Ingushetiya, 'if the president can remove the popularly elected head of a region or disband the regional legislature'?[60] Moreover, as Chuvash President, Nikolai Fedorov, has pointed out, the people have no way to democratically check the activities of the seven unelected presidential representatives.[61]

As we noted in chapter 1, in federations, regional autonomy is constitutionally guaranteed. The 'noncentralisation' of federations must be distinguished from the 'decentralisation' of unitary states. In other words, in federations there is a vertical separation of powers among federal and regional bodies of power, each of which have constitutionally guaranteed rights and powers. As Smirnyagin notes, in a federation, each tier of government is 'chosen at separate elections by the state's citizens, who give each its own legitimacy and make it independent of the others'.[62] Putin cannot legally centralise policy areas which have been constitutionally assigned to the regions or which come under the joint authority of the regions and the federal government. The federal government cannot simply ignore the rights of the federal subjects without itself violating the Constitution and undermining both federalism and democracy. Moreover, Putin's claim that his reforms are wholly within the ambit of the Constitution is patently absurd. His attempts to justify his reforms by stating that they are reforms of his presidential administration and not of the country, remind us of Yeltsin's cynical manipulation of the Constitution and his penchant for ignoring federal laws whenever it suited him (see chapter 9). Putin would appear to be following in the footsteps of a long line of previous Soviet leaders, who seek to justify the 'means' by reference to the 'ends'.

Finally, Putin faces the same dilemma as that of Gorbachev and Yeltsin before him, how to maintain the unity of the state without abandoning a commitment to democratisation. At present it would appear that Putin is willing to sacrifice democracy in order to win unity. However, his attacks on the sovereignty claims of the republics are surely just as likely to stir-up nationalist sentiments as to quell them. Putin will have to tread carefully if he does not want to lead Russia back to the chaotic days of the 'parade of sovereignties'.

Notes

1 See, Presidential Decree no. 765, July 23, 1992, 'Ob utverzhdenii polozheniya o predstavitele Prezidenta Rossiiskoi Federatsii v krae, oblasti, avtonomnoi oblasti, avtomnon okruge, goradakh Moskve i Sankt-Peterburge', *Vedemostii S'ezda Deputatov Rossiiskoi Federatsii i Verkhovnovo Soveta Rossiiskoi Federatsii*, 29 (July 23, 1992), 2163; Presidential Decree no. 186, February 5, 1993, 'O predstavitele Prezidenta Rossiiskoi Federatsii v krae, oblasti, avtonomnoi oblasti, avtomnon okruge, goradakh Moskve i Sankt-Peterburge'; Presidential Decree of January 17, 1995, 'O vnesenii izmenenii i dopolnenii v Ukaz Prezidenta Rossiiskoi Federtatsii ot 5 Febralya 1993 no. 186, 'O predstavitele Prezidenta Rossiiskoi Federatsii v krae, oblasti, avtonomnoi oblasti, avtomnon okruge, goradakh Moskve i Sankt-Peterburge'; Presidential Decree no. 696, July 9, 1997, 'O polnomochnom predstavitele Prezidenta Rossiiskoi Federtatsii v regione Rossiiskoi Federatsii', *Sobranie Zakonodatel'stva Rossiiskoi Federatsii*, 28 (1997), 3421. See also the accompanying statute to the 1992 Decree, 'O predstavitele Prezidenta Rossiiskoi Federatsii v krae, oblasti, avtonomnoi oblasti, avtomnon okruge, goradakh Moskve i Sankt-Peterburge', *Rossiiskaya gazeta* (July 24, 1992).
2 P. Kirkow, *Russia's Provinces: Authoritarian Transformation versus Local Autonomy?* (Basingstoke: Macmillan, 1998), p. 123.
3 M. Hyde, 'Putin's federal reforms and their implications for presidential power in Russia', *Europe-Asia Studies*, 53:5 (2001), 722. See also, W. A. Clark, 'Presidential prefects in the Russian provinces: Yeltsin's regional cadres policy', in Graeme Gill (ed.), *Elites and Leadership in Russian Politics* (New York: St Martin's Press, 1998), and I. Busygina, 'The President's representatives: problems of establishing and developing an institution', *Russian Politics and Law*, 35:1 (1997).
4 J. Helmer, 'Russia: regions pressure Kremlin into policy shift – an analysis', *Radio Free Europe/Radio Liberty, Daily Report* (November 4, 1997), 2.
5 V. V. Putin, 'Television address by the Russian President to the Country's citizens', *Rossiiskaya gazeta* (May 19, 2000), p. 3. Translated in *CDPSP*, 52:20 (2000), 5.
6 *Ibid.*

7 M. Evangelista, 'Russia's path to a new regional policy', Davis Centre for Russian Studies, Harvard University, *PONARS Policy Paper*, 157 (2000), p. 3.

8 Thus for example, Vladimir Gustov was appointed First Deputy Prime Minister in charge of regional issues. Primakov also established a new Ministry of Regional Policy headed by Viktor Kirpichnikov, the leader of the Union of Russian Cities.

9 N. Petrov, 'Russia's regions or regions' Russia?', *Carnegie Briefing Papers*, 3 (March 1999), 4.

10 See, Presidential Decree, no. 849, May 13, 2000, 'O Polnomochnom Predstavitele Prezidenta Rossiiskoi Federatsii v Federal'nom Okruge', and the accompanying Resolution, 'O Polnomochnom Prestavitele Prezidenta Rossiiskoi Federatsii v Federal'nom Okruge'. Published in *Rossiskaya gazeta* (13 May, 2001).

11 J. A. Corwin, *RFE/RL Russian Federation Report*, 2:9 (March 7, 2001), 5.

12 O. Oracheva, 'Democracy and federalism in post-communist Russia (relations between Moscow and the regions in the Russian Federation)', paper presented at the conference, 'The Fall of Communism in Europe: Ten Years On', May 14–17, 2001, The Hebrew University of Jerusalem, p. 11.

13 'Presidential administration's Samoilov on seven representatives', *EWI Russian Regional Report*, 5:30 (August 2, 2000), 4–6.

14 See, E. Teague, 'Putin reforms the federal system', and R. Sakwa, 'Federalism, sovereignty and democracy', in C. Ross (ed.), *Regional Politics in Russia* (Manchester: Manchester University Press, 2002), M. Hyde, 'Putin's federal reforms and their implications for presidential power in Russia', *Europe–Asia Studies*, 53:5 (2001), 719–43. The duties of the 'polpredy' were further outlined in Putin's Presidential Decree of January 30, 2001, no. 97, 'O Vnesenii dopolneniya I izmeneniya v polozhenie o polnomochnom predstavitele Prezidenta Rossiiskoi Federatsii v federal'nom okruge, utverzhdennoe ukazom Prezidenta Rossiiskoi Federatsii ot 13 Maya 2000 No 849'. Published in *Rossiskaya gazeta* (30 January 2001). According to this decree the presidential envoys were directly subordinate to the head of the Presidential Administration.

15 Speech by V.V. Putin at the Presentation of the Annual Message from the President of the Russian Federation to the Federal Assembly of the Russian Federation, *Rossiiskaya gazeta* (July 11, 2000), pp. 1, 3. Translated in *CDPSP*, 52(28) (2000), p. 7.

16 Interview with S. Kirienko, *Nezavisimaya gazeta* (October 25, 2000), p. 3.

17 D. V. Badovskii – 'Systema federal'nykh okrygov i institut polnomochnykh predstavitelei prezidenta RF: sovremennoe sostoyanie i problemy razvitiya', in *Polpredy Prezidenta: Problemy Stanovleniya Novovo Instituta* (MGU, Nauchnye Doklady, no. 3, January 2001), p. 5.

18 A. Slabov, 'Georgy Poltavchenko raises his voice', *Kommersant* (February 10, 2001), 2. *CDPSP*, 53:6 (March 7, 2001).

19 It is also interesting to note that the political movement 'Otechestvo' has begun to restructure its party-territorial structures in conformity with the new federal districts.

20 I. Gordeyev, *Vremya Novostei* (January 12, 2001), 1.

21 Badovskii, 'Sistema federali'nykh okrugov', p. 6.

22 R. Orttung and P. Reddaway, 'Russian state-building: the regional dimension', in *The Russia Initiative: Reports of the Four Task Forces* (New York: Carnegie Corporation, 2001), p. 100.

23 See, the Federal Law, no. 113–F3, August 5, 2000, 'O Poryadke Formorovaniya Soveta Federatsiya Federal'novo Sobraniya Rossiiskoi Federatsii'. Adopted by the state Duma July 19, 2000 and ratified by the Federation Council July 26, 2000, *Rossiskaya gazeta* (August 5, 2000).

24 A. Kostyukov, Obshchaya gazeta, 30 (July 27–August 2, 2000), pp. 1–7. Translated in the *CDPSP*, 52:30 (2000), 5.

25 The Governor of Kaluga, Vyacheslav Parinov appointed his predecessor Valerii Sudarenko; Chukotka Governor Roman Abramovich appointed his predecessor Aleksandr Nazarov. In Altai krai, Governor Aleksandr Surikov named Vladimir Germanenko, a deputy governor in the krai; Andrei Chirkin, the First Deputy Governor of Khabarovsk Krai, will represent the krai administration. And Viktor Stepanov, former head of Kareliya was selected to represent that Republic's presidential administration. J. A. Corwin, *RFE/RL Federation Report* (December 16, 2001) as cited in *Kommersant-Daily* (December 15, 2001).

26 The legislature in Buryatia selected Vladimir Bavlov, Deputy Chair of Buryatia's Committee on Natural Resources; legislators in Amur Oblast selected Galina Buslova, General Director of the Aviation Agency 'Aviatrast'; Deputies in Khabarovsk Krai's Legislature confirmed the selection of the former chair of the krai legislature, Viktor Ozerov as their representative. J. A. Corwin, *RFE/RL Russian Federation Report* (December 16, 2001), 2.

27 The head of 'Transaero', Aleksandr Pleshakov was nominated by the Governor of Penza oblast; Sergei Bekov, Vice President of the Russian Union of Industrialists and Entrepreneurs (Ingushetiya); Leonid Binder, a Norislk Nickel Executive (Taimyr AO); Ilya Lomakin-Rumyantsev, a former Federal Finance Ministry official (Marii-El). Oleg Deripasta, the Head of 'Siberian Aluminium' (Nizhnii Novgorod). J. A. Corwin, *RFE/RL Russian Federation Report*, 3:12 (April 4, 2001), 2.

28 'Ukaz Prezidenta Rossiiskoi Federatsii', no. 602, September 1, 2000, published in *Rossiiskaya Gazeta* (September 1, 2000).

29 I. Busygina 'Federalism and the administrative reforms of President Putin in the context of the democratic transition in Russia', unpublished have presented at the winter 2000 SRC symposium, p. 8.

30 Putin here would appear to be borrowing ideas from Russia's past. The State Council was the supreme consultative body in the Russian Empire from 1810 to 1917. And a State Council also functioned in the Soviet Union for just a few months after the failed August 1991 Coup.

31 The law on the removal of the governors and disbanding of legislatures takes the form of amendments to the Federal Law 'Ob Obshchikh Printsipakh Organizatsii Zakonodatel'nykh (Predstavitel'nykh) i Ispolnitel'nykh Organov Gosudarstvennoi Vlasti Sub'ektov Rossiiskoi Federatstii', which was ratified by the President on October 6, 1999. Published in *Rossiskaya gazeta* (October 19, 1999).

32 'Annual message of the President to the Russian Federal Assembly', *Rossiiskaya gazeta* (July 11, 2000), 3. Translated in *CDPSP* 52:28 (2000), 7.

33 J. A. Corwin, 'Vulnerability of governors to dismissal questioned', *RFE/RL Russian Federation Report*, 2:21 (June 7, 2000).

34 Orttung and Reddaway, 'Russian state building', p. 98.

35 Putin, 'Television address', 5.

36 A. Kostyukov, *Obshchaya gazeta*, 5 (February 1–7, 2001), p. 1. This amends a

previous law adopted in October 1999 which limited governors to two terms. The amendment counts the first term for a governor as the one starting after October 16, 1999.

37 M. I. Vil'chek, 'O klyuchevikh problemakh stanovleniya instituta pol-nomochnykh predstavitelei Prezidenta RF', in *Polpredy Prezidenta*, p. 20.

38 Resolutions of the Constitutional Court of June 7, and June 27, 2000 repudi-ated the sovereignty of the republics as not in line with the Federal Constitu-tion. See, M. V. Baglai, *Konstitutsionnoe Pravo Rossiiskoi Federatsii* (Moscow: Norma, 2001), pp. 305, 338–9. This same resolution also noted that it was against the Constitution for regional organs of power to appoint officials of federal bureaucracies in the regions.

39 K. E. Graney, 'Ten years of sovereignty in Tatarstan: end of the beginning or beginning of the end?', *Problems of Post-communism* (September/October 2001), 37.

40 J. A. Corwin, *RFE/RL Russian Federation Report*, 3:2 (January 10, 2001) as cited in *Obshchaya gazeta*, 52 (January 10, 2001).

41 Interfax (January 11, 2001).

42 J. Corwin, *RFE/RL Russian Federation Report*, 3:13 (April 11, 2001), 1.

43 R. Orttung, *EWI Russian Regional Report*, 6:18 (May 16, 2001), 2.

44 M. Shandarov, *EWI Russian Regional Report*, 6:5 (February 7, 2001), 5.

45 *Kommersant Daily* (May 8, 2001).

46 I. Rabinovich, 'Bashkortostani legal situation is worse than before campaign to bring laws into line', *EWI, Russian Regional Report*, 6:44 (December 12, 2001), 10.

47 *Ibid.*, 11.

48 *Ibid.*, 10.

49 Graney, 'Ten years of sovereignty', 37–8.

50 *Ibid.*, 38.

51 O. Yemelyanov, *EWI Russian Regional Report* 6:3 (January 24, 2001), 3.

52 *EWI Russian Regional Report*, 6:10 (March 14, 2001), 6.

53 R. Orttung, *EWI Russian Reional Report*, 6:18 (May 16, 2001), 4.

54 S. Pushkarev, *EWI Russian Regional Report*, 6:9 (March, 7, 2001), 4–5.

55 *EWI Russian Regional Report*, 5:47 (December 20, 2000), 5.

56 J. A. Corwin, *RFE/RL Russian Federation Report*, 3:21 (July 18, 2001), 2.

57 *Ibid.*, 3.

58 B. Berezovskii, 'Open letter to President Putin', *Transitions* (June 5, 2000), p. 1.

59 V. Putin, *First Person: An Astonishingly Frank Self-Portrait by Russia's President Vladimir Putin*, with N. Gevorkyan, N. Timakova and A. Kolesnikov; translated by C. A. Fitzpatrick (London: Hutchinson, 2000), pp. 182–3. Cited in R. Sakwa, 'federalism, sovereignty and democracy', in C. Ross (ed.), *Regional Politics in Russia* (Manchester: Manchester University Press, 2002), p. 18.

60 Graney, 'Ten years of sovereignty', 37.

61 N. Fedorov, *Nezavisimaya gazeta* (October 25, 2000), 2.

62 L. V. Smirnyagin, 'Federalizm po Putiny ili Putin po federalizmu (zheleznoi pyatoi)', *Carnegie Briefing Papers*, 3:3 (March 2001), 3.

From constitutional to political asymmetry: crafting authoritarian regimes in Russia's regions and republics

Russia's constitutional asymmetry has prevented the development of universal norms of citizenship and human rights in the federation. As long as republic and regional leaders pledged support for Yeltsin and 'brought home the bacon', in the way of ethnic stability, tax revenues and electoral support, federal authorities have been quite happy to turn a blind eye to the flagrant violations of the Russian Constitution by regional elites. Russia's 'federation' without 'federalism' has simply allowed the authoritarianism of the centre to be replaced by local level authoritarianism.

As we discussed in chapter 3 regional and republican elites have been able to adopt constitutions/charters and other laws which violate the federal constitution. And a number of the bilateral treaties signed between Moscow and the regions have sanctioned the transfer of unconstitutional rights and powers to the republics.[1] Thus, authoritarian leaders have been able to use the federal system as a protective shield in their quest to consolidate their various brands of authoritarianism. Moreover, the greater the degree of autonomy given to a federal subject in Russia the greater the degree of authoritarianism we find.

Below we discuss the various ways in which presidents and governors have been able to gain a dominant control over their political systems. In particular, we examine the way in which leaders of the ethnic republics have been able to maintain power by manipulating the electoral system.

Sartori has described the electoral system as the most specific manipulative instrument of politics.[2] As we discussed in chapter 1, free and fair elections are a major prerequisite for democracy. Moreover, Huntington's 'two-turnover test' for a consolidated democracy is centred on elections.[3] Certainly, democracy 'may entail more than a fair election' but as Blais and Dion note, 'without an election no democracy'.[4] And as Pammett stresses, only after elections 'allow power to be peacefully handed over to the opposition' can it be argued that, 'the initial phase of democratic construction is in some sense completed'.[5] According to Blais and Dion in a democracy:

1) All citizens must have the right to vote, with no exclusion based on sex, race, opinion or religion, 2) voting must be secret so as to minimize potential intimidation, 3) the election must be regular: it must be held at steady intervals, as prescribed by law, 4) the whole process must be fair, devoid of violence or fraud and, 5) finally, the election must be competitive, that is to say, all positions can be contested, all groups or parties may run candidates and are free to express their points of view.[6]

For O'Donnell elections can be considered institutionalised only when

1) Leaders and voters take for granted that in the future inclusive, fair, and competitive elections will take place as legally scheduled, 2) voters will be properly registered and free from physical coercion, 3) their votes will be counted fairly, 4) winners will take office, and will not have their terms arbitrarily terminated.

And he notes that countries 'where elections do not have these characteristics do not qualify as polyarchies'.[7]

As we shall document below, many of Russia's republics and regions patently fail to even meet Dahl's minimum conditions for polyarchy never mind the more stringent prerequisites for consolidated democracy as discussed in chapter 1. The fact that most deputies work part-time, that many work for the executive branch of government, and that parties are non-existent or very weak have all conspired to give regional executives a free reign to govern their regions as they see fit. In most regions there is no effective democratic opposition to challenge the authority of the executive branch.

In Russia, presidents and governors, as we discussed in chapter 8, have captured control over the nomination and appointment of heads of federal bureaucracies situated in their territories (including members of regional courts, law enforcement and security bodies etc.). And they have also been able to draw on the considerable financial resources of their administrations (local government printing presses, administrative staff, transport and hotels) to support their electoral campaigns. In addition, the press in most regions is firmly under the control of the executive.[8]

One of the most important powers of regional executives has been their control over the appointment of the chairs of local electoral commissions. Thus, for example, in Sverdlovsk, the governor (Rossel) was able to remove the chair of the regional electoral commission from power in 1995, and the President of Buryatiya (Potapov) saw to the removal of the chair of the republic's electoral commission in 1998. In Krasnodar the governor solved the problem by simply appointing himself chair of the krai electoral commission. And according to the central electoral commmission there were serious infringements of federal legislation with regard to the appointment of members of electoral commissions in eleven regions in the most recent assembly and gubernatorial elections which were conducted over the period 1998–2000.[9]

According to article 111 of Tatarstan's Constitution, the President has the right to nominate candidates for half the members of the republic central electoral commission and half the members of the Constitutional Court. The other half of both bodies are chosen by members of the Parliament. Thus, by packing the Parliament with his administrative subordinates (see chapter 8) the Tatarstan President can maintain control over the courts and the electoral process in the republic, which in turn guarantees the president's complete domination of the legislature. For Farukshin, 'therein, lies the roots of servile obedience, hypocrisy and flattery that the appointed officials abundantly exhibit for the person of President Shaimiev and for the Kazan Kremlin's policies'.[10]

Language, residency and age

Although federal legislation states that citizens of the Russian Federation may be elected regardless of their 'sex, race, nationality, language, origin, property and official status, place of residence, religion, beliefs, affiliation of public associations, and other factors',[11] as we discussed in chapter 4, ten republics require that presidential candidates posses knowledge of both Russian and the titular language.

Thus, for example, Valentin Lednev was prevented from standing in the 1997 Adygeyan Presidential election because he did not speak the Adegeyan language, even although Adygeyans make up only 20 per cent of the republic's population. Other republics have placed unconstitutional residency and age requirements on candidates.[12] Thus, for example, according to local electoral legislation, candidates standing for presidential elections in Sakha must have resided in the republic for fifteen years. In Adygeya, Bashkortostan, Buryatiya, Kabardino-Balkariya and Komi ten years; Kareliya and Khakasiya seven years. And in more than fifty regions of the Russian Federation local electoral laws place similar residency restrictions on candidates for regional assemblies. These laws have been used by incumbent presidents and governors to prevent opposition candidates from participating in elections. Local electoral laws also stipulate minimum and maximum age requirements for electoral candidates which infringe federal legislation.[13]

Nomination signatures

Chief executives have also manipulated the rules for collecting nomination signatures to squeeze out opposition candidates from the elections. According to the 1997 Federal Law on elections, 'The maximum number of signatures required for a candidate to be registered must not exceed two percent of the total number of voters' in the electoral district where the candidate is standing' (article 31.1).[14] However, in the republics of

Buryatiya, Sakha, Tyva; Stavropol' Krai, Orenburg and Tomsk Oblasts, electoral rules call for nomination signatures from 3 per cent; in Kurgan, Saratov, Chelyabinsk, 5 per cent, and in Dagestan and Kalmykiya, 10 per cent. The system of collecting signatures is often corrupt, with candidates paying for signatures with money, vodka or even other household goods such as sugar. As Fillipov notes, in rural districts it would quite literally be impossible to gather such a large number of signatures without the active support of the regional authorities.[15] In the 1997 law on elections a much stricter regime for regulating the collection of signatures and for checking their accuracy was introduced. Nonetheless, in elections under the new rules in Rostov oblast which took place in 1998, 38 of the 238 candidates (19 per cent) were still refused nomination, and in Kalmykiya 11 of 13 opposition candidates were refused registration for elections in that Republic.[16] In regional elections (for governors and assemblies) conducted in 2000, 22 regions violated federal legislation with regard to the collection of signatures.[17]

In Bashkortostan and Mordoviya the incumbent presidents (Rakhimov and Merkushkin, respectively) used identical ploys to stop popular opponents from standing against them in presidential elections. Special clauses were added to the local election rules which declared that candidates would be barred from the elections if more than 3 per cent of their nomination signatures were invalid. By this method, all but one 'bogus opposition candidate', was expelled from the presidential elections in both republics. In Bashkortostan the bogus candidate was a minor member of President Rakhimov's own cabinet, and in Mordoviya, the director of a factory. In Bashkortostan, a Russian Supreme Court order demanded that two of the expelled candidates be reinstated, but this decree was simply ignored by the Bashkortostan Republican Court which is under the control of the President. As Lussier notes: 'the electorate had little knowledge of these events since the local media offered a one sided support for Rakhimov, the independent newspaper and radio stations had been shut down, and the station director arrested'.[18]

Both Presidents easily won re-election, Rakhimov gaining 70 per cent and Merkushkin 96.6 per cent of the votes cast.[19] In Bashkortostan the protest vote against all candidates was 17 per cent, the highest ever in an election at this level.[20] In Ufa, the capital and a region of high sympathy for one of the expelled candidates, only 53.4 per cent of the voters participated in the election, and over one-third (34.6 per cent) voted against both the candidates.[21] The former Governor of Primorskii Krai, Nazdratenko, has also engaged in similar actions in elections which Yeltsin finally cancelled in October 1994. Nazdratenko also engaged in outright intimidation of rival candidates in the gubernatorial election of December 1999. The former mayor of Vladivostok, Cherepkov, withdrew from the race in November. His bank accounts had been seized by the krai administration.

Another rival for the governorship, Svetlana Orlova, was 'removed forty-eight hours before the election by the Krai Duma' leaving only one serious candidate. Nazdratenko, not surprisingly won the election, picking up 65 per cent of the vote.[22]

Single candidate uncontested elections

It is against federal laws to hold uncontested elections for the post of chief executive, but even so the republics of Tatarstan, Kalmykiya and Kabardino-Balkariya continue to flout this law. In Tatarstan where the republican constitution (article 77) states that 'any number of candidates can be listed on the electoral ballot', President Shaimiev simply interpreted this to mean that only one candidate may be nominated. Shamiev was subsequently elected President in uncontested elections in 1991 and 1996. Similarly, in the 1995 campaign for the Tatarstan legislature, twenty-one heads of local governments, who were the direct appointees of Shaimiev, were allowed to run unopposed.[23] In Tatarstan's presidential elections voters who supported Shaimiev simply had to place their ballots in the ballot box; however, if they wanted to vote against him they had to take the ballot paper, in the full view of members of the electoral commission, to a cabinet where they crossed out his name and then return to place this in the ballot box. This is exactly the way elections were conducted during the Soviet period.

Kalmykiya's law on elections permits presidential candidates to stand in single candidate races and to gain office with as little as 15 per cent of the vote, from a turnout of just 25 per cent of registered voters. Kalmykiya President Ilyumzhimov reportedly rejected suggestions from members of the parliament (Khural) that he should be elected for life, saying that 'for the time being, we must outwardly observe democratic procedures'.[24]

Manipulation of the date of elections

Presidents and governors have also not been averse to changing the date of elections to their own advantage. Thus, for example elections were called before their due date in Ingushetiya in 1994, Kalmykiya in 1995, Tatarstan in 1996, Orel in 1997, and Bashkortostan in 1998.[25] In a rather extreme case, in 1995 the President of Kalmykiya, Ilyumzhinov, called for new presidential elections to be held three years ahead of schedule where he stood as the only candidate, winning 85.1 per cent of the vote.[26]

In February 1999, Belgorod Govenor Yevgenii Savchenko managed to persuade the regional legislature to change the timing of the election from December 1999 to May 1999. And as Danielle Lussier notes, Savchenko's success in both moving up the date and winning his election inspired other regional leaders to follow suit. Soon after, Omsk Governor, Leonid Polezhaev, Novgorod Governor Mikhail Prusak, and Tomsk Governor Viktor Kress all managed to move their elections to September and secure landslide victories. Moscow Mayor Luzhkov opted to have the election for his post changed from June 2000 to December 1999 to coincide with the State Duma elections. As expected Luzhkov easily won another term, earning 71.5 per cent of the vote.[27] We should not forget, of course, that Yeltsin cynically brought forward the Russian presidential elections from July to March 2000 in order to ensure Putin's victory.[28]

Manipulating rules on election turnout

There are also wide variations in regional electoral laws over the minimum turnout required for elections to regional assemblies and executives to be valid. According to federal legislation a 25 per cent minimum turnout is the norm for legislative assemblies, but in some regions it is as high as 50 per cent (for example, republics of Altai, Kabardino-Balkariya, North Osetiya-Alaniya and Khakasiya) and in others as low as 15 per cent (Kalmykiya). In total contravention of federal law, no minimum turnout is stipulated for elections to regional assemblies in Stavropol' and Khabarovsk Krais; Belgorod, Volgograd, Kirov, Leningrad, Novgorod and Chita Oblasts.[29] In a similar manner minimum turnout requirements also vary considerably for gubernatorial elections. Thus, in fifty-six regions it was stipulated as 25 per cent; in two regions 33 per cent; four regions 35 per cent; and nineteen regions 50 per cent. In five regions no norm was noted.

Turnout for the 2000–1 round of gubernatorial elections averaged 51.8 per cent with the lowest registered in Vladimir oblast (34 per cent) and the highest in Nenetsk AO (73.8 per cent). However, unusually high turnouts may not represent a high level of democracy but quite the opposite. High turnounts may indicate that political pressure was put on citizens to participate in the elections much as happened during the Soviet period (see discussion on 'guided elections' below).

Turnout is generally lower for elections to regional assemblies than for gubernatorial elections. In some cases where turnout has been very low the legitimacy of the assemby has been weakened and in extreme cases it has made it impossible for the legislature to gain the necessary quorum to function. Thus for example, In Kaluga in the election of August 25, 1996 turnout was less than the minimum requirement in nineteen electoral districts out of forty. In Ryazan oblast in the election of March 30, 1997 in ten of thirty-six electoral districts turnout was also below the 25 per cent minimum. This was a marked improvement over 1994 when because of political apathy at the elections the assembly did not have the necessary two-thirds complement of deputies for a quorum, and it required a special edict from the President to function. The Chuvash elections which first took place in March 1994 were followed by seven further rounds of elections over the course of the following two years, as the regional assembly desperately sought to raise its electoral turnout.[30] In Khakasiya in the election of December 1, 1996, twenty electoral districts out of seventy-five had turnouts of less than the required 50 per cent and a hurried executive order to lower the minimum turnout requirement to 25 per cent was quickly adopted in the midst of the electoral campaign! In July 2001 legislators in Primorskii Krai made an even more drastic amendement to their law on elections by abolishing the requirement for a minimum turnout altogether. In perhaps the most infamous case of all, it took until May 2001 before the citizens of Vladivostok were finally able to elect a city Duma. There had been no representative body in the city since Yeltsin disbanded the soviets in 1993. The previous twenty attempts had all failed due to low turnout.[31]

Gerrymandering

A number of regional executives have also sought to redraw the boundaries of their electoral districts to favour their candidacies. Federal law states that variations in the size of electoral districts must not vary by more than 10 per cent. But a number of regions have simply ignored this law when drawing up their electoral registers. In the regional elections of 1995–97, of the 3,154 electoral districts, 350 had variations in size of more than 10 per cent and 124 more than 15 per cent. In Novgorod oblast the difference between the largest and the smallest electoral district varied by a magnitude of 5.6 times, in Tula a magnitude of 6.8. In the 1999 elections for the State Council in Tatarstan some districts were 100 times larger than others. The Russian Supreme Court declared these district boundaries illegal, and opposition groups called for the legislature to be disbanded.[32] In Rostov oblast almost one-quarter of the rural districts are flat plains which many railways and roads traverse, and the population in these rural districts are predominantly communist in political orientation. In drawing up the boundaries of the electoral districts the anti-communist governor was able to dilute the communist vote by artificially joining some of the rural districts with the more 'reformist oriented' urban districts. The new electoral districts now include combined rural and urban districts which do not even have borders with one another.

Changing the rules on tenure of office

Once in office, regional leaders have also used their considerable autonomy to manipulate local election rules in order to hold on to power.

Thus, for example, on November 27, 1996 the Tatarstan parliament made changes to article 108 of the Republic's Constitution, which stipulated that a person may be elected Republic President for only two five-year terms in a row. The parliament also removed the age limit for presidents which had been set at 65 years. This allowed President Shaimiev to run for a third term in March 2001 which he won easily with 80 per cent of the vote (this time the election was competitive, with four other contenders).

More recently new legislation promoted by President Putin has sanctioned the further infringements of such tenure rules. Thus, on January 25, 2001 the State Duma (with Putin's express wish) approved a law that allowed sixty-nine regional leaders to stand for a third term and a further seventeen to seek a fourth term in office. According to this new legislation a governor's term is now considered to start after October 1999. The new rules will permit President Shaimiev of Tatarstan to run for a fourth term. Also eligible for a fourth term will be the leaders of the republics of Kalmykiya, Ingushetiya, Adygeya, Tyva, Kabardino-Balkariya, Buryatiya, Bashkortostan, Sakha, Komi and Chuvashiya, as well as the governors of Tomsk, Omsk, Novgorod, Sverdlovsk, Belgorod and Orel oblasts.[33] The law was a concession to regional leaders for their loss of membership in the Federation Council (see chapter 8).

Electoral fraud

If all else fails, republican elites have not been loath to resort to outright fraud and the falsification of election returns. As Lowenhardt notes, during the 1996 presidential elections in Tatarstan the republican leadership illegally transferred somewhere between 35–45,000 votes from Zyuganov, Lebed, Yavlinskii and Zhirinovsky to Yeltsin.[34] According to Lowenhardt the following foolproof methods of falsifying election results were common practice in the Republic:

1) Widespread tampering with voters' registers: voters' registers contain considerable numbers of 'dead souls' (deceased or non-existent people); others vote in their name;
2) Pressure of local officials on voters to vote for the establishment candidate;
3) Fictive voting (particularly in the countryside);
4) 'mistakes' made by polling station members during counting, in favour of one particular candidate;
5) Intimidation of local election observers;
6) Replacement of ballots during or after counting in favour of a particular candidate;
7) Outright falsification of counting protocols in cases where all other methods have failed.[35]

Guided elections

Governing elites are also not averse to using coercion and/or persuasion to mobilise their citizens to come out and vote for their choice of leaders. The votes of the electorate in these 'guided' elections always coincide with the interests of the local elites.[36] A first clue to the phenomenon of guided elections is where the electorate always cast their votes for the dominant political force in Moscow, the 'party of power'. Thus, for example in the 1991 Russian presidential elections the majority of citizens in Dagestan, Kabardino-Balkaraya, Karachaevo-Cherekessiya, Tatarstan, North Osetiya, Ingushetiya, Bashkortostan, Kalmykiya, Sakha, and Tyva, rejected Yeltsin who, at that time, was the representative of the democratic opposition, and they cast their votes in favour of Nikolai Ryzhkov, a leading member of the CPSU. But in 1996 citizens in these republics were called upon by the governing elites to support Yeltsin as he now represented the 'party of power' and they duly voted according to the wishes of the regional elites.

Another indication that we might be witnessing a guided election is the presence of a high election turnout figures, far above the national average. Thus, for example, in the 1996 Russian presidential elections turnout was over 90 per cent in 60 electoral districts: 25 of these districts were in Bashkortostan and 24 in Tatarstan. Such figures smack of a throwback to the Soviet period where mobilization of the electorate was common practice.

A major study of voting patterns in the lowest level of electoral commissions, the Territorial Election Commission (TIK) in the 2000 presidential elections showed that there were just 121 out of 2,748 commissions where turnout was above 90 per cent. And once again the majority of these were in the republics of Bashkortostan (31 out of 70) and Tatarstan (35 out of 62). In Ingushetiya all 6 of its TIKs had high turnouts; Kabardino-Balkariya (8 of 11) and Mordoviya (7 of 27).[37]

According to official election figures, in the Kaibitsk district of Tatarstan, of the 11,676 voters on the electoral register only 20 did not participate in the elections! In Dzheirakhskoi electoral district there was supposedly a 100 per cent turnout!, which was higher than that reported for election turnout in Soviet times.[38] According to Mikhailov such high turnouts are the result of mobilisation campaigns directed from above, and in some instances the outright falsification of data by electoral commissions under the guidance of regional elites.

According to Kozlov and Oreshkin further evidence for the existence of such 'guided' elections can be seen in election data for those regions which radically changed their political orientation between rounds of presidential elections or across time between different elections. Thus, for example, major changes took place in voting patters in Bashkortostan,

Tatarstan and Dagestan between the two rounds of the 1996 Russian Presidential elections.[39] In forty-one rural electoral districts in Tatarstan (all but two) the share of the vote for Zyuganov dropped sharply. In thirty-four districts by more than 15 per cent, and in several others 30–50 per cent. Thus, for example in Zaynisk district in the first round Zyuganov polled 68 per cent of the votes and in the second round only 18 per cent (Yeltsin polled 76 per cent).[40] Such variations in voting can only be explained with reference to the work of the local elites and their ability to mobilise the population behind their choice of candidates.

A third source of evidence for guided elections is related to the level of support given by citizens to candidates in republican presidential elections. Where a candidate receives a very high percentage of the vote, much higher than the average, this is likely to suggest that the electorate has been subjected to some form of extra-legal coercion or 'persuasion'. This applies even to uncontested elections (e.g., in Tatarstan, Kalmykiya and Bashkortostan). Thus for example (in elections conducted over the period 1995–98), the President of Kabardino-Balkariya Republic, Valerii Kokov received 99.35 per cent. In Tatarstan Mintimer Shaimiev received 97.14 of the vote. Over 80 per cent was received by Moscow Mayor Yurii Luzhkov (88.49 per cent), the President of the Republic of Kalmykiya, Kirsan Ilyumzhinov (85.09 per cent), head of the administration of Krasnodar Krai, Nikolai Kondarenko (82 per cent), the governor of Vologda Oblast, Pozgalev (80.69 per cent), and the governor of Saratov Oblast, Ayatskov (80.19 per cent).

Finally, we can learn a great deal by studying the number of wasted ballot papers. Thus, Mikhailov in his study of the March 2000 presidential elections found unusually high percentages of wasted ballots in a number of TIKs. Thus, for instance, in Mamadyshskii TIK (Tatarstan) 11.19 per cent of all ballots were deemed wasted; in Chernozemel'skii TIK (Kalmykiya), 8.26 per cent, Shemyrshinskii TIK (Chuvashiya), 6.87 per cent, El'nikovskii TIK (Mordoviya), 5.01 per cent, Relyubskii TIK (Saratov), 4.05 per cent, Bokovskii TIK (Rostov), 3.98 per cent, Maiskii TIK (Kabardino-Balkariya), 3.35 per cent, Chaa-Khol'skii TIK (Tyva), 3.27 per cent.[41] Moreover, further study of these TIKs showed that turnout was not particularly high. So another explanation is needed to explain why there were so many wasted ballots in these particular districts. As Mikhailov notes, the most likely explanation is that there was a deliberate process of falsification in favour of the candidates supported by the regional elites.

Taking into consideration factors such as extraordinary high turnout levels, higher than average numbers of wasted ballots and extraordinary levels of support for one candidate, Mikhailov argues that the most serious infringement of electoral laws and the highest levels of falsification took place in the following regions: Bashkortostan, Dagestan, Tatarstan, Saratov Oblast, Mordoviya, and Kabardino-Balkariya.[42] And the overall picture confirms that it is in the ethnic republics where such infringements are most common. Thus, in a study of elections for regional heads of administration (1995–97) the following twelve federal subjects (all ethnic republics) were found to be the least democratic: Dagestan, Kabardino-Balkariya, Karachaevo-Cherkessiya, Tatarstan, Bashkortostan, North Osetiya-Alaniya, Ingushetiya, Kalmykiya, Sakha, Mordoviya, Adygeya and Altai.[43]

Furthermore, Stepan's study of over a hundred gubernatorial and presidential elections conducted over the period June 1991–99, shows the dominant power of incumbents, and particularly incumbent presidents. As can be seen from table 9.1, the higher the status of the federal subject the less competitive the elections. Thus, for example, 'in 7 of the 34 republican elections (20.5 per cent) only one name appeared on the ballot' whereas 'in none of the 72 elections in the other two hierarchical categories did this occur'. Moreover, 'the highest percentage of victories, by

Table 9.1 Comparative prima facie evidence of electoral competitiveness and non-competitiveness in elections for the chief executive in the eighty-nine subjects of the Russian Federation, all elections held between June 1991 and May 1999 (%)

	Elections in titular republics (N = 34)	*Elections in titular autonomous units (N = 11)*	*Elections in non-titular oblasts, krais and federal cities (N = 68)*	*All elections (N = 106)*
Prima facie evidence of competitiveness: incumbents contested and were defeated	23.7	40	50.8	2.5
Prima facie evidence of non-competitiveness: only one candidate on the ballot	20.5	0	0	6.2
Victory by incumbent by more than 85% of valid vote	20.5	0	4.1	8.5

Source: A. Stepan, 'Federalism and democracy: beyond the U.S. model', *Journal of Democracy*, 10:4 (October 4, 1999), 153.

more than 85 per cent, [were] also found overwhelmingly in the republics'.[44]

The development of authoritarianism in the regions

As O'Donnell notes, in democracies accountability runs not only vertically, making elected officials answerable to the ballot box, but also horizontally, across a network of relatively autonomous powers that can call into question, and eventually punish, improper ways of discharging the responsibilities of a given official.[45]

The inability or the unwillingness of the Russian Constitutional Court, the central electoral commission and other federal law enforcement agencies, to step in and declare such elections null and void, has fundamentally undermined the Constitution and set back the development of a legal culture in Russia. The politicisation of the judiciary, electoral commissions and the courts, is a particularly worrying development. The law of 30 September 1997, 'On the Basic Gurantees of Electors to Participate in Elections and Referendums' which reiterated the dominance of federal electoral laws over regional ones, has so far failed to bring uniformity to electoral rules and practices. As Dmitri Oreshkin noted with regard to the latest round of gubernatorial elections conducted over the period 2000–01, 'elections in Russia have not become an institution for the electors to control the governors, [rather] it is the governors who control the electors'.[46] The unwritten message from the Yeltsin and Putin administrations to the Russian Central Electoral Commission, has been, to turn a blind eye if those infringing electoral laws are their supporters.

Politics in Russia's regions is epitomised by the domination of informal over formal rules. The 'politics of uncertainty'[47] still dominates the political landscape of most regions. Regional elites are not fully committed to the democratic 'rules of the game', and in many of the ethnic republics, in particular, they have 'crafted' authoritarian regimes rather than consolidated democracies.

Notes

1 As Löwenhardt notes, in 1995 the Secretary of Tatarstan's Central Eelectoral Commission declared that 'since Tatarstan is part of the Russian Federation but not as one of its subjects, the federal law, "On Basic Guarantees of Electoral Rights of the Citizens of the Russian federation", is not in force on the territory of Tatarstan'. Löwenhardt, 'The 1996 presidential elections in Tatarstan', *Journal of Communist Studies and Transition Politics*, 13:1 (March 1997), 135.

2 Cited in R. G. Moser, 'The impact of parliamentary electoral systems in Russia', *Post-Soviet Affairs*, 13:3 (1997), p. 284.

3 S. Huntington, *The Third Wave: Democratisation in the Late Twentieth Century* (Norman and London: University of Oklahoma Press, 1991), p. 263.

4 A. Blais and S. Dion, 'Electoral systems and the consolidation of new democracies', in D. Ethier (ed.), *Democratic Transition and Consolidation in Southern Europe, Latin America and Southeast Asia* (Basingstoke: Macmillan, 1994), pp. 251–2.

5 J. H. Pammett, 'Elections and democracy', 45.

6 Blais and Dion, 'Electoral systems', p. 251.

7 G. O'Donnell, 'Illusions about consolidation', *Journal of* Democracy, 7:2 (April 1996), 37.

8 One of the most graphic examples of media control was in Primorskii krai where Governor Nazdratenko closed down the local television channel after its editor compromised the Governor's reputation. Later an assassination attempt was made on the author of the programme. See, P. Kirkow, *Russia's Provinces: Authoritarian Transformation versus Local Autonomy* (Basingstoke: Macmillan, 1998), p. 133. For other examples of corruption and dictatorial power in Primorskii krai, see J. Hahn, 'The development of political institutions in three regions of the Russian Far East', in C. Ross (ed.), *Regional Politics in Russia* (Manchester: Manchester University Press, 2002).

9 Buryatiya, Marii El, Chuvashiya, Khabarovsk, Lipetsk, Novgorod, Ryazan, Samara, Smolensk, Chelyabinsk and Yaroslavl'. V. A. Malyshev and V. I Raudin, 'Neobkhodimo sovershenstvovat' poryadok formirovaniya izbiratel'nykh komissii', *Vestnik Tsentral'noi Izbiratel'noi Komissii*, 8:122 (2001), 49.

10 M. Kh. Farukshin, 'Federalizm i demokratiya: slozhnyi balans', *Polis*, 6:42 (1997), 171.

11 Federal Law, 'Ob Osnovnykh Garantiyakh Izbiratel'nykh', as amended March 30, 1999, article 4.2.

12 *Kommersant Daily* (March 13, 1997), p. 2.

13 In a similar manner whilst the law does allow regions to add some age restrictions for candidates it firmly states that these must not exceed a minimum age of 21 for candidates in legislative elections, and 30 for candidates in gubernatorial elections. But again these federal norms have simply been ignored. In some republics presidential candidates must have a minimum age of 35 (Adygeya, Bashkortostan, Kabardino-Balkariya, Kareliya, Komi, North Osetiya, Tatarstan, Khakasiya, Chechnya) whilst in others they must be at least 40 (Sakha). In other republics candidates must be under the age of 65 (Bashkortostan, Kabardino-Balkariya, Kareliya, Komi, Tatarstan, Krasnoyarsk Krai) and in others, under 60 years of age (Kalmykiya, Sakha, Khakasiya, Stavropol Krai, Ivanovo, Kirov, Kurgan, Nizhegorod, Tambov oblasts, Taimyr AO).

14 *Vybory v zakonodatel'nye predstavitel'nye*, p. 34

15 A. Fillipov, 'Vybory zakonodaltel'nykh (predstavitel'nykh) organov gosudarstvennoi vlasti sub'ekotov Rossiiskoi Federatsii (1990–98)', in *Vybory i Partii*, p. 120.

16 *Ibid.*

17 T. N. Bukhanova, 'Vydvizhenie i registratsiya kandidatov na regionalnykh vyborakh v 2000', *O Vyborakh*, 2 (2001), 19.

18 D. Lussier, 'Bashkortostan's president re-elected in campaign plagued by violations', *EWI Russian Regional Report*, 3:25 (1998), 13.

19 *Ibid.*

20 *Russkii Telegraf* (June 16, 1998).

21 D. Lussier, 'Bashkortostan's president', 14. See also J. Grävingholt, 'Bashkortostan: a case of regional authoritarianism', in C. Ross (ed.), *Regional Politics in Russia* (Manchester: Manchester University Press, 2002), pp. 177–92.

22 J. Hahn, 'The development of political institutions in three regions of the Russian Far East', in C. Ross (ed.), *Regional Politics in Russia* (Manchester: Manchester University Press, 2002), p. 153.

23 Farukshin, 'Federalizm i demokratiya', p. 171. See also, M. Farukshin, 'Tatarstan: syndrome of authoritarianism', in Ross, *Regional Politics in Russia*, pp. 193–206.

24 Ya. Tregubova, 'Kirsan Ilyumzhinov dreams of a stable and peaceful Kalmyk Khanate within Russia', *Sevodnya* (17 October 1995), p. 3. Translated in *CDPSP*, 47: 42 (1995). 16. Ilyumzhinov was first elected President in April 1993, he then won a second term in a hastily called election in October 1995 – with a 7-year term.

25 N. Petrov and A. Titov, 'Vybory glav ispolnitel'noi vlasti regionov', in *Vybory i partii*, p. 59.

26 Following amendments made on January 17, 2001, Kalmykiya's Law on the Presidency has now been brought into line with federal norms.

27 D. Lussier, *EWI Russian Regional Report* (January 2000), 16.

28 *EWI Russian Regional Report*, 6:15 (April 25, 2001), 2.

29 *Vybory v zakonodatel'nye predstavitel'nye*, p. 11.

30 J. Kahn, 'A federal façade: problems in the development of Russian federalism', D. Phil. thesis (University of Oxford, 1999), p. 252.

31 O. Zhunusov, *EWI Russian Regional Report*, 6:20 (May 30, 2001), 4.

32 *EWI Russian Regional Report*, 6:16 (May 2, 2000), 10–11.

33 *Kommersant Daily* (January 25, 2001).

34 J. Lowenhardt and R. Verheul, 'The village votes: the December 1999 elections in Tatarstan's Pestretsy District', *Journal of Communist Studies and Transition Politics* 16:3 (September 2000), 118.

35 J. Lowenhardt, 'The 1996 presidential elections in Tatarstan', *Journal of Communist Studies and Transition Politics*, 13:1 (March 1997), 138.

36 R. F. Turovsky, *Politicheskaya Geografiya* (Moscow and Smolensk: MGU, Geofraficheskii Fakul'tet, 1999), p. 337.

37 V. Mikhailov, 'Demokratizatsiya Rossii: raslichnaya skorost' v regionakh', in *Osobaya Zona*, p. 54.

38 *Ibid.*

39 V. N. Kozlov and D. B. Oreshkin, 'Regional'nyi analiz resul'tatov vyborov i tipologiya regionov po politicheskim predpochteniyam izbiratelei', in *Vybory Prezidenta Rossiiskoi Federatsii 1996* (Moscow: Ves Mir, 1996), p. 190.

40 *Ibid.*, p. 42.

41 *Ibid.*, p. 58

42 *Ibid.*, p. 72.

43 D. B. Oreshkin, 'Elektoral'naya demokratiya i tselostnost' politicheskovo

prostranstva Rossii', *O Vyborakh*, 2 (2001), 29. For other interesting recent studies of regional elections, see D. B. Oreshkin, 'Geografiya eletoral'noi kul'tury i tsel'nost' Rossii', *Polis*, 1 (2001), 73–93; E. V. Popova, 'Problemy izmereniya elektoral'noi politiki v Rossii: gubernatorskie vybory v sravni-tel'noi perspektive', *Polis*, 3 (2001), 47–57.

44 A. Stepan, 'federalism and democracy: beyond the U.S. model', *Journal of Democracy*, 10:4 (October 4, 1999), 152.

45 G. O'Donnell, 'Delegative democracy', *Journal of Democracy*, 5:1 (January 1994), 61.

46 D. Oreshkin, Seminar, 'Russia's regions: the results of the year 2000', Carnegie Centre, Moscow, January 19, 2001.

47 See, M. McAuley, *Russia's Politics of Uncertainty* (Cambridge: Cambridge University Press, 1997).

10

Conclusions

Article 1 of the Russian Constitution states that the Russian Federation 'is a democratic federative rule of law state with a republican form of government'. However, as this study has shown, whilst many of the structural prerequisites of a federal state have undoubtedly been formed, a federal and democratic culture has still to emerge. Thus, as Kempton notes, 'although Russia inherited a federal structure, it did not inherit a federal tradition'.[1] Centre–periphery relations in Russia have been determined principally by political and economic factors rather than constitutional norms.

The difficulties of creating a democratic federation in Russia have undoubtedly been made much more problematic by the nature of its origins as a quasi-federation within the USSR. One of the most destructive legacies which Russia inherited from the Soviet Union was its ethno-territorial form of federalism. The 'dual nature' of Russian federalism, which grants different constitutional rights and powers to different subjects of the federation, has from the outset created major tensions and divisions between federal subjects. Indeed, the demands for legal separatism and the development of bilateralism can be seen as logical responses to the constitutional inequalities inherent in the system.

The foundations of Russia's constitutional order

The manner by which Russia's constitutional foundations were laid down have also had a major impact on its transition. As we have seen the foundations of Russia's constitutional order were born out of conflict and coercion rather than dialogue and consensus. And the Constitution was largely imposed from above on a weak society, which was still suffering from the after-shocks of Yeltsin's violent assault and dissolution of the Russian parliament.

Moreover, Yeltsin's victory over the parliament was a pyrrhic victory. For although a 'presidential Constitution' was officially ratified in

December 1993, the Constitution was fundamentally weakened by questions over its legitimacy. As we discussed in chapter 1, one of the central preconditions for a democratic federation is the voluntary membership of its subjects. But in December 1993, forty-two subjects out of eighty-nine failed to ratify the Constitution. And many of those ethnic republics which had rejected the Constitution soon went a step further, and declared that their own constitutions were to take precedence over the Russian one. Chechnya demanded outright secession and Tatarstan declared that it was only an 'associate member' of the federation. Others republics, such as Bashkortostan, Kalmykiya, Sakha and Tyva were able to forge confederal relations with the centre.

Since December 1993, federal relations in Russia have largely been determined by a 'war of laws'. There was no 'elite pact' or 'elite settlement' in Russia. Nor was there a post-revolutionary 'circulation of elites' as happened in many of the states of Eastern Europe in 1989. Russia's 'revolution' was both a 'revolution from within' and 'from above', whereby members of the Russian 'nomenklatura' largely took over the reigns of power from members of the Soviet nomenklatura. And elite continuity rather than elite circulation was even more the norm in Russia's twenty-one ethnic republics. Former Communist leaders here were able to swap their 'Communist spots' for nationalist ones.

Over the period 1991–93 there was a fierce struggle for power between the Russian parliament and President, which soon gravitated, downwards to the republics and regions. And in 1992 Yeltsin was forced to concede major powers to the federal subjects in the Federal Treaty. Yeltsin needed the support of the regions in his struggle with the Russian parliament. In the period between the signing of the Federal Treaty in March 1992 and the adoption of the Russian Constitution in December 1993 the republics were able to make the most of the political impasse in Moscow. Thus, the constitutional foundations, that were to determine the future direction of these republics for many years to come, were laid down during a time of great turmoil and uncertainty, and before the Russian Constitution was formally adopted. During this period of weak and divided central powers, the republics were able to carve out for themselves ever-greater amounts of national autonomy.

Problems over the legitimacy of the federal Constitution weakened the authority of the federal government and the status of federal laws in the federal subjects. And, as we discussed in chapter 3, Yeltsin further undermined the authority of the Constitution by signing forty-six bilateral treaties with the regions. Before long there was a 'war of laws' between federal and republican constitutions. Indeed, federal relations have been regulated by five competing and contradictory sources of law: (1) the federal Constitution, (2) the Federal Treaty, (3) federal laws, (4) bilateral treaties, and, (5) the constitutions and charters of the republics and regions.[2] Thus, unity and diversity both exist in Russia but in contradiction rather than harmony. Indeed, there would appear to be as many kinds of federal relations as there are subjects of the federation.

From ethnic to legal and economic secessionism

Fearing that demands for secession would spread from Chechnya to other parts of the federation, Yeltsin tolerated a high degree of regional autonomy in the ethnic republics. By backing moderate nationalist leaders and promoting bilateral treaties with the most troublesome regions, Yeltsin was able to marginalise the more radical nationalists and bring the 'parade of sovereignties' to an end.

However, as we discussed in chapter 4, the dangers of ethnic separatism spreading across the federation were never, in fact, very high. In only 7 of Russia's 21 republics does the indigenous population make up a majority. And of the 11 autonomous there are only 2 where the indigenous population predominates. Furthermore, in those 7 subjects where the indigenous population comprises a majority, 1 is landlocked and the remaining 6 are dependent on the centre for their economic survival.

It is the development of legal separatism, not ethnic secession, which has proved to be the greater threat. Over the period 1996–97 Yeltsin lost his control over the appointment of regional governors and his ability to control the federation Council was therefore also substantially weakened. And by 1997–98 many of Russia's governors and presidents had successfully carved out personal fiefdoms. Legal separatism was soon a de facto reality for many regions. Thus, as we noted in chapter 8, by 2001 just under a quarter of all legal acts adopted by the regions and republics contradicted the federal Constitution and federal laws. Regional governors and republican presidents were also able to capture control over the appointment of the heads of federal bureaucracies situated in their territories.

President Putin came to power with a mandate to win back power from the governors and to create a unified legal space across the federation. However, Putin's success has been only partial. In many regions and republics the number of laws which violate the Constitution have actually risen. As we noted in chapter 8, in December 2001, 72 per cent of Bashkortostan's laws still violated federal norms, a figure which was actually higher than it was in May 2000 at the beginning of Putin's reforms. Moreover, new constitutions adopted in Bashkortostan and Tatarstan still include the full texts of their bilateral treaties, many of whose provisions violate the Russian Constitution. And in defiance of a Constitutional court ruling, Bashkortostan, Sakha, Tatarstan and Tyva have all steadfastly refused to renounce their sovereignty claims.

Federalism and democratisation in Russia

As we discussed in chapter 1, scholars of federalism have stressed the positive relationship between federalism and democratisation. Thus, for example, Daniels argues that, 'by distributing power, federalism curbs arbitrary rule, both at the centre and locally. It decentralizes responsibility while providing a mechanism to restrain potential local conflicts and abuses. It provides a school of democracy, and it quite literally brings government closer to the people'.[3] Similarly, for Elazar, 'Federalism by its very nature must be republican in the original sense of *res publica* – a public thing; a federal polity must belong to its public and not be the private possession of any person or segment of that public, and its governance therefore requires public participation'.[4]

And for Elazar, public participation is the key factor which distinguishes federalism from feudalism. Feudalism entails, 'a series of contracts among fiefdoms, in which authority is arranged hierarchically and power is usually organised oligarchically'. On the other hand, 'true federal arrangements must rest upon a popular base'.[5] For King, as we have seen, federation and democracy are synonymous, and for true federalism to function relations between the centre and regions must be grounded in constitutional law and democratic representation. For, King, only liberal democracies can be truly federal.[6]

Such theories are fine for liberal democracies, but what of transitional regimes such as Russia where federalism and democracy need to be constructed and consolidated simultaneously, and where constitutionalism and the rule of law are, as yet, only weakly developed in Russian society. The Russian federation's unique blend of constitutional, socio-economic, and political asymmetry, far from promoting democracy, has bolstered authoritarian regimes in the regions. High levels of regional autonomy have led the regions more often in the direction of dictatorship than democracy. The constitutions of the republics and the charters of the regions have been forged out of fire and the struggle for power between regional executive and legislative bodies of power. Whoever wins the struggle imposes their form of political system. Thus, we would appear to be in a conundrum, for federalism, it is argued, is impossible without democracy, but in Russia's multi-national state, democracy is impossible without federalism.

As the Russian proverb states 'the fish rots from the head down'. In a bid to bring in regional votes and to ensure tax returns and ethnic quiescence, Yeltsin often turned a blind eye to the development of authoritarian regimes in the regions. Likewise, Putin's reforms of the federal system have made a mockery of both federalism and democracy. The constitutional powers of the regions have been usurped by seven unelected presidential representatives. And Putin's powers to dismiss popularly elected governors and assemblies is a highly retrograde step. Moreover, Putin's attack on the sovereignty claims of the ethnic republics may weaken the powers of moderate leaders in the republics and give greater degrees of popular support to more radical nationalists and separatist movements.

The development of such high levels of constitutional and political asymmetry in Russia has weakened the federal government's ability to protect and promote democracy across the federation. Paradoxically, it is in those subjects of the federation which have been granted the most autonomy, the ethnic republics, where we find the highest levels of authoritarianism. Presidential leaders in the ethnic republics have been able to use their considerable levels of political autonomy to carve out authoritarian regime. Thus, as Whitmore notes: 'Many of Russia's 89 regional executives have indeed become brazenly authoritarian, flaunting the law, ignoring the country's constitution, and routinely violating human rights and democratic norms. Regional leaders have fixed elections, emasculated parliaments, bribed the courts, strong-armed the media, and bullied opposition figures'.[7]

Such practices have enabled regional leaders to pack regional assemblies with their loyal supporters. And in many of the ethnic republics, assemblies are nothing more than an appendage of executive power. And by controlling the parliaments regional leaders have been able to control other key bodies such as the police, courts and electoral commission all of which are highly politicised.

There can be no consolidation of democracy in Russia without a nation-wide consolidation of parties and the party system. The chronic weakness of political parties in regional assemblies has intensified the clientalistic and corporatist nature of politics in Russia and it has allowed regional governors to virtually rule alone without any effective opposition. And in the absence of parties and party competition regional assemblies have been swamped by economic and administrative elites.

Moreover, Putin's reform of the party system is yet a further blow to the development of local-level democracy. Regional parties will no longer be able to operate from 2003. The President's 'party of power' (Unity) will undoubtedly be one of the few beneficiaries of the new law on parties. And the centralisation of the party system will undoubtedly bolster Putin's quest to centralise power in the state and restore the 'power vertical'. Finally, as we have stressed in chapter 6, it is very difficult to consolidate parties in weak and fragmented federal systems, but it is doubly difficult to build federal systems in the absence of strong and territorially comprehensive parties.

Local democracy is also surely a necessary prerequisite for democratisation at the national level. And the provision of certain basic democratic procedures should, in a democracy, be universally available to all citizens across the federation regardless of their place of residence. But, in Russia this has been far from the case, and there are wide regional variations in the development of civil society, electoral practices and adherence to constitutional norms and the exercise of human rights. Regional and republican parliaments have blatantly adopted legislation violating human rights and they have openly carried out policies which discriminate against the rights of ethnic minorities.

Whilst we have not conducted a systematic study of politics in all eighty-nine subjects of the federation it is clear from this study that, according to the definitions given by Dahl, O'Donnell and Beetham, (see chapter 1), very few, if any, of Russia's regions, and none of its ethnic republics qualify as democracies. Authoritarian regimes dominate Russia's regional landscape.

For Montesquieu, large states must choose between tyranny and federalism. But as Petrov stresses, 'True to its habit of choosing both evils, Russia has taken the path of building a "federation of tyrannies"'.[8] In a vicious circle, authoritarianism at the centre has been nourished by authoritarianism in the regions and vice versa. To conclude, Yeltsin and Putin, unlike Gorbachev, may have succeeded in maintaining the unity of the state, but only by sacrificing Russia's democratic transition.

Notes

1 D. Kempton, 'Russian federalism: continuing myth or political salvation', *Demokratizatsiya*, 9:2 (2001), p. 202.

2 A. Umnova, *Konstitutsionnye Osnovy Sovremennovo Rossiiskovo Federalizma* (Moscow: Delo, 1998), p. 50.

3 R. V. Daniels, 'Democracy and federalism in the former Soviet Union and the Russian Federation', in P. J. Stavrakis, J. DeBardeleben and L. Black (eds), *Beyond the Monolith: The Emergence of Regionalism in Post-Soviet Russia* (Baltimore: Johns Hopkins University Press, 1997), p. 233.

4 D. Elazar, *Exploring Federalism* (Tuscaloosa and London: University of Alabama Press, 1987), p. 107.

5 D. Elazar, *Federalism and Political Integration* (Israel: Turtledove, 1979), p. 47.

6 P. King, *Federalism and Federation* (London: Croom Helm, 1982), p. 94. Cited in Burgess and Gagnon, *Comparative Federalism*, p. 5

7 B. Whitmore, 'Power plays in the provinces', *Transitions* (September, 1998), 72.

8 N. Petrov, 'Russia's regions or regions' Russia? prospective realignment of the nation's political subdivisions', Carnegie Institute, *Briefing Papers*, 3 (March, 1999), 1.

Index

Note: main entries are given in **bold**.